The Modernity of Sanskrit

The Modernity of Sanskrit

Simona Sawhney

MINNESOTA
University of Minnesota Press
Minneapolis
London

Portions of chapter 2 were previously published in "Who Is Kalidasa? Sanskrit Poetry in Modern India," *Postcolonial Studies* 7, no. 3 (2004): 294–312, and in "Ethics and the Writing of Experience: Kalidasa in the Work of Mohan Rakesh," *Journal of Contemporary Thought* (India) 14 (2001): 41–53.

Published by the University of Minnesota Press
111 Third Avenue South, Suite 290
Minneapolis, MN 55401–2520
http://www.upress.umn.edu

Library of Congress Cataloging-in-Publication Data

Sawhney, Simona.
The modernity of Sanskrit / Simona Sawhney.
p. cm.
Includes bibliographical references and index.
ISBN 978–0–8166–4995–2 (hardcover : alk. paper)
ISBN 978–0–8166–4996–9 (pbk. : alk. paper)
1. Sanskrit literature—History and criticism. 2. Hindi literature—Sanskrit influences. I. Title.
PK2903.S375 2008
891'.2—dc22

2008028724

Printed in the United States of America on acid-free paper

15 14 13 12 11 10 09 10 9 8 7 6 5 4 3 2 1

For my parents
Bhupinder and Sewak Singh Sawhney

Contents

Preface and Acknowledgments

I started studying Sanskrit quite late, after I had already spent a few years in graduate school. Although I had become interested in Sanskrit texts earlier, the decision to learn the language crystallized only in the aftermath of December 6, 1992. For me, as for many Indians of my generation, the destruction of the Babri masjid, a sixteenth-century mosque allegedly built on the remains of an earlier Hindu temple, and the violence that both produced and followed that destruction became signposts toward a destination so abhorrent as to be virtually unthinkable. Less than a decade after the massacres of Sikhs in 1984, we had once again witnessed a massive wave of violence directed against members of a minority community, and its horrific scope had indelibly altered the landscape of India.

At that time, studying Sanskrit seemed a way of engaging the phenomenon we call Hindu nationalism. While this phenomenon has no doubt been shaped by diverse political forces, various strategic initiatives, and detailed calculations, it could not have attained its power if it had not also fed on a cultural and libidinal shift. A significant aspect of this shift has been the almost total appropriation of the Sanskrit tradition in India by the Hindu right. The destruction of the Babri masjid became a manifest symbol of such appropriation: it demonstrated the success of the fantastic welding of a Sanskrit epic text (popularized over the centuries through adaptations in vernacular languages) with twentieth-century electoral politics and a distinctly modern cult of masculine prowess.

Traditions, of course, wither away if they are not appropriated. But in a crucial sense they also decay when their appropriation is no longer contested. In writing this book, I have attempted to contribute, in a small academic way, to the work of those who are engaged in contesting the appropriation of the Sanskrit tradition in our times. Writing it has been a daunting task, partly because I am still a student rather than a scholar of Sanskrit and partly because of the immense complexity of the texts about which I want to write. But I have also received much guidance, often from teachers whom I have never met. At one moment of panic—the kind of panic that is doubtless familiar to all who attempt to write about canonical and monumental texts—I came across a wonderful line in a novel by Hazariprasad Dvivedi: "Kisī se na darnā, guru se bhī nahīn, mantra se bhī nahīn, lok se bhī nahīn, ved se bhī nahīn" (Do not fear anyone, neither the teacher, nor the mantra, nor the world, nor the Veda). The words inspired courage, and in the course of writing this book, and thinking about Dvivedi's own work, I often returned to them.

It would not be possible to list here all such guides; I only hope that the impress of the works that have influenced me over the years will be legible in the pages of the book. But I will take this opportunity to thank at least a few teachers and friends. Among my professors at University of California, Irvine, I am especially indebted to J. Hillis Miller, who communicated to his students his great love for reading and thinking, Ellen Burt, Jacques Derrida, Julia Lupton, and Andrzej Warminski. At Berkeley, Sally Sutherland Goldman and Robert Goldman taught me Sanskrit—I will always be grateful for their generosity and especially for the time Sally spent reading Sanskrit texts with me outside of class. For their warm encouragement and interest in this project, I thank Rajeswari Sunder Rajan, Clinton Seely, Antoinette Burton, Hans Hock, Vasudha Dalmia, Suvir Kaul, Ania Loomba, and Eduardo Cadava.

Several friends, at Minnesota and elsewhere, took the time to respond to parts of the manuscript. Christine Marran, Dan Brewer, Mike Molasky, Mark Anderson, Vinay Gidwani, and Maki Morinaga read an early draft of the first chapter; Ajay Skaria read drafts of two chapters and became an instructive and most challenging interlocutor; Andrew Norris and Diane Detournay provided perceptive comments on early drafts of chapter 3; Emily Rook-Koepsel and Julietta Singh helped edit drafts of chapter 4; and Paul Rouzer provided incisive and swift advice on a muddled draft of chapter 5. Joe Allen and Ann Waltner read the entire manuscript; without their support and that of Douglas Armato, my editor at the University of Minnesota Press, the book may never have seen the light of day. I would also like to thank Andrea Patch, Nancy Sauro, Rachel Moeller, and everyone else at the Press, especially Lynn Walterick for amazing copyediting. Thanks also to an anonymous reader for the University of Minnesota Press for helpful comments and to Rukun Advani of Permanent Black for his interest in the work. Among those whose friendship sustained me through years of working on this book I must name Guy Pollio, Linette Davis, Rainer Nagele, Trish Loughran, Usha Jain, Lee Zimmerman, Kyle Cuordileone, Ali Mir, Jimmy Wallenstein, Andreas Gailus, Qadri Ismail, Sithara Shreen, Anke Pinkert, Alka Hingorani, Sharad Chari, Preeti

Chopra, Divya Karan, Rachel Schurman, Dan Brewer, Juliette Cherbuliez, Shiney Varghese, and my cousins, Timmi Suri and Raman, Raju, and Pammi Sethi.

Bruce Braun and Sabina Sawhney read drafts of several chapters, asked many questions, demanded changes, and took on the tiresome task of persuading me to continue whenever I wanted to give up in despair or exhaustion. I am differently, and immeasurably, indebted to each of them.

Finally, I'd like to thank my parents for their patience, care, and trust through the years.

Introduction

From what are the phenomena to be saved? Not only, and not so much from the disrepute and contempt into which they have fallen as from the catastrophe that a certain kind of tradition, their "valorization as heritage" very often entails.—They are saved through the disclosure of the breach in them.

—Walter Benjamin, *Gesammelte Schriften*

Reading Sanskrit

At the center of U. R. Anantha Murthy's Kannada novel *Samskara* (1965) is a clearing in the forest where the protagonist, the learned and ascetic Brahmin Praneshacharya, gets clumsily entangled with the beautiful lower-caste Chandri, cries out "Amma!" (mother!), and sleeps with her, just as we've been expecting him to do since the beginning of the novel. Once this moment of initiation has passed, he recalls the words of Naranappa—his old adversary and Chandri's old lover—who had scandalized the entire Brahmin community with the ingenuity of his transgressions: "Naranappa had said mockingly: to keep your brahminhood, you must read the Vedas and holy legends without understanding, without responding to their passion." The narrator then goes on to say, "Embedded in his [Praneshacharya's] compassion, in his learning, was an explosive spark, which was not there in the others' stupidity. Now the tamed tiger is leaping out, baring its teeth."[1]

What does "responding to the passion" of the Sanskrit texts mean here? At one level it means not reading them as spiritual or moral allegories but as stories about desire and sensuality. This is how both Praneshacharya and the narrator seem to understand Naranappa's words. The Sanskrit stories themselves become "explosive" in this reading as they ignite the spark that convention and fear had rendered dormant in Praneshacharaya. Thus the living vitality of the ancient texts is reconfirmed and generations of austere, priggish readers are suitably dismissed. But at another, more earthly level, "responding to the passion" of the Sanskrit texts simply means here that an upper-caste man finds, in these texts, a sanction, or even an invitation, for sleeping with a lower-caste woman. In that case it means—if one may be so perverse—that responding to the texts entails internalizing the hierarchies of caste, gender, and power rendered erotic in them. Would that be the same as "understanding" these texts, as Narannapa's words imply?

It seems to me that this passage draws our attention to the curious ways in which the reader's passion and the text's apparent passion become alibis for one another. The privileged spontaneity and immediacy of passion provides a means for distinguishing between mere reading and *real* reading or "understanding." In the modern Indian response to Sanskrit texts, this distinction sometimes asserts itself with exceptional force, perhaps because so-called traditional readers, unlike their modern counterparts, often valorized what we may today call mere reading—the act itself of reciting and articulating the holy words—over what they perceived as the transient, trivial, and individual comprehension of the work. The work itself was considered infinitely more significant than its comprehension by the paltry individual. This was of course more true of the ritual texts, the Vedas, than of others, but if we keep in mind the fact that in different periods and for different classes of people, the act of reading itself carried rather different meanings (recitation, memorization, interpretation, performance, and so on), we would be better able to perceive how the very being of the Sanskrit texts, their manner of existing in the world, has changed in fundamental ways over the centuries.[2]

Modern readers rarely perceive these texts as the enigmatic sign of a profound and vital mystery; indeed, that may be precisely what makes them modern.[3] On the contrary, whatever mystery the texts might disclose or withhold has to be granted them by the reader. That is why the act of reading becomes significant in an entirely new way. The passage I cited from *Samskara* discloses how, in attempting to bring early texts within our own horizons, we tend to read them as allegories of our own concerns. Sometimes, as in the case of Narannapa—whom I would call the passionate but also deluded reader—we then become captivated by what *appear* to be moments of transgression, even when these moments are entirely enmeshed within a conservative political structure. Anantha Murthy's novel shows us at several junctures how a mimetic reproduction of certain scenes from Sanskrit texts may masquerade as rebellious innovation or as a challenge to tradition, as long as these scenes focus, for example, on the breaking of sexual taboos, while more or less preserving their patriarchal or caste-engendered frame.

But the passage from *Samskara* also indicates something more interesting about the act of reading. Praneshacharya recalls Naranappa's words after he has slept with Chandri and hence "lost" the spiritual merit that he had worked so hard to accumulate—even going to the extent of marrying an invalid woman so as to get "ripe and ready" for salvation.[4] He thus recalls these words at a moment when they offer a hope that the "sin" he has committed might not be a sin at all, but instead a symptom of a closer and more insightful reading of the Sanskrit texts he reveres. If, in being touched by Chandri, he has been truly touched by the Vedas, then his act is not a lapse but a new mark of progression in his spiritual journey. The passage thus reveals something about the way readings are shaped, transformed, or discarded. The words of the dead Naranappa, which had apparently glided ineffectually over Praneshacharya earlier, return to him with new authority at just this moment of bewilderment, to offer hope and affirmation. Thus the passage suggests not only that reading is inextricably affected by the interests and desires of the reader but also that it continually reacquires significance in contestation with other readings.

I begin with this passage because it dramatizes so vividly the question that initiated this book and retained its significance through each phase of writing: How may we read Sanskrit texts today? The "we" in this question refers to all those who are, in a manner of speaking, modern—that is to say, those who can no longer take reading itself for granted but are provoked to consider its presuppositions, limits, and effects. It thus includes scholars as well as general readers, Indians as well as non-Indians. The question has at least two dimensions, one concerning the very activity of reading, and especially of reading ancient texts, and the other concerning the status of Sanskrit in contemporary India.

Texts that come to us from a world long vanished indeed arouse specific kinds of doubts about reading. Our grasp of the language never seems adequate, and we wonder how much of the historical context we need to understand in order to make sense of the work. Once articulated and considered, however, these turn out to be questions that inevitably belong to the activity of reading. For when examined, they reveal the assumption that provokes them: that contemporary texts, written in a familiar language, are intelligible to us in an immediate manner, and that we share with them a common time and a common understanding of the world. There may be some degree of truth to this assumption. Insofar as in reading a text we are attempting to determine its referential burden, to decide, for instance, what it represents, or even how it represents something, we will indeed find it easier to do so with texts whose references (to events, places, people) are recognizable and whose idiom seems immediately comprehensible. But contemporaneity also gives us the *illusion* of familiarity, and likewise the illusion of the transparence of language. For whenever, in reading, we foreground what we might call the rhetorical dimension of a work, or the density and resistance of its own language, then the apparent transparence of the medium becomes manifestly clouded. We are then forced to confront the work as a text and to recognize that its language does not offer itself immediately as communication. Texts that are remote from us present this phenomenon most vividly. Their language vividly strikes us as *a mode of apprehending the world;* the movement of its tropes has not yet been effaced for us by habit or daily use. We encounter such a language in the process, as it were, of translation: as a language that, in the words of Walter Benjamin, "envelops its content like a royal robe with ample folds," instead of forming "a unity like a fruit and its skin."[5] In studying early texts we may be most powerfully exposed to the unfamiliarity that lies at the heart of language and from which we are usually shielded by our own habitation in contemporary languages. That is one of the reasons why reading early literature, an act that appears so fraught with historical problems, might turn out to be instructive for the act of reading in general.

Indeed, the more attentively we focus on our engagement with language, the more clear it becomes that in this regard, contemporaneity and remoteness may be categories that obscure rather than clarify the problem. One of the characteristic features of all writing is its potential to survive its author and to live on, sometimes for many centuries. This capacity for apparently surviving intact distinguishes texts from all other objects in the world. As Peggy Kamuf writes in a different context, "We call 'text' . . . that which bears its name not as the mark of mortality but rather as the very possibility of its living on and continuing to be called by its name."[6] The text survives, not as a ruin but as the sign of a world that has been ruined. Indeed, we could say that the very act of writing positions a text to be destined toward the future. From the moment writing begins, it is placed ineluctably in flight, already moving elsewhere, away from the writer, away from the room and the place and the year. Thus writing in some way always speaks of a world that has ended, about the passing away of that world, not only because it is made of words that signal the end of immediacy—or perhaps the birth of immediacy as an impossibility and a dream—but also because it comes into existence first in defiance of the moment and as a rupture in the moment.

Being attentive to that rupture, which indicates the institutional, linguistic, and cultural work of representation, becomes particularly urgent at a time when Sanskrit texts appear in our world as signs of themselves, allegories of

(Hindu-Indian) antiquity. Today, when these texts elicit attention, they elicit not reading as much as passion: the love of those who are driven by fidelity to an origin, for whom Sanskrit becomes a prop in the staging of a violent drama of cultural continuity, and the hatred of all those to whom both origin and history appear as a relentless saga of injustice. Indeed, the very question of what India is—a question that has, from the moment of its first murmur, given rise to not only unease and disagreement but also repeated horrific violence—is deeply connected to the status and place of Sanskrit texts in the life of the modern nation.

Thus we arrive at the second dimension of the question with which we began: How may we read Sanskrit texts today? This dimension concerns the political charge that Sanskrit, as a language as well as a tradition, has accumulated during the nineteenth and twentieth centuries. Frequently recruited in the service of Hindu nationalism during the anticolonial struggle, Sanskrit has, in the past few decades, again been energetically yoked to the new Hindu nationalism that has been gathering force in India and abroad. Such appropriation has meant that a divisive political agenda, formulated on the basis of a religio-nationalist identity, precedes the reading of texts and determines their import in advance. Among Indian students who learn Sanskrit today, many do so at camps and schools run by Hindu nationalists, and thus, in learning an ancient language, the students also imbibe the language of a modern ideology. The corollary to this is that those who do not subscribe to that ideology often see no reason to study the language either, so strongly has it become associated with cultural conservatism. Perhaps one could go so far as to say that nothing has been so detrimental to the life of Sanskrit literature in our times as the appropriation of the Sanskrit tradition by Hindu nationalists and the corresponding reinstatement of Sanskrit as the mark of orthodoxy.

I say "reinstatement" because, as we know, Sanskrit has always carried the stamp of orthodoxy; it might be more accurate to say that it *is* the stamp of orthodoxy. No one who studies Sanskrit or reads Sanskrit literature can afford to overlook this vividly pronounced strain in its history and lineage; a strain that makes Sanskrit a kind of metaphor for institutional violence and the preservation of hierarchy. The word *saṃskṛta* itself indicates something that has been refined, purified, or polished—something that has been "worked" by culture. In this it is opposed to the languages that were called "Prakrits," literally designating those that are natural or first-made, made at the beginning—in a state that has a more intimate relation to human beings and that must also, paradoxically, be disavowed as a mark of the human. Sanskrit, on the other hand, has been associated with the performance of ritual, the study of the sacred texts, and, later, with "classical" literature. Upper-caste ("twice born") men learned to speak it, but usually not lower-caste men nor any women.[7] In early India, however, the two manners of speech must have been comprehensible beyond each group of speakers: in Sanskrit drama, women generally speak Prakrit and upper-caste men Sanskrit, and they seem to understand one another about as much as their modern counterparts do.

It is not certain when the language we know as Sanskrit acquired that name. In the work of the great grammarian Panini (fifth century BCE), the language is simply called *bhāṣā*—language. He makes a distinction between this language and the language of the Vedas but does not use the word "Sanskrit" to refer to either. According to the Sanskrit scholar Ashok Aklujkar, "the earliest Brahmanical authors who can be said with certainty to use *saṃskṛta* as a noun having a language as its referent do not seem to be much earlier than the beginning of the Christian Era."[8] He considers Bharata's *Nāṭyaśāstra* to be the earliest text that explicitly makes a distinction between Sanskrit and Prakrit. Two other early uses of the word *saṃskṛta* with reference to language are found in the *Rāmāyaṇa* and in Kalidasa's *Kumārasambhava*. The former is particularly interesting: it occurs in the *Sundara Kāṇḍa* when Rama's emissary, the monkey Hanuman, has succeeded in locating Rama's abducted wife Sita in Lanka and is wondering how to speak to her. Which language would enable him to win her confidence? At first he thinks that since he is a little monkey, it would be best to speak *saṃskṛta vāc* (the *saṃskṛta* or refined language) to her, for it is the language of "humans"—presumably opposed to the language of monkeys. But he is also concerned that if he speaks this refined language, she might take him for the demon Ravana and become afraid.[9] Here *saṃskṛta* is used as an adjective, perhaps showing us that it might be more accurate to think of Sanskrit as a particular *use* of language rather than a particular language.

The distinction between a correct or grammatical language and the language of the world *(loka)* is evident from very early texts. Thus it seems quite clear that grammatical rules were part of the distinction between the two. But the ideological difference is perhaps more significant. Madhav Deshpande notes that "even a casual reading of Patanjali's *Mahābhāṣya* (circa 100 BCE)" would allow one to grasp the fact that "there was a fierce competition between Sanskrit and Prakrit, and that in this competition the Prakrit had already surpassed Sanskrit as the language of the world *(loka)*. Under these circumstances, the Sanskrit grammarians defended Sanskrit as the language of dharma, rather than as a language of worldly communication."[10] Deshpande thus describes the valorization of Sanskrit as an attempt to create and preserve Brahmin hegemony. He suggests that from the perspective of the grammarians, the Prakrits were not so much original or "first-created" languages as *degenerate* languages—those that had suffered a decline from the perfection of Sanskrit. Sanskrit, as the only eternal language, was considered impervious to socio-historical changes.[11] Though the idea of Sanskrit as the divine and eternal language may not have originated with the grammarians, their work enables an epistemological taxonomy such that Sanskrit itself remains shielded from the movement of history. The Prakrits were susceptible to historical change and influence; they belonged to the world where space and time matter, but Sanskrit belonged to the timeless time of divinity; it thus functioned as a figure for a conception of language that guarantees an eternal relation between word and meaning. Deshpande notes that such a distinction conferred on the Prakrits an inescapably dependent status: they could only be conceived in relation to Sanskrit: "The only relation that held between the eternal Sanskrit and Prakrits, according to Indian grammarians, was that of successive degeneration of Sanskrit at the hands of incapable speakers" (73).

A comparison is often made between Sanskrit and Latin in this context. And in many ways it is an apt comparison, insofar as we are considering the status of a classical but effectively "dead" language. However, as we know, in the case of Latin, the change from its status as secondary and acquired to its status as primordial and "dead" took place much later, after Dante. Until the fifteenth century, Latin was considered a later development of the vernacular; as Giorgio Agamben puts it, "The greater nobility of Latin does not exclude the primogeniture of the vernacular."[12] The change, when it occurs, radically affects the European orientation, not only toward Latin, but toward language itself:

> In a decisive turning-point in European culture, Dante's antithesis between the vernacular and grammar—that is, between the experience of the originary and secondary status of the event of language . . . comes to be replaced by the antithesis between living language and dead language. The humanist opposition then conceals and, in fact, even overturns the meaning of the earlier distinction. *For the essential bilingualism of human speech is now resolved through a diachronic separation by which one language is pushed backward, as "dead," prior*

> *to "living" language.* Yet the language that thus dies—Latin—is not Dante's imperishable grammatical language but rather a mother tongue of a new kind, which is already the *lingua matrix* of seventeenth-century philology—the original language from which other languages derive.[13]

In referring to the "essential bilingualism of human speech" Agamben points to the distinction that always asserts itself between the institutional and inherited structure of language as grammar on the one hand and its dimension as a creative or expressive medium, a "living" medium, on the other. This distinction, whose political and conceptual resilience poststructuralist thought has mapped, is most obviously parsed out, as it were, in the distinction between classical and vernacular language. In the plot of the story of Sanskrit, a temporal tension appears: on the one hand, the institution of grammar and the language's deeper relation to the sphere of the ritual is constantly invested with divine and primordial characteristics, while on the other its very name indicates its connection to *saṃskāra*—that is to say, to an essentially belated act of refinement, cultivation, or consecration. In some of the chapters that follow, this book will trace how this paradox programs a powerful and remarkably predatory narrative that reappears in different forms in literary and philosophical texts: for instance, in the concurrent valorization of both the natural *and* the conquest of the natural; in the concept of law; in the mixed dread and envy of "natural" passion; in the ambivalence toward asceticism; and in the alternating affirmation and suspicion of rhetoric. One of the strands I pursue in this book follows the different itineraries of this narrative in Sanskrit texts as well as in modern readings of those texts. The three themes I have focused on, love, violence, and poetry, thus refer not only to the concerns of the particular texts discussed in the book but also to varying engagements with figures of the natural, the spontaneous, and the immediate. Love, violence, and poetry, as perhaps the most powerful fantasies of immediacy, both in Sanskrit literature and in modern readings of this literature, set in motion defensive and recuperative movements that alert us to the complex political forces traversing each text.

Colonial Agent

It is not surprising that "progressive" Indians have often protested against Sanskrit and all that it represents. When they do not read it as the sign of orthodoxy, they read it as the sign of a dead knowledge: something that has no place in a democratic modern world. Early-nineteenth-century debates among "orientalists" (those who supported the teaching of classical oriental languages and literatures in India) and "anglicists" (those who wished to focus, instead, on English and modern sciences) provide ample evidence that Sanskrit was already being declared, at that time, the medium of reactionary and useless knowledge. Instead of discussing here the utilitarian writings of James Mill and Charles Grant, or Macaulay's notorious Minute (1835), let us instead consider a letter written by one of the most remarkable Indian intellectuals of the period, Rammohun Roy, most often remembered for his articulate opposition to the practice of sati. Roy wrote this letter to Lord Amherst (governor-general, 1823–28) in December 1823, in protest against the Bengal government's decision in 1821 to establish a new Sanskrit College in Calcutta, and argued that an education in Sanskrit and Sanskritic methods of learning would only result in perpetuating the ignorance of native students. Canonical Sanskrit texts on grammar, metaphysics, and law, he asserted, have virtually nothing to teach the young student eager to participate and succeed in the modern world:

> We now find that the government are *[sic]* establishing a Sanskrit school under Hindu pundits, to impart such knowledge as is already current in India. This seminary (similar in character to those which existed in Europe before the time of Lord Bacon) can only be expected to load the minds of youth with grammatical niceties and metaphysical distinctions of little or no practicable use to the possessors or to society. The pupils will there acquire what was known two thousand years ago, with the addition of vain and empty subtilties since produced by speculative men, such as is already commonly taught in all parts of India.[14]

Though it appeals to "that enlightened sovereign and legislature which have extended their benevolent care to this distant land" (*Education Debate,* 113), the letter expresses a distinct suspicion that using the funds allocated for the education of Indians to establish a Sanskrit college may be a colonial ploy to keep colonial subjects "in darkness." Roy makes a persuasive case, and it is certainly not hard for us today to understand, and perhaps endorse, his arguments. When I cite his letter here, I do so not in order to register my disagreement with Roy's position but to reflect upon what the letter demonstrates.

It shows us that on the one hand, in the nineteenth century, the Sanskrit language had already become associated with a limited kind of traditional learning (grammar, law, and religion), and consequently, with a kind of knowledge that had been decisively surpassed. On the other hand, in Roy's letter, Sanskrit also becomes curiously associated with modern colonialism: with a system that guards its wealth and keeps it in reserve for the select few, hence becoming an ally of the new colonizers who, having themselves embarked on the path to enlightenment, secretly wish to keep others from following thereon. Roy's letter implicitly suggests that like the colonial system, Sanskrit is inherently elitist, functioning to limit rather than diffuse knowledge: "The Sanskrit language, so difficult that almost a life time is necessary for its acquisition, is well known to have been for ages a *lamentable check on the diffusion of knowledge;* and the learning concealed under this almost impervious veil is far from sufficient to reward the labour of acquiring it" (*Education Debate,* 112; my emphasis).

Although the General Committee of Public Instruction declined at the time to respond to Roy's letter, observing instead in its minutes that Roy's views were not representative of the general Hindu opinion (*Education Debate,* 19), a few years later Thomas Macaulay found in Roy's letter encouragement for advancing his own arguments about education, and he even borrowed from it examples of the futility of Sanskrit education. An extended response to Macaulay and the Anglicists was written by H. H. Wilson, himself a Sanskrit scholar and secretary of the General Committee of Public Instruction until 1833. In a letter to the editor of the *Asiatic Journal* dated December 5, 1835, Wilson expresses his fear that a departure from the committee's earlier orientalist position may be the "first stage of a very feasible project for the annihilation of all the languages of India, vernacular or classical" and the universal spread of English throughout the East (*Education Debate,* 207). With this extreme scenario in view, the letter makes several arguments for continuing government support for traditional Sanskrit and Arabic education. It argues that it is the government's duty to provide financial support for the learned classes of India, whose traditional patrons the British have replaced, and, indeed, to enlist these classes in the work of educating the country. Wilson perceives no incompatibility between the teaching of native and English literatures, observing that both could be pursued concomitantly. While all the knowledge imparted by traditional texts may not be current, he writes, such texts are still useful insofar as they help to maintain "amongst the natives of India a high tone of civilization," teach methods of close argument, and cultivate literary style. Toward the end of the letter, Wilson recurs to the relation between the vernacular and classical languages. The development of vernacular languages, he argues, is inconceivable without the aid of the classical, and modern literature in India can only come into being if it finds a ground and a foundation in the classical languages.

> It is in this latter particular, their effect upon the vernacular languages, that the cultivation of those considered in India as classical, is of indispensable necessity. The project of importing English literature along with English cottons into Bengal, and bringing it into universal use, must at once be felt by every reasonable mind as chimerical and ridiculous. If the people are to have a literature, it must be their own. The stuff may be in a great degree European, but it must be freely interwoven with home-spun materials, and the fashion must be Asiatic. In their present state, however, the vernacular dialects are unfit for the combination; they are utterly incapable of representing European ideas,—they have not words wherewith to express them. They must, therefore, either adopt English phraseology, which would be grotesque patch-work; or, they must have recourse, as they have been accustomed to do, for all except the most every-day terms, to the congenial, accessible, and inexhaustible stores of their classical languages. Every person acquainted with the spoken speech of India, knows perfectly well [. . .] that no man who is ignorant of Arabic or Sanscrit can write Hindustani or Bengali with elegance, or purity, or precision; and that the condemnation of the classical languages to oblivion would consign the dialects to utter helplessness and irretrievable barbarism. (*Education Debate,* 221)

In this account, the vernacular languages are deficient because they are incapable of representing European ideas, which would of course provide the "stuff" of any modern literature. The classical languages are paradoxically better equipped to do so, because they have a more nuanced and abstract vocabulary. Sanskrit and Arabic hence become implicitly analogous with English in this argument. They are necessary in order to save the dialects from "utter helplessness and irretrievable barbarism."

It does not require a great deal of imagination to discern, behind this passage, the specter that provokes it: the specter of an Indian modernity gone berserk for lack of husbanding. It is this modernity, at once helpless and barbaric, that would fester if left to its own devices. To rescue it, Europe must enter into a partnership with the Indian past, defeated and dead but fortunately still graced with elegance. Almost a hundred and fifty years later, G. N. Devy wrote a short book called *After Amnesia: Tradition and Change in Indian Literary Criticism* that we may read as a belated response to Wilson's orientalism.[15] Locating as "cultural amnesia" the colonial phenomenon that has severed the modern Indian intellectual from the long and complex history of the development of vernacular literatures and literary discourses, Devy argues that the crisis in Indian literary studies can only be addressed by taking these literatures seriously, by being attentive to their own structures and alignments and not reading them in terms of categories that emerged either in Sanskrit poetics or in European criticism. To do so, he contends, would be to willfully negate the very impetus that often animates these literatures. The new *bhāṣās* that emerged at the beginning of the millennium "expressed regional and heterodox aspirations in protest against the hegemony of Sanskrit and the culture developed through that language, sanskriti" (6). All *bhāṣās*, he claims, had become literary languages by the end of the fifteenth century: "The emergence and survival of mature literary traditions is the greatest phenomenon in Indian cultural history" (7). The contemporary Indian critic, however, is usually unable to gauge the significance of this phenomenon, for such a critic "feels a false emotional proximity to Western and Sanskrit ideas, while he tends to repress the *bhāṣā* tradition and to overlook the 'colonial' side of the colonial experience" (49). In contemporary India, the study of Sanskrit, Devy proposes, takes place in a strangely ahistoric space, detached from the immediate past. That is why Sanskrit texts often contribute to the flowering of cultural fantasies: "The worst part of the colonial impact was that it snatched away India's living cultural heritage and replaced it with a fantasy of the past. This amnesia, which has affected our awareness of native traditions which are still alive, is perhaps the central factor of the crisis in Indian criticism" (55).

Devy makes a spirited argument for recovering the memory of native literary traditions. Although his book sets itself the task of addressing a specific crisis in literary criticism, its purview is obviously wider and the literary scene becomes metonymic of far-reaching epistemological and psychic phenomena in the postcolonial condition. I cannot but agree with Devy's general analysis, though we part ways when he states that "what Indian literatures need at present is a realistic historiography and not so much of a theoretical discussion" (124). Beginning with the premise that historiography always carries with it its own theoretical underpinnings, whether articulated or not,

I would suggest instead that conceiving an abstraction called "theory" as a new form of Western imposition would be a mistake. To the extent that what is called "theory" teaches us to attend to the conceptual and figural frames within which we work, it may be best conceived not as something to be discarded or "applied" but rather as an interrogative self-reflexivity to be developed as a practice. Far from being irrelevant to postcolonial concerns, such reflexivity, in all its political and epistemological dimensions, perhaps becomes even more necessary when we address the consolidation, displacement, or restructuring of colonial and postcolonial hierarchies.

Though *bhāṣā* literatures have continued to grow in India, their life at present is often lived as a continual struggle against the Anglicization of the globe. At the same time, what have come to be known as "regional" languages must contend with the status of Hindi and with periodic attempts by the Indian government to give Hindi a dominant position in a spectacularly multilingual country. The Hindi officially promoted often has little to do with the spoken language of various north Indian regions; instead, it acquires its distinction from being severely differentiated from Urdu and Persian and forcefully aligned with Sanskrit. "Hindi nationalism" in the twentieth century has thus frequently functioned as a kind of proxy agent for *Hindu* nationalism.[16] Keeping in mind this broader context enables us to understand how the relation between Sanskrit and modern Indian languages—already uneven and often antagonistic, shaped by caste, region, and religion[17]—may have become, since the 1980s (and the reassertion of Hindu nationalist politics) even more strongly inflected by political concerns.

Modernity

In his influential book *Imagined Communities* Benedict Anderson proposes that the rise of national consciousness in various parts of the world was predicated on the erosion of "three fundamental cultural conceptions": the privileged status of a particular script-language (its access to ontological truth); the naturalized status of the monarch and his divine right to authority; and a conception of temporality that perceived the origin of the world as identical with the origin of humankind.[18] The phenomenon that most effectively facilitated the search for new conceptions of power, community, and temporality was the phenomenon Anderson names "print capitalism." While such explanations provide a compelling account of the rise of nationalism in broad historical terms, they inevitably present a master narrative that constitutes the relation between a prenationalist past and modern nationalism as a relation between two distinct and homogeneous worldviews. Such narratives, though persuasive, often represent the premodern in ways that obscure its close—and in many ways, constitutive—relation to the modern.

My own project begins with the speculation that because the moment of nationalism itself was often responsible for giving shape and name to the nation's past, and in particular to its "classical" age, that past is now accessible to us only as the past *of* modernity: one that belongs to it and cannot be dissociated from its own projects and conceptions. There is some obvious reciprocity here: cultural modernity itself becomes what it is by way of a confrontation with tradition—that is to say, with various contesting narratives about tradition. Given the directions taken by colonial and nationalist historiography in India, as well as the politics of cultural identity I have briefly discussed earlier here, it is not too surprising that "tradition" became closely meshed with the idea of Sanskrit for many writers and thinkers. Nineteenth- and twentieth-century intellectuals thus demonstrate a wide-ranging concern with canonical Sanskrit texts—with their status, relevance, and interpretation. This book concentrates on instances where modern texts explicitly position themselves as readings or rewritings of early texts, thus exposing the complex relation between the two. Such readings prompt us to reconsider sequential narratives of history by disclosing how modern readers have apprehended early texts—the elisions or transformations performed by them—and how their own work has been fundamentally affected by these apprehensions. To this end, I juxtapose, in each chapter, a particular Sanskrit text and selected modern readings and attempt to read them together—each in a historically constitutive relation to the other.

During the past two centuries, Sanskrit texts were alternately invested with the sharp and sometimes shrill energies of colonialist, nationalist, and Hindu nationalist discourses, as they were called upon to shape and legitimize competing narratives of Indian history. As I have noted, in our own time, Hindu nationalism has attempted a sweeping appropriation of both the Sanskrit language and Sanskrit literature in seeking to create an Indian nation gathered around the idea of *Hindutva* or Hindu-ness; indeed, it sometimes appears that the popular appeal of this enterprise might succeed in foreclosing in South Asia the very possibility of a politics that "does not stem from the will to realize an essence."[19] My book is structured partly as a response to this appropriation; therefore I have focused on modern readings that bring to the Sanskrit texts an engagement that opens, rather than limits, the possible world of these texts. The modern intellectuals and writers I discuss—Rabindranath Tagore, Hazariprasad Dvivedi, M. K. Gandhi, Mohan Rakesh, Dharamvir Bharati, Buddhadeva Bose, and Jaishankar Prasad, among others—had a complex relationship to Sanskrit texts and exhibited in their own work varying degrees of self-consciousness about the very activity of interpreting early texts. Their readings and rewritings of Sanskrit texts make apparent the political stakes of their work. In each case, we detect that the turn to Sanskrit texts was perceived as a necessary task, even a culturally and politically urgent task. At the same time, most of them allude, in one way or another, to the allegorical or metaphorical aspects of their reading as they attempt to accommodate the Sanskrit texts to their own projects. That is why, in thinking about modern readings, I attend to recurring tensions between impulses that we may name as historicist and hermeneutic on the one hand and more overtly *activist* on the other—that is to say, more overtly concerned with the text's use for, and impact on, the present. Such tensions show us very clearly how closely linked "methodological" or theoretical considerations—themselves often unarticulated—may be to political ones. Chapter 3, on Gandhi's reading of the *Bhagavad Gītā*, focuses most explicitly on these questions.

The book is written as a way of asking how we might read Sanskrit texts today, not to present a hypothesis about how they may have been read two thousand years ago. In a curious way, these texts appear to us at once as testaments from a world that has disappeared *and* as our own contemporaries. However, it is the very nature of the survival of Sanskrit texts that draws my interest. For example, the Sanskrit epics have become powerful contemporary political actors in India, especially since the immensely popular versions of their televised productions. As Arvind Rajagopal argues in his book *Politics after Television: Hindu Nationalism and the Reshaping of the Indian Public* (2001), the scene of Indian politics in the twentieth century was irreversibly changed by the impact of these televised productions. Of course, Hindu nationalism has not been the only player in this field. There have been many attempts to represent the epics in more imaginative, critical, and creative ways in art and literature. Moreover, the work of historians such as D. D. Kosambi, Romila Thapar, and D. N. Jha has made enormous contributions by critically reading the epics and other Sanskrit texts in terms of the relatively new field of social history. As will be readily apparent in many of the chapters of this book, I am especially indebted to Romila Thapar's pathbreaking work, which has brought tremendous vitality to the entire field of early Indian studies. Western Indologists have also often brought to Sanskrit texts a kind of critical engagement that perhaps could not have arisen within India. But for the most part, such scholarship is limited to a rather narrow space, even within the academy. Toward the end of this Introduction, I attempt a brief analysis of this phenomenon, which I take to be related to a larger question regarding the space of the humanities in the contemporary academy.

However, I am not interested only in the academic life of Sanskrit texts. This may seem an odd claim, especially since some of the modern writers I discuss have been part of the academy in India, and their work continues to have an institutional presence. What draws me to these particular texts is their deep engagement with Indian cultural modernity. The choice of texts is obviously limited by other factors as well: for example, the book focuses entirely on North Indian readers of Sanskrit works and privileges Hindi language reproductions of, and commentaries on, Sanskrit texts. This obviously has to do with the limits of my own training and ability, for which I cannot provide a coherent rationale. Given these unavoidable constraints, however, I have focused on modern texts that dramatize, in some way, their own act of intercepting Sanskrit texts as a politically resonant act. It is precisely because these texts themselves present the reading of Sanskrit texts as a specifically postcolonial task that I am interested in them. The title of this book thus has, for me, three distinct implications.

The "modernity" of Sanskrit refers, first, to the appearance and status of Sanskrit texts in modern India and to the ways in which they have contributed to reflections on literary, political, and cultural modernity. This is most easily apparent in the sphere of theater: modern theater in India, and particularly Hindi theater, began its career with acknowledging and reshaping its relation to Sanskrit theater. But it is also apparent elsewhere, for instance in those politico-philosophical writings that feel compelled to address Sanskrit texts in order to articulate and defend their ideas about the modern nation or the community. Partly because of the way "Sanskrit" had been framed by colonialism and nationalism, for many Indian writers the very question of the modern involved a dual negotiation: with European literature and the colonial experience on the one hand, and with the Sanskrit tradition on the other. Simon Gikandi's observation about modern Caribbean literature is apt here. For African and Asian writers, he claims, "the central categories of European modernity—history, national language, subjectivity—have value only when they are fertilized by figures of the 'other' imagination which colonialism has sought to repress."[20]

But I am also interested in the "modernity" of the Sanskrit texts themselves—that is to say, in how some of these text were themselves responding to debates, making changes and interventions, and otherwise engaged in asserting the rights of the new against the established and sanctioned old. Kalidasa's words in *Mālvikāgnimitra* give us some indication of this: "Purāṇamityeva na sādhu sarvaṃ na cāpi kāvyaṃ navamityavadyam" (The old is not always laudable, nor the new poem contemptible).[21] Such an appeal is of course inseparable from a corresponding sense of belatedness—from the burdens of a tradition that lies behind one. I am thus interested in noticing how classical Sanskrit texts, which often seem to us to be situated in the hoary stillness of an origin, were also part of a dynamic world of political and cultural change: a world where the foundations of political authority and of war were being profoundly interrogated, and which itself often evinces nostalgia for a more stable and simpler period.

Finally, I wish to draw attention to the modernity that may yet be possible for Sanskrit: a modernity in which it is neither neglected nor revered. A few decades ago, the work of the Konstanz school in Germany as well as the work of reader-response critics in the United States had forcefully argued that the literary text is neither "an object that stands by itself and that offers the same view to each reader in each period" nor "a monument that monologically reveals its timeless essence."[22] This is true, I would add, not only of the so-called literary text but of any text that is read in terms of its literariness. Unfortunately, the space for such reading seems to be steadily shrinking, not only because a displaced anxiety about political commitment sometimes pushes us to take positions rather than read texts but also because the very architecture of such space seems to be at odds with the aims of contemporary geoplanners. Creating such space in the American university would mean comprehensively challenging many of the assumptions and structures that organize the study of non-Western literatures. Although these literatures are more likely now than before to find a place in the humanities curriculum, it is surprising how often they continue to be read as *symptoms* or *examples* of an already-given cultural or historical moment rather than as texts whose very reading might disclose the lingering instability—or the violent stabilization—of that moment. The assumption regarding the transparency (or its inverse, the opacity) of the non-Western text remains a potent sign of the imperial university.

Because it suffers from the doubly plagued condition of being non-Western as well as ancient, Sanskrit occupies a most peculiar position in the academy.

If, in Indian schools and colleges, it is most often presented as a language that preserves a moral discourse about great origins, in America it becomes a tool for conducting cultural and historical anthropology. This may be symptomatic of a larger quandary regarding the very function of the humanities in the modern world. These two discourses, the moral and the anthropological, appear to have divided between them the field of the humanities. The one announces, in varying tones, that the value of the humanities lies primarily in their ability to retain a sense of the human as a moral (and not only a rational or scientific) agent, and the other privileges, instead, the analytic function of the humanities. The analytic humanities may appear preferable to their older cousin, the moral humanities, but they nevertheless arrive with their own prejudices. These almost invariably find their basis in the belief that only the most *current* knowledge, the one most recently born, may be considered knowledge, properly speaking: that is to say, something that has the capacity to instruct and teach. All other knowledges exist only as *archives* of knowledge; representations of the intellectual immaturity of other cultures and times. Undoubtedly such a hierarchy arises from the very idea of knowledge, which would be meaningless if it did not disavow other knowledges. The more the modern university sees itself as a site for "knowledge-production," the more stridently it will follow this logic, with all its attendant offshoots, including the problematic espousal of a multiculturalism that becomes the compensatory space for cultural diversity, "tolerance," relativism, and so on. "Multiculturalism" often becomes the site to which the moral humanities are relegated, so that the analytic humanities may continue with their more serious business. Simply questioning the peculiar status of Sanskrit in the university would not amount to much if we did not also note the larger frame which supports its marginalization. In a fundamental way, nothing will change until the very task of the humanities is redefined.

At present, at least in the United States, there seems to be a prevalent idea that Sanskrit texts may only be studied by those with highly specialized interests, usually in religious studies or anthropology. Thus the reading of Sanskrit texts, when it occurs in the university, takes place in limited arenas that have themselves acquired some of the characteristics long associated with Sanskrit. The most striking of these characteristics is the isolation—the protection, if you will—of Sanskrit literature, both from other literatures (whether Indian or non-Indian) and from current concerns regarding the possibility and the politics of interpretation. Barring some notable exceptions, modern scholarship has not engaged with the literariness of these texts and has usually discussed them from a historical, philological, or anthropological perspective.

This book suggests that a specifically literary approach—by which I don't mean an approach that "applies" something called literary theory but simply an approach that foregrounds the act of reading itself—might enable us to engage these texts differently. It might lead us to perceive them as neither antiquarian pieces of archival interest nor the testaments and guards of a severely hierarchical community but rather as texts whose import and significance always leaves something to be determined. A literary reading, in this sense, would not be a reading that is more attentive to the generic or the aesthetic attributes of texts but instead a reading that remains attentive to what, in a text, *constitutively* exceeds or even unravels the production of knowledge. It would be a reading that may at times be contradictory or incoherent, not because it is careless but because it *gives itself* to a text that itself follows, in fragmentary or fleeting ways, several uneven itineraries.

Part of the impetus for writing this book came from a desire to cross the boundaries that still seem powerful in the university: between area studies and comparative literature; "Indology" and postcolonial studies; "classical" and modern literatures. It seems oddly befitting that the story of Sanskrit—the great legislator of divisions—be told in the hope of fracturing these, and other, institutional divisions.

1

Smara: The Memory/Love of Kalidasa

An idiot aspiring to a poet's fame
I shall go to ridicule,
Like a dwarf with outstretched arms
Greedy for fruit up high.

—Kalidasa, *Raghuvaṃśa*

But Kalidasa cannot be spared from the suspicion of foreknowledge and dexterity. As soon as we begin reading him we know that he is far more self-conscious than Valmiki—perhaps even than Ashvaghosha—and also more sophisticated and decadent.

—Buddhadeva Bose, *Modern Poetry and Sanskrit Kavya*

In an essay first published in 1907, the Bengali writer Rabindranath Tagore presents a reading of Kalidasa's best-known play *Abhijñānaśākuntala* (*The Recognition of Sakuntala;* also often referred to as *Śakuntalā,* after the name of its heroine). Tagore's essay is concerned with articulating the particular strengths of Sanskrit drama by emphasizing its difference from Western drama, and to this end Tagore compares Kalidasa's play with Shakespeare's *The Tempest.* For Tagore, Kalidasa's work is singular in its ability to unite nature with law on the one hand and humanity on the other. Thus nature mediates between the realm of principle and the realm of the human, allowing us to see a world perfectly and beautifully cleansed of dissonance. Of *Śakuntalā,* Tagore writes: "In this poem, as there is the union of nature with rule and principle, there is also the union of nature with humankind. I think no country other than India could have brought about this sense of implicit union between dissimilarities."[1]

In retrospect, we perceive how such a reading contributes to the romantic reconstruction of Indian antiquity that was part of the nationalist response to colonialism. Indeed, the ambivalent position taken by the essay in its evocation of Europe is telling: on the one hand, Goethe's admiration for *Śakuntalā* is mentioned as desirable validation, and on the other, the essay is concerned with foregrounding a specifically Indian ethos that is fundamentally different from a Western worldview. One of the distinctive marks of this ethos, as described by Tagore, lies in its conception and representation of nature. It is easy today to critique Tagore's implicit orientalism, but we should not ignore in his remarks a postcolonial analysis that attempts to establish a decisive connection between the politics and the aesthetics of imperialism.[2]

Thus Tagore proposes that in *The Tempest,* nature is presented as an adversary that must be conquered through power and force, but in *Śakuntalā,* it appears as part of the human world, linked to human beings through ties of fellowship. The value of the Sanskrit play lies in its ability to present a synthesis between nature and "rule," both in its depiction of the forest hermitage, "a place where nature and contemplation, beauty and restraint are united," and in its portrayal of the love between King Dusyanta and the forest-dwelling Sakuntala—a love that must learn to accommodate natural passion to the restraint of social life. The Indian play thus provides a better, less violent, and more refined model of government. Tagore writes that "placed at the meeting point of constraint and freedom, the play *Śakuntalā* has acquired a rare quality. Its joys and sorrows, unions and partings are all brought about through the encounter of these two elements."[3]

The move from the pair nature/rule to the pair freedom/constraint appears to be a characteristically modern move in this context, for it would be hard to find in Sanskrit poetry an equivalent valorization of "freedom"—one strong enough to render it a categorically privileged term. Indeed, the opposition between freedom and constraint, and the concomitant desire for a harmonious mediation between them, gain particular intensity precisely in modern reflections on democracy and law. Elsewhere in his work, Tagore makes a distinction between "society" and "nation" that similarly evokes this opposition: "society" restrains individual freedom harmoniously, it provides a "natural regulation" of human relationships, whereas the nation exercises a merely "mechanical" regulation, being itself an expression of the "organized self-interest of a whole people."[4]

How would Kalidasa's work respond to this concept of "natural regulation," that is to say, to a rule that is at once the rule *of* nature, and rule *by* nature? Or at an even more primary level, how are "nature" and "rule" figured in this work? These terms allow us to discuss several related dimensions of the text: its representation of passion, immediacy, gender, kingship, and, most significantly, love. Reading the play along with some of the commentaries it has elicited, I will suggest here that the play performs a complex cultural task. Taking our cue from Tagore, we could say that one of its projects may indeed be to represent rulership as a moral, rather than a politically-violent, institution. A dual nature is summoned to perform this task: a nature that is to be mastered (associated, of course, with femininity) and a nature that provides sanction for mastery and law (associated with masculinity). Love emerges in the play as the aesthetic movement that relates these two aspects of "nature" and renders seductive the authority of the king. It does so by producing a wide-ranging heterosexual economy and by eroticizing subjection. The appearance of courtly love is thus fundamentally linked to the ideology of rule, power, and kingship. However, the inscription of love in the text may be more complex. The "nature" that is variously associated with instinct, animality, femininity—that which is *available* to mastery—also resonates as a figure for a lost world of immediacy and, by association, for the experience of a full, spontaneous, and pure love. Thus the feminine and the instinctual are at once subordinated and circuitously privileged, linked to a world that is desired but lost. Indeed, *Abhijñānaśākuntala* may be read as a play whose very plot unfolds the dual associations carried by the Sanskrit word *smara,* which may signify *both* love and memory and indeed indicates an intimate semantic relation between the two. The play suggests that love may constitutively share with memory its focus on a lost presence. It is like memory insofar as it depends on the power of the past moment (of passion) to survive and to affect the future. Keeping this in mind, I have attempted to remain attentive to the backward glance of love in Kalidasa's work and to those gestures in the text that repeat this glance.

The plot of *Abhjñānaśākuntala* is briefly as follows. King Dusyanta goes hunting in the forest and, chasing after a deer, enters the hermitage of a sage. There he meets the beautiful Sakuntala, daughter of an *apsarā* (a divine seductress), and falls in love with her. The sage, Sakuntala's adoptive father, is away on a journey, and in his absence Dusyanta convinces Sakuntala to contract a "gandharva" marriage with him—to sleep with him without formal rites. Leaving his ring with her, he goes back to the city, promising to send for her in a few days. After he leaves, a visiting sage, Durvasa, known for his formidable wrath, comes to the hermitage, but Sakuntala, apparently absorbed in a reverie of her lover, fails to notice his arrival. Enraged by her lack of hospitality, he curses her, saying that the object of her contemplation will forget her and will not even recognize her on sight. Sakuntala's distraught friends plead with the sage to ameliorate the curse, and finally he relents, stipulating that Dusyanta's ring will enable the recognition of Sakuntala.

Her friends decide to shield Sakuntala from knowledge of both the curse and its remedy, only advising her to show Dusyanta his ring if he seems unsure of her identity. She eventually goes to the city to meet the king, who, of course, does not recognize her and alleges that the child she carries in her womb cannot be his. When Sakuntala attempts to show him his ring, she realizes that she has lost it at a river shrine on the way.[5] Humiliated and grief-stricken by the king's public rejection, she appeals to the earth to rescue her and is transported away to a celestial hermitage by the aid of her divine mother.

Meanwhile, a fisherman finds the ring in the belly of a fish, and it is brought to the king. On seeing the ring, the king recalls everything and is consumed by remorse. Now he begins pining for his lost love and castigating himself for his cruelty. In the last scene, he visits the divine hermitage where Sakuntala now lives with her son and is reunited with her.

Turning Neck, Backward Glance

At the very beginning of the play, in the transition between the prologue and the play, we are introduced to some of the major motifs in the text in an exchange between one of the female actors and the director (*sutradhāra,* literally: one who holds the threads). The conversation, foregrounding the self-conscious theatricality of the production, is of a kind often found at the beginning of Sanskrit plays. The director requests the woman to sing a song in praise of the charms of summer to entertain the audience, and she complies by singing a verse about young girls adorning themselves with bee-kissed flowers. First expressing his enchantment with the song, the director then asks her which play they should now present for their audience and the actress reminds him that they had already decided to perform the new play called "The Recognition of Sakuntala." In response, the director says:

> Oh yes, I am reminded. For a moment I forgot. Because:
> I was forcefully carried away by the attractive rhythm of your song,
> Just as King Dusyanta was by the swiftly moving deer. (1.5)[6]

At this point, the two of them leave the stage, and we see King Dusyanta entering, as though on a chariot, chasing a deer.

Let us pause here to take note of the language of this brief passage. The moment of forgetting, which will assume central importance in the play, is presented here as a moment of being diverted or distracted by beauty. Commenting on these lines, Barbara Stoler Miller writes, "The actress' singing, like the beautiful movements of the magical antelope, or the art of poetry, makes the audience 'forget' the everyday world *(laukika)* and enter the fantastic *(alaukika)* realm of imagination that is latent within it. The entire play is a reenactment of this idea."[7] We might add, however, that this "entering" into the fantastic realm is no light transport. The director claims that he forgot his earlier mention of the play because he was forcefully or violently carried away *(prasabhaṃ hṛtaḥ)* by the woman's song. The adjective *hāriṇ* (attractive, captivating), which describes the song, is related to the past participle *hṛta* (carried away or abducted). Both derive from the verb *hṛ:* to take or carry away, to lead, to rob, plunder, to captivate, charm, subdue, or influence.[8] The word occurs frequently in the text, and like many of the words through which the vocabulary of attraction, desire, and love crystallizes in Kalidasa's work, this one also presents a drama of seizing and transporting, of forced migration, played out between an active and a passive actor.

In the brief verse recited by the director, his own captivation by the song is compared with the king's captivation by the deer. This may be, of course, simply an elegant device used to convey the audience from the prologue to the play itself, a means to usher in Dusyanta's entry. But the comparison is so odd that it demands to be read more carefully. For though the analogy presents the king as the one who is affected, as if despite himself, drawn or led away by the charm of the deer, we also know that the deer is in fact the hunted one in this scene—the one who is vulnerable, who is being driven away and forced to flee by the advancing chariot of the hunter. Keeping in mind this moment of reversal, where the hunted is figured as the hunter, and the act of violence as the act of helplessness, let us consider the king's first verse, which turns the terrified deer into an object of aesthetic wonder and seduction. Entering the stage, the king exclaims that he and his charioteer have traveled a long way, *ākṛṣṭāḥ* (pulled or attracted) by the deer, and then goes on to describe the fleeing deer's backward turning neck as being *abhirāmaṃ* (delightful or charming):

> Look, with gaze fixed on the chariot following him, his neck
> gracefully turning again and again,
> From fear of the arrow falling, his hind quarters seem almost to
> enter his chest.
> Half-eaten grass falls on the path from his open mouth
> So swiftly he leaps that he appears to belong to the sky, not the
> earth. (1.7; 14)

The deer is beautiful, desirable *(abhirāmaṃ)* because of the grace of his neck, repeatedly turning to gauge the proximity of the chariot. The verse begins with the following compound: *grīvābhaṅgābhirāmaṃ* (one who is charming because of the turning of the neck), and immediately the veiled cruelty of the image becomes apparent. For not only is the deer's terror read as charming; the word used to describe the turning of the neck, *bhaṅga* (stretching out or turning) is itself noticeable, since its primary meaning is to break or shatter. Thus barely concealed in the grace of the turning neck lurks the shadow of the broken neck, the very fracture interrupting the motion of the verse and making space for analysis.[9] Once we perceive the silhouette of the broken neck, everything about the deer begins to disintegrate: the fixed gaze appears now a sign of death, and the beauty of the leaping body turns grotesque. The deer, it seems, has already been carved and reassembled: it has indeed become a creature of the other world, of the sky and not of the earth.

Let us begin our analysis of the play and of Kalidasa's work in general by focusing on this turning/broken neck and on some of the intersecting narratives that converge at this juncture. How does the turning of the deer become an object of aesthetic wonder? How does this turn come to signify seduction? The relation indicated here between the king/hunter and the deer allows us to follow a particular narrative of the erotic through the text and through Kalidasa's work as a whole. This narrative has to do with the feminization of the animal, the attempt to present even the violence of hunting—and correspondingly of kingship—as a desirable violence, and so on. But the movement of the body that turns toward the very point from which it moves away also draws our attention to the *figure* of ambivalence—the image, shape, and *gesture* of tension—which itself becomes a mark of the erotic in the play and in turn demands attention. Though it is clear that this figure functions more or less as a convention in Kalidasa's work, its conventionality does not erase its energy. By marking the necessity of resistance it correspondingly reveals the element of force in Kalidasa's depiction of desire.

Dusyanta's encounter with the deer is the first of a series of encounters staged between absolute power and absolute vulnerability, a contrast that is an integral part of the drama of the erotic in Kalidasa's work, as in many other works of Sanskrit poetry. Here, the encounter between power and vulnerability depends on the backward glance of the fleeing deer, for only that glance can convey to the hunter the terror of the deer and, correspondingly, the desired affirmation of his own power. This contrast is explicitly signaled a few lines later, when the king is prevented from killing the deer by a hermit who tells him that the deer belongs to the hermitage and is therefore inviolable. The hermit's words linger on the contrast between the force and brutality of the king's arrow and the softness and vulnerability of the deer's body, thus unavoidably rendering seductive the very act they appear to prohibit:

> Do not let your arrow fall on the tender body of the deer, like fire on a heap of flowers. How fragile the life of the deer, and how sharp your arrows, fierce like thunderbolts. (1.10; 18)

The hermit then goes on to counsel the king, saying that his weapon is meant for the protection of the distressed, not for injuring the innocent. "Protection" thus appears as the sublimation of aggression, but of course the work of sublimation can never be complete. Indeed, the constant confusion between the two generates a narrative that at once produces a new figure of the "romantic" hero—compassionate, protective, sensitive—and at the same time relies on the erotic potential of the aggressive hunter to fulfill this task. The king's relation to the animal thus becomes the charged locus where several discourses meet: it becomes the site where the ascetic's challenge to the king's temporal authority, deepened and inflected by the influence of "heterodox" (Buddhist or Jain) discourses, intersects with the generic requirements of courtly romance. At the beginning of *Śakuntalā,* the king is described as *mṛgayāvihāri* (1.30–31; 69): one whose diversion is the hunt, and it is the burden of the play to question and transform this epithet, even as it reinforces the ideal of kingship and masculinity that has generated it.[10]

A debate on the merits of hunting later in the play is of interest in this context, for while it presents an occasion for the king to relinquish his earlier passion for the hunt, it also lists, among the benefits of hunting, the fact that the chase allows the hunter to see the minds of animals transformed through fear and anger (2.5; 64). The full weight of the assumption that such a sight would be desirable in and of itself can only be gauged if we read it as referring not so much to an advantageous gain in knowledge as to an increase in pleasure. We may understand this pleasure by taking into account the various ways in which the hunted animal is feminized and femininity is eroticized specifically in terms of the hunt in numerous texts of Sanskrit poetry. The particular drama of the hunt is significant in these texts precisely because it combines so inextricably the elements of pursuit with the elements of violence. A most striking passage of this kind occurs in another of Kalidasa's texts, in a section from sarga 9 of the *Raghuvaṃśa,* which provides an extended description of King Dasaratha hunting.[11] Here, hunting is presented as a courtesan who seduces the king (9.69), and the king's addiction to the sport is implicitly critiqued by the events that unfold in the narrative. I will mention just one verse here, which describes how the king, poised to release his arrow, refrains from doing so when he sees the eyes of the gazelles, agitated by fear *(trāsa),* reminding him of the eyes of his lovers. These lovers are not shy and timid girls, as one might expect, but *prauḍhapriyā,* older, bold women who would not be afraid of "making eyes": "The beautiful eyes [of the gazelles] trembling in terror, reminded him of the fluttering eyes of bold lovers" (9.58). Mallinatha's fourteenth-century commentary says that the king withdraws his arrow at that moment because of "an excess of pity born from the memory of the confusion *(vibhrama)* of the beloved [women]."[12] The verse vividly exposes the close association between signs of mortal fear in animals and signs of feminine desire. We see how the two are intimately connected for the king, his perception of the animal's fear immediately turning into a reminder of his lovers' desire. If the hunt is addictive because it provides affirmation of one's mastery over the natural world (Dasaratha kills lions, we are told, because he resents their supposed kingship over other animals),[13] this addiction is explicitly linked to the fundamentally sexual aspect of mastery.

Thus Kalidasa's work draws our attention to the way the hunted animal merges with the figure of the desirable woman, and the deer in the opening scene of *Śakuntalā* presents a striking example of this. But the image of the fleeing deer, with its neck turned around, does not only suggest vulnerability. That turn or twist stages an image that is repeated in the text. The physical motion of the deer mirrors, in this instance, the inner motion of the king's own mind, which is pulled, on the one hand, by a desire to preserve the deer as an object of beauty, and on the other, by a desire to kill it. Hazariprasad Dvivedi, one of Kalidasa's most devoted readers, has also noted this ambivalence. He writes that the opening verse, which draws our attention to the charm of the turning neck, shows us that the king who wishes to hunt is at the same time a lover of beauty.[14] Correspondingly, we may say that the deer, turned back even as it runs forward, signals both a seduction and a retreat, or in a different register, both a desire for life and for death. Thus read, nothing would be accidental about the occurrence of the word *bhaṅga* in the verse, which superimposes the graceful turn on the violent break of the neck.

I dwell on the deer because this figure of a turning body, or of a body caught between two trajectories or two motions—in other words, a body that dramatizes, in its very movement, a tension or ambivalence—appears several times in Kalidasa's work and, in a particularly striking manner, in the work of at least one of his predecessors, the Buddhist writer Ashvaghosha. The production of a body pulled in two directions must be seen as a significant element of the textual emergence of desire. Desire, in these texts, or rather in the cultural lexicon inscribed within and by these texts, is recognized as that which gains its own luminosity only through being pitted against some other force, whether that force be external or internal. There must be an impediment, an obstruction, or an opposing pull, for desire to come into play. In *Śakuntalā,* the deer draws the reader's attention retrospectively, once we begin to notice how often this motion is repeated in the first act of the play. At the conclusion of the act, after the first meeting between Sakuntala and the king, when Sakuntala is about to leave with her friends, she pretends that her clothing has been caught on the branch of a tree, so as to turn back to steal one more glance at the king, and when she finally leaves she is described as turning back over and over again, thus echoing the image of the hunted deer. This passage follows one where the king has already described his own state of conflict with regard to her departure, saying that though he wishes to follow her, he is held back by *vinaya,* restraint or modesty:

> The movements of a desiring person follow his mental impulses.
> Thus, wishing to follow the Muni's daughter, I am suddenly checked
> by restraint. Though I have not moved from my place, it is as
> though I have [already] gone and returned. (1.26; 46)

And after her departure, in the last verse of the act, the king again expresses a similar feeling, this time by way of a striking simile:

> Like the Chinese cloth [silk] of a flag, being carried against the wind,
> The restless mind runs back, as the body moves forward. (1.31; 54)

In each of these three moments, the king's and Sakuntala's bodies appear to repeat the turning motion of the running deer. Though these images invite us to think of desire and restraint as symmetrical, we know, of course, that there is nothing symmetrical about them, and that the only function of restraint in this narrative is to heighten the experience of desire. In order to perceive how this might be an intervention on the literary scene and how Kalidasa might have significantly changed the economy of romance, let us briefly recall a verse written by his predecessor Ashvaghosha.

This verse occurs in the play *Saundarananda* (first century CE), which tells the story of the younger brother of the Buddha, Nanda by name. The full couplet is as follows:

> Taṃ gauravaṃ budhagataṃ cakarṣa bhāryānurāgaḥ punarācakarṣa
> Soaniścyānnāpi yayau na tasthau turaṅstaraṅgeṣviva rājhaṃsaḥ.
>
> The devotion due to the Buddha drew him and passion for his wife drew again;
> From indecision he could neither go nor stay, like a royal swan caught among the waves. (4.42)[15]

A verse following soon after continues the same theme:

> He was bound by attachment to desire, and drawn by passion for the law
> Turned around by sorrow, he went, like a boat in the cross-current of a river. (4.44)

Nanda's ambivalence takes a classic form here: he is pulled in one direction by sensual desire and in another by dharma: religion, law, righteousness. Ashvaghosha uses the same word, *anurāga* (passion), to describe Nanda's attachment to his wife in the first verse, and his attachment to the moral law in the second one. Both exert an equal pressure, so that he is turned around, revolved, twisted by sorrow. Finally he leaves his home to become a Buddhist monk, but he will continue to be tormented by his (in)decision for a long time.

It seems to me that this verse reveals something about the turning figure that throws light on the verses we find in Kalidasa's work. Ashvaghosha's verse, like Kalidasa's, appears to dramatize subjection to *both* the law of restraint and the law of desire. But for Ashvaghosha, the purpose of the tension is to highlight Nanda's eventual "victory" over passion. For Kalidasa, it is exactly the reverse. We know all along that it is the "other" force that will be negated and conquered—it indeed exists only to highlight the eventual "victory" of desire. This is most vividly illustrated by a verse from Kalidasa's *Kumārasaṃbhava* (The Birth of the Prince), which repeats a brief phrase from Ashvaghosha's text. The verse appears at the conclusion of the central episode in *Kumārasaṃbhava,* where the god Siva has finally been won over by Parvati, the daughter of the mountain, who has been practicing austerities to gain his love. In this decisive episode, Siva tests Parvati's devotion to him by appearing in the guise of a young ascetic who is scornful of Siva. With consummate skill, the scene plays out one of the most enduring relays of romantic love: between the one who knows and the one whose pleasure ultimately comes from not knowing. After the young Parvati has proved her fidelity by a spirited defense of Siva and is about to leave in anger and agitation, the god reveals himself to her:

> Saying, then I will go from here, the girl started moving, her bark-bodice slipping from her breasts,
> When the bull-bannered lord, assuming his own form, held her, with a smile.
> Seeing him, the daughter of the mountain-lord, all trembling and covered with perspiration, and having one foot raised to walk away, was uncertain whether to go or to stay, like a river obstructed by a mountain in the path. (5.83–84)[16]

"Na yayau na tasthau," She could not move or stay. We note exactly the same language—the same phrase—of ambivalence, as in Ashvaghosha's verse, yet Parvati's trajectory is perfectly opposed to Nanda's. The text makes it quite clear that Parvati's hesitation is not so much a sign of emotional or ethical ambivalence as of modesty; as Mallinatha's commentary succinctly says: "From shyness, this is the meaning." Unlike Nanda, for Parvati there is no essential conflict between law and desire, since what she desires is in fact the law—and not just any law, but the law of laws, the law of death, Siva himself. Whereas Nanda has to give up the life of the householder and of sensual gratification to become a renouncer, Parvati becomes an ascetic in order to gain sexual pleasure and domesticity. That is why, in describing the penance she undergoes, the text remains fascinated by her delicacy and youth, repeatedly dwelling on the contrast between the tenderness of her body and the harshness of the penance she performs. Indeed, it seems that even in describing Parvati's austerities, the real aim is always to present her as a sexual figure. Thus we see that at the moment when her strength and perseverance as an ascetic are most visible, when she has rebuked her arrogant visitor and asserted her own convictions, the narrative voice is compelled to draw attention to her femininity by mentioning that her bark garment has slipped—presumably because of her agitation—and revealed her breasts. In that moment of confusion, all determination and strength fall away, she becomes again a young girl *(bālā)*, tremulous, uncertain, perfectly embodying the vulnerability that constitutes this particular image of eros. She is a river impeded by a mountain: what more need be said?

We may then surmise that though Kalidasa's plays, like most love stories, revolve around some obstacle or prohibition, the function of such obstacles is always to enhance the movement of love. For his female protagonists in particular there is never an essential conflict between law and desire. Legitimate desire—that is to say, desire for the beloved who will be a husband, or for the husband himself—is in fact the duty of the woman, and nothing pulls her from this duty.[17] Dharma (religion, law, righteousness) for her is inseparable from the figure of the male beloved, and her subjection to that figure is endlessly eroticized, not only in Sanskrit drama but also in innumerable other texts of Indian literature. When the figure of Parvati becomes, for an instant, indistinguishable from the figure of Nanda, it impresses upon us this fundamental gap between the two texts. Not for Kalidasa the dread of the female body, the fear of treacherous desire, that is so central a part of Ashvaghosha's Buddhist text. Asceticism plays a role in Kalidasa's work only insofar as it can contribute to the drama of love. When Parvati becomes the double of Nanda, she in fact inverts Nanda's "decision" and places the ascetic impulse in the service of eros. In other words, she rewrites the narrative of asceticism and desire as it has been authorized from the ascetic perspective. We could therefore say that in Kalidasa's work, these figures which turn longingly, or pause hesitantly, do not so much enact as *mime* a conflict between duty and desire. Reframing the "pull" of duty as the pull of modesty, they reframe it now at the service of the erotic impulse.

The King and His Beloved

In this way romance comes on stage; it is no longer merely one element—a welcome but slight distraction—in the narrative of origin myths, wars, or struggles for succession but must generate on its own some of the suspense, tension, and antagonism of battle. Along with romance enters the romantic heroine, a creature quite unlike her epic counterpart. This distinction is particularly pronounced in the case of Sakuntala, whose story changes considerably in the passage she makes from the *Mahābhārata* to Kalidasa's play. In the *Mahābhārata,* before agreeing to sleep with Dusyanta, Sakuntala first asks the king to promise that the son born of their union will be his heir. Later, when she goes to meet him with their son, and he pretends not to recognize her, she delivers a sharp and spirited rebuke, which reminds the king of his moral duties and impresses upon him the value of wives. The story ends with a celestial voice confirming the truth of Sakuntala's story. The king now admits that he had gone through this ruse only to ensure that Sakuntala's son be recognized by the people as his legitimate heir. In this version we find no ring, no curse, and no loss of memory.

Kalidasa's Sakuntala has changed quite remarkably. Commenting on this change, Stephanie Jamison writes:

> The Sakuntala of the epic is a strong-minded girl, distinguished by her learning in the law. Before she sleeps with the king, she evades his verbal tricks and insists on extracting an agreement to recognize any child of the union as heir . . . The Sakuntala of Kalidasa is at first too awed by the king to speak to him; when she falls in love, she also falls into an almost catatonic languor; and when she is later rejected by the king (not by his own fault, in this version), she simply slinks away. . . . The play is a wonderful piece of poetry, but the bleaching of Sakuntala's character from her epic model is unsettling to some of us.[18]

Romila Thapar likewise comments on the contrast between the epic Sakuntala, whose "attitude is not that of a submissive subject" and who is "a forthright, free, assertive, high-spirited young woman,"[19] and Kalidasa's Sakuntala, who is "extremely shy and retiring, the romanticized persona of a woman of upper caste culture" (52). While the difference between the two figures is unmistakable, it may be a mistake to explain it by a hypothesis concerning the "actual" change of status of women. Instead, we should consider the role and function of the female beloved in Kalidasa's work. This role becomes most visible in the context of Kalidasa's focus on the court. Therefore I'd like to pay more attention to Thapar's observation that "there is in the play a rhetoric of political power based on the monarchical state" (48). As she notes, the "up-grading" of monarchy is a feature shared by several literary texts of the time. If we read Kalidasa's work in general as participating in the writing of kingship and its ideology, the function of the female beloved becomes more clear. Usually associated with some other lineage or place, and thus with a realm over which the king may not have direct power, the female beloved who submits to desire becomes also the effaced but nevertheless legible emblem of subjection itself.

The plays thus create an overdetermined scenario where erotic and political functions happily coincide. Indeed, most of Kalidasa's plays stage the female protagonist's susceptibility to the power of the king/lover in a rather unambiguous way. The master-servant relation is most vividly articulated in *Mālvikāgnimitram*, where the heroine Malvika is destined to spend a year as a servant in order to gain a suitable husband. She spends that year in the court of King Agnimitra, where her status as a servant gives rise to some discussion as the romance between the servant and the king develops. None of Kalidasa's other heroines occupies this space in quite so marked a manner, but most of them are in some way debased or punished, if not directly by their lover, then by some other power. All these heroines have to go through a period of debasement/punishment in order to gain the one they love; culpability and servitude become interchangeable since what is significant is not guilt as such but rather the structural position of being susceptible to the force of authority.

Much of the erotic charge of the text is generated when this susceptibility to force shades into a vulnerability that requires protection. The beloved woman, like the land or the city under threat, is the one who most needs protection, *and therefore* her acute vulnerability is essential to her relationship to the king. Thus descriptions of sovereign power, of the king's relation to his subjects and to his city, all indicate that perhaps the most significant function of the figure of the beloved in these texts is to eroticize subjection to sovereign power: that is to say, to both sovereign protection *and* sovereign violence. It is in this light that we must understand why the king, who is supposed to be everyone's protector, almost invariably wounds the woman who loves him. As in his relation to the city, assault and protection sometimes become indistinguishable and reveal themselves as twin aspects of the same relation. In *Raghuvaṃśa*, when King Dasaratha goes to Mithila, where his sons will be married, his power over the king of Mithila is thus expressed: "He reached Mithila and surrounded it with his troops, damaging (tormenting) the trees in its gardens. The city, like a woman, endured the siege of love as a wife like the desired embrace of her beloved" (11.52). We would perhaps miss the significance of Kalidasa's work if we glossed over the immense rhetorical task performed by such passages. The king's claim to the land is at once naturalized and sexualized by way of the most powerful of all "naturalized" institutions, that of marriage. Thus, whether the female beloved is associated with "natural" landscapes or with the city—in each case, her function is to render seductive, by strength of association, the king's claim to the land.

We may also notice another feature these female protagonists share. Except for Parvati in *Kumārasaṃbhava,* all of Kalidasa's heroines marry kings who already have other wives, and the question of fidelity becomes significant in each work in one way or another. Indeed, in each text we find a moment of disclosure when the romantic ideal of (monogamous) love is exposed as a kind of strategic fantasy, and the king's access to other women is juxtaposed against the heroine's unwavering fidelity. This is true not only of Kalidasa's work but of several Sanskrit plays from that time. Though polygamy might be at odds with the ideal of courtly romance, it is also necessary for the erotic dynamic of the plot. The female lover's jealousy (like her fear) remains an integral part of the vocabulary of desire.

In all these instances, the representation of romance relies on a particular aestheticization of subjection. By rendering desirable the authority of the king, the female beloved assumes the place of the ideal subject, whose desire has merged perfectly with her duty. She thus enacts the appeal of subjection itself. If Kalidasa was indeed a poet at the court of Chandragupta II, as is widely believed, and if he lived at a time when imperial conquest was often sealed by a marriage alliance between the emperor and a princess of the conquered land, the sociopolitical power of such an appeal would become even more vivid.[20] In other words, given our current understanding of the historical context, the association of the female beloved with the imperial subject appears to be both a plausible and a far-reaching move. One may easily imagine how the figure of the subjected yet desired (and desiring) woman comes to play a complex role in the political aesthetics of empire. Because her subjection is dramatized through a series of metonymic associations, Kalidasa's work is also able to eroticize the king's (violent) power over the forest, the animal world, and the city through the implicit feminization of these domains.

Doubtless we now inhabit a different terrain, yet we have not entirely escaped the political space opened in this way. I would speculate that the figure of the perpetually vulnerable (and constitutively apolitical) "civilian" in contemporary discourse is among the modern heirs of this figure of the beloved woman. Like the beloved, the civilian is the figure in whose name, and for whose protection, sovereign violence may be exercised with impunity. It is not accidental that women and children are most often mentioned in news and human rights reports as civilians par excellence. The division between the soldier and the civilian not only highlights the femininity of the civilian but also serves to eclipse the stronger and more capable figure of the citizen. In contemporary discourse, the civilian inevitably emerges as the *noncitizen*:

the one who seems to have disavowed political responsibility, whose political function is to require protection and hence to legitimize the exercise of state violence. Like Kalidasa's deer, who calls forth the king's protection at the same time that he tempts the hunter, or like the heroines who elicit, in the tropes of heterosexual romance, both violence and protection, the civilian is the necessary counterpart of contemporary state power.

Cursed Love

In focusing on the symbiosis between nature and rule, readers of *Abhijñānaśākuntala* wish often to foreground in the play a transition from a worse to a better desire, from a degraded to a privileged model of love. According to this reading, Sakuntala is cursed by the ascetic Durvasa because she is too absorbed in her love to be mindful of the demands of hospitality. Both Rabindranath Tagore and Hazariprasad Dvivedi thus read the play as a moral parable—as a lesson that cautions against immediate passionate attachment and valorizes, instead, an attachment born of discipline and true longing for the beloved. Are there other ways of reading the moments of prohibition on which Tagore and Dvivedi focus: the pivotal moment of Durvasa's curse, for instance, or the even more violent moment in *Kumārasaṃbhava* when Kama, the god of love, is burned to death by the ascetic Siva?

Like Tagore, Dvivedi reads both texts as portraying the "harmony between love and asceticism." In both *Śakuntalā* and *Kumārasaṃbhava,* Dvivedi writes, Kalidasa has shown that "love born of physical attraction is unstable; a single stroke may bring it to an end."[21] *Kumārasaṃbhava* describes the seduction of Siva and his marriage to Parvati, daughter of the Himalaya mountain. In the fourth canto of the poem, Kalidasa narrates an episode from a popular myth: the burning of Kama, god of love, by Siva, the supreme ascetic. Kama has been asked by the god Indra to help in Siva's seduction by Parvati, for the son born of their union will help the gods to vanquish their adversaries. Just as Kama is about to shoot his arrow at Siva, Siva spies him and with a single glance reduces him to ashes. Later Kama will be resurrected, but in the interim Kalidasa presents us with the lament of Kama's wife Rati, who expresses not just her own despair but the despair of all embodied beings, whose happiness depends on Kama (4.10).

Dvivedi's response to the burning of Kama is closely connected to Tagore's reading of *Śakuntalā.* Both make evident a paradox concerning the concept and representation of nature. On the one hand, Kalidasa is extolled because he is a poet of nature, and the human relation to nature, as described in his work, is one of close kinship and affection. On the other hand, nature in these readings is also presented as that which must be purified and purged *of itself* in order to play a suitably beneficent role in human life. This is a familiar logic, but one so powerful and far-reaching that we may still be living within its reach. Nature, or more accurately, the "first making"— that which is made first *(prakṛti)*—is an impossible figure for that which is to be at once emulated *and* overcome. It is the figure for that which is prior to, or outside of, institutionality itself, and the positing of this priority becomes necessary both to legitimize and to question the "work" of culture and institution. Analyses associated with "deconstruction," and most of all the texts of Jacques Derrida, have rigorously exposed the movement of such a logic in Western metaphysics and politics. The series of oppositions put into play by Kalidasa's work (nature/culture, female/male, lust/asceticism, instinct/mastery) exhibits such a pattern. The first term of each pair must at once be maintained (for without it the second would be meaningless) and, at the same time, rendered subordinate. The task of the second term is to diminish, and not to erase, the first. Keeping this in mind, let us return to the moments of prohibition in these plays.

In reading Kalidasa's work in terms of a distinction between a love that is prohibited and one that is extolled, Tagore and Dvivedi themselves rely on a less apparent distinction between a bad and a good nature. The latter is consonant with hegemonic human institutions, and the former subversive of them. As we know, the project of uniting nature with law perhaps always entails naturalizing and elevating a *particular* custom to the status of law. However, "nature" may not ultimately be the real focus of concern. Indeed, it seems that the most significant aspect of Tagore's and Dvivedi's reading is its attachment to a certain "asceticism" as the ideal of culture. Asceticism, understood as the ideal of internalizing prohibition, of internalizing the law *as* prohibition, functions here as a way of warding off the threat posed by "nature"—that is to say, by the custom/culture consigned to immediate life.

Discussing the moment after the burning of Kama in *Kumārasaṃbhava,* when Parvati becomes an ascetic herself in order to win the love of Siva, Dvivedi writes,

> Parvati understood that her naturally beautiful figure was of no avail, and started to prepare for penance. Having reduced all the ostentation of eternal spring to ashes in a single moment, Kalidasa

> occupied himself with describing Parvati's penance. Penance (asceticism) is the purification of nature. *(Tapasyā prakṛti kā saṃskār hai).* Destroying perversion, Kalidasa raised the palace of culture. Misguided yearning for consummation is the perversion of life; penitential prayer for love is the purification of life. Solitary renunciation is fruitless like solitary love. A fruitful love is only possible (only takes birth) in an ascetic grove *(tapovan).* The fifth section of *Kumārasaṃbhava* presents us with a glimpse of that ascetic grove. It is as alluring as it is peaceful. The ascetic grove is the source of Kalidasa's inspiration. *Abhijñānaśākuntalam* starts with the ascetic grove and ends there as well.[22]

A little later in the same essay he writes,

> Kalidasa has seen the completion of the human being in the fellowship of nature. Where the human being moves in oblivion, at the behest of natural instinct, there he invites destruction; but when he transforms himself through asceticism in such a way that nature in all its forms conducts itself at his behest, then he invites immortality. Kalidasa has made manifest the indication-following form of nature. Here, nature follows the mind purified by penance *(Yahān prakṛti tapasyā dvārā saṃskṛt chitt ki anuvartini hai).*[23]

The passage reveals the uncertain status of nearly all its principle terms: nature, humanity, and fellowship. For Dvivedi, the burning of Kama comes to signify at once the vanquishing of unruly nature, of lust, and of female pride in beauty. Though the close link established here between renunciation and the conquest of nature is not surprising, we must also examine what exactly is being valorized under the names *saṃskṛt* (literally: made together or assembled; also: purified or refined) and *saṃskṛti* (culture/purification). It seems clear that these terms are linked to mastery—over that which has been consigned to immediate life, whether internal or external—and that this mastery is implicitly associated with masculinity. Both Parvati and Sakuntala become worthy by renouncing their "feminine" charm in favor of the hardships of penance; according to Dvivedi, Parvati "understands that her naturally beautiful figure is of no avail."

But as we have seen, this figure is indeed *of* avail. In the last section, I suggested that Kalidasa's work does not really inhabit the frame that privileges asceticism as internalization of prohibition. The eroticization of asceticism is perhaps most vividly articulated in *Kumārasaṃbhava* as it draws on the repertory of myths concerning Siva and Kama. Although Kama is "killed" by Siva, it is clear that the burning of Kama is also a sign of Kama's victory. Here, Kalidasa's work connects itself with a strand that runs through other versions of this myth and that celebrates precisely the erotic aspect of the severe, solitary ascetic who "accumulates" and holds in reserve his sexual energy. As Wendy Doniger writes in her study of Siva narratives, "Even without the description of the manner in which Siva is 'burnt' by Kama before he can return the attack, the very act of burning Kama betrays Siva's vulnerability and his innately erotic nature."[24] The burning of Kama—the fact that he must be destroyed by burning, rather than by any other means—forcefully reveals the shape of revenge, by showing us that the one who burns has already been burned—and indeed, branded by Kama. It is not that Kama now exists in a sublimated state (the heat of lust metamorphosed into the heat of asceticism or transformed into a tranquil and disinterested appreciation of beauty) but rather that the very act of destroying Kama—of apparently staging his disappearance—will position Siva as Parvati's suitor and, eventually, as her magnificently virile husband. In combining great asceticism and great eroticism in the figure of Siva, the myth responds to the following question: How is it possible to enjoy (absolute) desire without losing (absolute) mastery? It seems to me that Kalidasa's work, and in particular his representation of this episode, draws our attention precisely to this aspect of the burning of Kama. The violence directed against Kama, which Dvivedi reads as the destruction of "perversion," of unstable and unreliable lust—as violence *against* (a kind of) love—should instead be read as the violence *of* "love"; that is to say, the violence through which Siva establishes himself as a properly aggressive and masterly figure, and hence as the proper object of Parvati's (and the reader's) desire. Thus Siva's rejection of Kama—the ascetic's rejection of desire and instinct—is incorporated as a pivotal moment in the very trajectory of desire.

Durvasa's curse in *Abhijñānaśākuntala* may be similarly analyzed. The story of Sakuntala is also found, in different and much abbreviated form, in the epic *Mahābhārata*. The curse, however, is Kalidasa's innovation: in the epic narrative, the king has not in fact forgotten Sakuntala but only pretends to do so, until a divine voice confirms the paternity of Sakuntala's son. Then the king claims that he adopted the ruse in order to allay any doubts his subjects might have entertained about the child's claim to the throne. The curse and other changes introduced by Kalidasa have been read in different ways by modern critics. The dominant nationalist reading remains inscribed within a patriarchal economy. It reads the curse as the condemnation of lust, of single-minded passion—in brief, of a love that obliterates and forgets duty. But this reading has also been questioned. In an extended discussion of Kalidasa's play in comparison with the text of the epic narrative, Romila Thapar notes that the curse is "the stereotypical impediment of the folk-tale; its object is a woman and therefore she becomes responsible for the turn of events."[25] She goes on to ask whether the curse and the ring might have been introduced because "they gloss over the real tension between Sakuntala and Dusyanta, namely, the paternity of her child." On this account, the curse is brought into the picture in order to absolve Dusyanta of blame; his love for Sakuntala can no longer be called into question and thus the curse enables him to fulfill the ideal of the romantic hero. Thus Thapar writes that "romantic love hides the loss of empowerment [of women.]"[26] Indeed, the significance of the curse can scarcely be overestimated, for besides shifting the blame (for Sakuntala's desertion) from the king to the heroine herself, it also allows the poet to introduce in the story the period of separation and longing *(viyoga)* often considered necessary for the aesthetic representation of love in Sanskrit poetry.

Rabindranath Tagore, in his reading of the curse, also reflects upon its relation to the character of Dusyanta. He points toward one of the most revealing moments in the play: the moment before Shakuntala's arrival at court, when we hear one of Dusyanta's other wives singing a song about the king's infidelity: "O honey-bee! Greedy for new honey, you are now pleased only by the lotus. Having earlier kissed the mango-blossom, how have you now forgotten her?" In a most perceptive move, Tagore calls this moment " a small rent in the veil through which we can get an idea of the royal sin" and notes that "the desertion of Sakuntala by the amorous Dusyanta, which in real life would have happened as the natural consequence of his character, is here brought about by the curse of Durvasa."[27] Like Thapar, he reads the curse as a ploy that protects Dusyanta's status as a romantic hero. This is persuasive, but perhaps we can take it a little further.

Like the burning of Kama by Siva, Durvasa's curse may be read as the ostensible prohibition on eros that intensifies the movement of eros. Not of a more pure or selfless eros, as Tagore and Dvivedi suggest, but rather of an eros even more profoundly attached to its secret inner exigence: in this case, the production of female abjection as delectable. If, following Romila Thapar's indication, we consider the ascetic Durvasa as the double of King Dusyanta,[28] we could say that together they enable the staging of Sakuntala's helplessness in the face of male desire and demand, and that this helplessness is indeed a necessary element of the erotic drama itself.

To read Durvasa's curse in the moral register—whether as an indictment of Sakuntala's *or* Dusyanta's lapses—would be to miss something crucial about the heterosexual economy that is articulated here. Through different avenues, I have been trying to suggest that the ascetic's "no" in this economy is entirely aligned with *affirming* the woman's subjection to the king/lover. The ascetic's prohibition is not a real prohibition, for in the end, the ascetic/father's desire is not different from the king's. In fact, there is no conflict between the ascetic and the king, who are co-conspirators here. Rather than "hiding" the woman's loss of power, romantic love actively produces the (desirable) woman as powerless.

So far, I have investigated the various ploys by means of which a particular figure of desire is articulated in Kalidasa's work, and I have proposed that the task of this figure is to eroticize a (necessarily heterosexual) relation between sovereignty and vulnerability, and hence to legitimize and naturalize the power of the king. But does this analysis exhaust the force of these texts? In accounting for the most compelling figures and gestures through which the text foregrounds its manifest or latent themes, have I succeeded in accounting for the text itself? On the contrary, does not reading the work as a text entail precisely an awareness of that which escapes the logic not just of sovereignty but also of any single interpretation? If, like generations of other readers, we still find it possible to remain enthralled by Kalidasa's work, it is not only because we continue to be produced, as it were, by the political economy inscribed by that work, or simply because of the "beauty" of its language. I would suggest that it is rather because the work does not *let itself be accounted for:* the closer we draw to it, the more swiftly it escapes, somewhat in the manner of the tantalizing deer chased by King Dusyanta in the opening scene of *Śakuntalā.*

For instance, a reflection upon love in *Śakuntalā* would surely have to consider, in addition to what I have discussed so far, the theme of memory and forgetting. Durvasa's curse also becomes a means for Kalidasa to introduce this theme, which may play more than an expedient or strategic role. Indeed, in suggesting that love remembers, re-creates, or stitches together something initially lost or forgotten, the play recalls us to the intimate relation between love and memory already inscribed in the Sanskrit word *smara*—which may mean both love *and* memory. Keeping this in mind, we might consider the hypothesis that it is not so much sin and penance that is essential to love but forgetting and remembering. What would be specific to a concept of love that is intrinsically linked to recollection? How would we understand this concept? As several readers have noted, this is indeed one of the central preoccupations of the play.[29] Here, I will focus on what seems to be the most insistent element of this connection between love and memory—one that may also be connected to the status of the natural that I've been attempting to delineate.

In *Abhijñānaśākuntala*, the one who is forgotten is the early Sakuntala, so deerlike as to be almost a doe herself, so akin to the creeper, the leaf, the petal, as to be simply one more instance of the natural world whose submission to the king is eroticized by the movement of the drama.[30] When the king remembers her later, however, he paints a picture of her: she is still standing amid trees and creepers but is now explicitly a work of representation. In the fifth act of the play, after the king has seen his ring and remembered his marriage to Sakuntala, he is consumed by sorrow and remorse. Now, in the city, amid the palace environs, he recalls the hermitage, the forest, and his beloved, recalls all those incidents that had already been described in the first act, and paints a picture that would allow him to see an image of his beloved. The *apsarā* Sanumati, a friend of Sakuṇtala, secretly watches all of this and astutely notes that the king's experience now follows the lines of the painting (*yathālikhitānubhāvyeṣaḥ*, 6. 20–21; 236); meaning that he experiences again his meeting with Sakuntala as he paints her, the act of inscription now governing the movement of memory.

Thus we see that it is essential for the play that the pastoral love be forgotten and later remembered—as a text. Indeed, this excessive and violent rupture with immediacy seems almost gratuitous, given that even in the first act Kalidasa's evocations of nature had already marked "natural objects"—bees, flowers, creepers, and deer, as well as "natural passion"—as *conventions.* All those images that recur, not just in this play but in Sanskrit poetry in general—the creeper entwined around the tree, the bee's cruel flirtation with all and sundry blossoms, the river's amorous embrace of the sea—far from persuading us about the "naturalness" of a heterosexual economy with its concomitant laws of strength and weakness, force and vulnerability, power and subjection, in fact persuade us of nothing so much as the *impossibility* of the appearance of a "natural" landscape. All of nature has already been cultured, gendered, heterosexed; the natural cannot appear, except within the terms of this economy, just as the forest cannot appear, except as marked by the hyperculture of ascetic will to power. How is it possible to conceive of Sakuntala as an archetype of pastoral innocence, as generations of German (and Indian) readers have insisted, when her cognition has never been anything other than a *recognition,* even within the structure of Kalidasa' play?

Perhaps Sanskrit classical drama reveals a peculiar recognition of its own highly stylized and wrought presentation of love when it foregrounds the connection between love, memory and loss. The inscription of love as memory may signal that what is called love can only appear in these texts as a sign of its own absence. The "nostalgia" of Kalidasa has not gone unmarked by modern critics, though they might account for it in somewhat different terms. Thus Romila Thapar writes, "In romanticizing the *āśrama* [hermitage], one may well ask if Kalidasa is not reflecting a nostalgia for the forest which seems to have already overtaken urban culture."[31] In a different vein, Stephanie Jamison focuses on the retrospective element in "classical" Sanskrit poetry when she discusses the "creative nostalgia" of poets like Kalidasa: "Sanskrit in the classical era, the classical moment, involves a self-conscious revival, a deliberate appropriation of the language of an earlier era, and a way to restore the gold of a previous golden age . . . The conservatism of the early Guptas, their conscious harking back to previous days of imperial glory, specifically from the Mauryan empire of the fourth to the second century B.C., . . . have frequently been commented on."[32]

Jamison's argument concerns Sanskrit literature's political evocation of the past and the revival of the Sanskrit language itself as a "carrier of culture" during the so-called classical period. It is a provocative argument for thinking historically about the symbolic political status of the Sanskrit language. In terms of our concerns, it may be most significant for indicating how the past, as the figure of lost authority, becomes mapped onto the past as the figure of immediacy and of a passion that can only be recalled. Even at the level of the plot, we notice that in this corpus of texts, love is frequently that which is remembered, and remembered as loss. In his brilliant reading of love and memory in Sanskrit poetry, Charles Malamoud draws our attention to this configuration:

> *Smarasi Smara* . . . "You Remember, Love . . .", the alliterative construction which opens a passage of Kālidāsa's *Kumārasaṃbhava,* is a symbol of sorts for all poetic reflection on the subject of love as remembrance. Love is itself called upon to recall that which it once was, in a formula that leads one to understand that *it only is when it has been.*[33]

The repetition of *smara* in the opening phrase of the verse cited by Malamoud is particularly poignant since it is part of the lament of Rati, Smara's wife, after his death. The phrase, which may also be read as a question—"Do you remember?"—also carries a grain of censure. It suggests that the person to whom it is addressed has forgotten (love itself), and that the one who remembers is now alone in remembering. Love comes to be in all its emotive finery only when it is recalled, and it is recalled only when it has been lost. Bilhana's *Caurpañcāśikā,* with its haunting refrain, "Even now. . . I remember," testifies precisely to this melancholic aspect of love. This may be one reason why the period of separation, *viyoga,* is so essential to Sanskrit poetry, and why these poems repeatedly stage the narrative of love as an act of representation and remembering.[34] Though *viyoga* obviously fulfills some narrative or generic requirements ("union" by itself cannot produce a story), it also becomes structurally complicit in producing "love" as that whose recognition depends on its recollection.

Durvasa's curse may now acquire a different dimension. An instance of the power of language, a curse (like a blessing) attests to that dimension of language that enables it to be productive rather than merely mimetic. However, in the play the curse becomes, in the most comprehensive sense, the curse of language itself—that is to say, the curse of (a theatrical or conventional) language that would render impossible the appearance of love, except as memory. Indeed, the curse—Kalidasa's innovation and addition to the received tale—is in many ways the most overdetermined element of the text. From a moral perspective, it is the antidote to excess. It befalls the lover who is entirely occupied with her love, who is *ananyamānasā*—one whose mind has no room for another—and robs her of her love. From a psychoanalytic perspective, it enacts the Father's apparent prohibition, which in fact intensifies the movement of love and becomes a crucial element of the story of desire. And on the narrative level, it enables love to emerge as memory by staging the banishing of love.

I would like to suggest that for us, there may be yet another way of reading the curse. This would not entail reading it as a moral rebuke that becomes part of a satisfactory story about the protagonists' education. Instead, it would entail reading it in terms of our own "education." What if we took Durvasa's call to hospitality seriously? That is to say, if we did not read it as the call of an imperious, disgruntled, or jealous father but rather as the call of hospitality itself? In some ways we are closer here to Dvivedi's and Tagore's readings of the play, but not entirely so. In remaining attentive to the difficulties of writing about a text entangled in several incompatible affiliations and commitments (for which the names "political," "emotional," or "aesthetic" can never suffice), the call of hospitality can assume a significance beyond cultural ethics. Let us recall here that the Sanskrit word for guest, *atithi,* designates not the stranger or the enemy, as the Latin *hostis* does, but rather the one whose arrival is not fixed, the one who may arrive without warning. *Ātithyam,* hospitality, would thus name that which is due to the undated; it would indicate a relation to the other and to the time of the other that may be at odds with the retrospective temporality signaled by *smara.* The other interrupts, without warning. The curse may thus reveal the tension between a love predicated on loss and recollection, and a hospitality connected to openness to the untimely. This tension, which is integral to the text, must become linked today to our own encounter with the text. I would suggest that beyond the apparent moral parable, and even beyond the political allegory I have attempted to sketch out above (following and extending the comments of Romila Thapar), we may find inscribed in this tension two different modes of relating to a work whose temporal relation to us remains uncertain, historical time notwithstanding. Kalidasa's work cannot be read only as coming from a past that is forever inaccessible: a past that can only be recalled as the lost past of a nation, a language, or a culture. It only remains a text insofar as it receives the various and sometimes incompatible responses, readings, and investments of its readers. The fertile tension between *smara* and *ātithyam* sustains the structure of not only love but also reading and thinking.

Exile

Abhijñānaśākuntala is not the only one of Kalidasa's texts where a curse sets the plot in motion. Always pronounced by an older, powerful male figure, curses are also pivotal in *Vikramorvaśīya* and *Meghadūta.* In the latter, the one who is cursed is also male; a Yakṣa, a semidivine being, who is also the central character of the poem. The poem implies that like Sakuntala, he fails in the performance of his duties because he is distracted by love and is therefore cursed by his master, Kubera, the god of wealth, to spend a year in exile, away from his beloved wife. Longing for her, he sees a cloud and begs it to convey his message of love to his wife. He then goes on to describe the path the cloud will traverse to reach his wife, and the journey is presented as an elaborate saga of love, each section of the landscape being imagined in erotic terms. The most curious verse in the poem occurs at the very beginning; just as the Yakṣa is about to address the cloud, the poet says:

Dhūmajyotiḥ salilamarutāṃ sannipātaḥ kva meghaḥ
Sandeśārthāḥ kva patukaraṇaiḥ prāṇibhiḥ prāpṇīyāḥ
Ityautsukyadaparigaṇayanguhykastaṃ yayāce
Kāmārtā hi prakṛtikripaṇāścetanācetaneṣu

Where the cloud, a swirl of smoke, light, water, and wind
And where the import of messages, meant for vital beings,
  nimble hands.
Forgetting this in his eagerness, the Yakṣa pleaded with the cloud:
Those tormented by love are by nature rendered blind
And cannot tell conscious from unconscious.[35]

How can the cloud, a mix of smoke and water, be the recipient of a message? The Yakṣa, in his eagerness, did not take account of that, for those tormented by love are pitiful, idiotic by nature, insofar as they cannot distinguish between conscious and unconscious objects. Condensed in this verse is the dilemma of the poet of love, at once envious and derisive of the love he describes. The poet's text must mark its own distance from the deluded consciousness of the Yakṣa, even as it imitates it; repeatedly performing the same "error" of which it accuses the Yakṣa, in its own personification of rivers, flowers, bees, and mountain. Since the poem would not exist without the Yakṣa's "blindness," such blindness may be obliquely extolled by the very lines that appear to mock it.

In a short lyrical essay about this poem (published in 1907), Rabindranath Tagore identifies the modern reader with the figure of the exiled Yakṣa. The reader is banished from the India of the poem, just as the Yakṣa has been banished from his homeland:

> The Yakṣa's cloud thus sails over hills, rivers, and cities, and with it go the sighs of the reader, afflicted by the sorrow of separation from his loved one. It was the India of the poet, where the loving-tender eyes of village wives had not yet learnt the artful play of eyebrows, and the town wives' long-lashed dark eyes, adept at beguiling play, sent out curious glances like swarms of bees. We are banished from that India. We have only the poet's cloud to send there as a messenger.[36]

Brief though it is, this is perhaps the most striking of all of Tagore's essays on Kalidasa. Though it describes a nostalgia for a romanticized past, it also cautions us against such nostalgia by reframing and transforming it. Representing time as space, Tagore suggests that the ardent modern reader perhaps imagines his relation to an earlier time—to Kalidasa's India—as similar to the Yakṣa's relation to his distant beloved. The language of exile and banishment accentuates the spatial dimension of loss, as it situates the modern reader as the homeless one, longing for something he can only sense as a fleeting shadow. But as the essay progresses, this beloved is recast: now it becomes the figure of the perfect one, "that deathless, most beloved being at the heart of infinity." Tagore suggests that it is not the passage of history but human destiny itself that compels us to long for her, though we can never reach her: "Not only in the past or the present as a whole: in each man there is the bottomless sorrow of separation. She whom we pine for lives by the inaccessible shore of her own Manas Sarovar, the lake of her solitary mind.[37] We can only send our imagination there, never reach it in the flesh. Look where you are, and where am I! What lies between us? Nothing less than infinity."[38]

At the beginning of the essay, it seems that "early" India, as evoked by Kalidasa's poetry, is the "home" from which the modern reader has been banished: "From Ramgiri to the Himalayas ran a long stretch of ancient India over which life used to flow to the slow, measured mandakranta metre of the *Meghadutam*. We are banished from that India, not just during the rains but for all time." Here, modernity is presented as a state of exile and homelessness. But as the essay progresses, it becomes clear that a profound sense of loss and separation is an aspect of the human condition itself. Now it appears that modernity, with its constitutive and "historical" sense of loss, might therefore be the true and natural "home" of humanity, the state most able to represent something essential about the fact of being human. By the conclusion of the essay, the Yakṣa has come to be a figure for the loneliness of the human condition:

> You on the lonely mountain top, sorrowful in separation—who has assured you that on a clear autumn night under a full moon, a night of such beauty as was never seen before, you will have everlasting union with her whom you embrace in your dreams, to whom you send messages through the cloud? You cannot distinguish between the sentient and the inanimate. Who knows, you may also have lost the distinction between reality and imagination.[39]

If Kalidasa's work enacts a desire for lost immediacy in its representation of love, as I have suggested in my reading, then Tagore's reading has significantly recast that loss. What is emphasized in his work is the yearning for the abstract, the spiritual, and the divine. Of course, it is not accidental that a decadent love—that is to say, a love that (implicitly) mourns the loss of its fullness and immediacy and obsessively recounts the lost or remembered pleasures of the body—be itself recalled, in the nationalist period, as a love that looks forward to a union with the divine. It is not hard to see why an essentially spiritual (and indeed, modernly spiritual, if one may say so), "ancient" India would be more attractive at this time, even—or perhaps especially—for a critic of nationalism such as Tagore. But Tagore's essay may be more fruitfully read as an analysis of the modern reader's nostalgia. For the essay does not begin by asking what Kalidasa's work is about but instead by asking why the modern reader responds to this work in a certain way. In asking that question, and beginning with the modern reader's sense of banishment, the text in a sense attempts to compensate that reader, "afflicted by the sorrow of separation from his loved one," by *giving* him, precisely through the trope of a universal and ahistorical longing, the connection he wishes to have with the past:

> From this narrow sea-girt present, when we look at the shores of that ancient land described in the poem, and think of the women gathering flowers in the jasmine groves beside the Shipra, the old men who told tales of Udayana in the town squares of Avanti, and the sojourners away from home, who, looking at the first clouds of Asharh, yearned for their wives—we feel that between them and us there ought to have been a bond. Our common humanity binds us intimately together, but remorseless time separates us. Not only in the past or the present as a whole; in each man there is the bottomless sorrow of separation. (223)

The last sentence in this passage heals, as it were, the rift caused by "remorseless time" by internalizing it within the human condition, and hence negating precisely the temporal distance/difference that is the source of anxiety. To feel separated from an imagined ideal relation, is common to all humans. Just as his beloved embodied, for the Yakṣa, the prototype of the most desired (but inaccessible) one, so too for the modern reader—especially one from a colonized country—a primeval India may appear as the (impossible) cure for his alienation. Thus the aim of the essay is finally to question the nostalgia that causes the modern (presumably Hindu) reader to ascribe his sense of homelessness to his "separation" from early India—his forced exile, if you will, from the imagined beauty, wholeness, and intimacy of that world. "We feel that if we could only find our way back to Avanti or Vidisha, on the bank of the Reva, the Shipra, or the Nirvindhya, we would be freed of the vulgar cacophony that surrounds us today" (222).

By suggesting that it is precisely the modern reader's sense of loneliness, desire, and yearning that in fact brings him closest to the Yakṣa, the essay attempts to free such a reader from the perceived curse of having a history instead of living a culture. This it can only do by reading metaphorically the longing, loss, and separation of which Kalidasa's text speaks, and by thus turning the text into a parable. Indeed, the essay strongly indicates that perhaps the act of reading is in some ways always a metaphoric act, depending on the metaphoric dimension of language in order to carry or "translate" a text from one time to another, or even from one consciousness to another. As we know, Kalidasa himself had wondered about the strangeness of messages and what they may be capable of conveying. This may be related to the textual being of the message and thus to its propensity to overflow or transgress the very categories it constructs.

In *Meghadūta,* when Kalidasa questions the sanity of sending messages through clouds, he in fact draws our attention to a more fundamental dilemma: the dilemma of sending messages through language, which posits the terms "sentient" and "insentient" but itself seems to remain outside these categories. By remaining outside, it forces us to question the rigor of that distinction. That is to say, if that which becomes an exemplary sign of consciousness (the ability to convey or receive messages) depends on something "insentient" or, indeed, something material (language itself), then how reliable would be the distinction between sentient and insentient, conscious or unconscious? But that is not all. In looking at that verse again, we notice that perhaps "nature," the apparent beloved of language, is also a liminal category. The first part of the verse makes a distinction between the cloud—a mix of smoke, light, water, and wind—and the import of messages. What relation could possibly exist between two such diverse things, the poet asks incredulously. In other words, how could the cloud, a material object, an object of nature, a mere natural thing, be the recipient of a message, which is meant for conscious beings? In the second part, however, we learn that the Yakṣa is *prakrtikṛpṇaḥ,* pitiful by (his own) nature, or rendered pitiful by nature. Nature here designates a kind of law—the presence of an inescapable logic. That law, like language, escapes the distinction between sentient and insentient. It does not simply govern the impersonal properties of natural things, such as clouds, but also governs consciousness (those tormented by love are rendered pitiful by nature) and hence produces a psychic logic about such "cultural" abstractions as love and pity. "Kāmārtā hi prakṛtikṛpṇāḥ" has the form of an aphorism but also of a "natural" law that exceeds and hence reshapes the domain of nature. A message—perhaps from Kalidasa—that starts by proclaiming the insentience of "nature" turns almost imperceptibly into a message about the way nature provides the law for sentience itself.

One might of course object that "nature" *(prakṛti)*, like language itself, has a particular valence in early Sanskrit literature, which must be considered in such discussions. My own sense is that while no reader of Sanskrit texts can afford to be unaware of the way these concepts have been thought in that tradition, neither can contemporary readings of these texts be limited by any given or stable meaning that has been assigned to these terms. On the contrary, the task of the reader is precisely to determine what these concepts come to signify in particular texts, not as they were read two thousand years ago (that would be an impossible endeavor) but as they appear to us today. For us, reading Kalidasa's work today, this verse from *Meghadūta* seems to be situated at the very heart of the oeuvre. Like Tagore, we cannot help reading it metaphorically: as a meditation, not only on the very act of sending and receiving messages but also on love, nature, and poetry. Such moments in Kalidasa's work—and there are several—show us that there is a complexity and density to all these terms that we must attempt to read, without immediately subsuming them within available representations of the culture, theology, or philosophy of something called "ancient India." Only then will we perceive what is untimely or unexpected in them.

This is not to say that the text is an ahistorical object but rather to indicate that it *cannot* be simply historical either. The act of reading texts produces a temporality for which available temporalities of "history" cannot account, since the entities on both ends of the spectrum—the text and the reader's consciousness—are themselves changed through this act. Even this change is not easy to categorize temporally: occasionally it occurs in a flash, but more often it emerges dimly through the years in slow, slumbering ways. In the next chapter, I will examine how Kalidasa's work was "transformed" by some of the Hindi writers who loved him best and how this work, in turn, had a profound impact on the way modernity itself was represented and apprehended by the postcolonial generation of Hindi writers. As we know, Kalidasa himself wrote almost obsessively about a kind of love that shapes—and indeed *produces*—the loved object as the object of memory. But at the same time, he draws our attention to a hospitality that would remain attentive to the intrusion, however violent or unseemly it may be, of the unexpected and the untimely. Such an attention may interrupt our inclination to turn Kalidasa's work into a lost beloved object and instead cause us to question our own investment in nostalgia. Perhaps we have yet to learn how to love Kalidasa.

2

Literary Modernity and Sanskrit Poetry: The Work of Mohan Rakesh

Modernity turns out to be indeed one of the concepts by means of which the distinctive nature of literature can be revealed in all its intricacy.

—Paul de Man, *Blindness and Insight*

In a short essay written in 1946, the renowned Hindi writer Hazariprasad Dvivedi describes a dream in which he saw the fourth-century Sanskrit poet Kalidasa sitting in front of Dvivedi's house in Shantiniketan, looking at a Kanchnar tree.[1] Kalidasa would now gaze at the tree in full bloom, now close his eyes, as though in reverie. Dvivedi wonders if Kalidasa is reminded of flowers from his own time—that is to say, from Sanskrit poetry: "In his mind, was he remembering that cluster of flowers from his own time, floating on the tremulous waves of the Sipra river, set afloat by someone's desire, or was he recalling some little flower bouquet, curl-offered *(alakārpit)*, which had, at some time, graced palace windows in Ujjayini."[2] The dream astonishes Dvivedi. Full of curiosity about its meaning he goes out the next morning and sees two figures near the tree: one, an artist "copying" the Kanchnar tree on his sketch pad, and the other a Santhal (tribal) girl who plucks a few flowers from the tree, sticks them in her hair, and walks on. Drawn to finding and reading signs, Dvivedi wonders which one of them could represent the poet he had seen in his dream the night before.

For anyone with even a passing acquaintance with Dvivedi's work, there is nothing surprising about the dream. Kalidasa is a strong presence in this work, as he is in the work of several Hindi writers of the early and mid-twentieth century. Their sense of a new beginning, of the urgency of that particular historical moment, not only provoked reflections on tradition, identity, and nationalism but also led to a new and often passionate interest in Sanskrit literature. They are no longer simply writing poetry on the model of Kalidasa's work, as people had been doing for several centuries. Instead, they are self-consciously seeking to understand their relation to Kalidasa and, by association, to the tradition of Sanskrit poetry and drama they had inherited. In this chapter, I will discuss what Kalidasa had come to represent for modern Hindi writers such as Dvivedi, Srikant Verma, and Mohan Rakesh, focusing on the work of the dramatist, novelist, and short story writer Mohan Rakesh (1925–72). Rakesh is by no means a "representative" Hindi writer of his period, but for several reasons his work is of particular interest in this context. On the one hand, he was intensely engaged in thinking about modernity and literature, and on the other, his work exhibits a serious concern with Sanskrit texts. Examining his first two plays in relation to the Sanskrit texts that partially inspired them—the works of Kalidasa and the first-century Buddhist writer Ashvaghosha—I attempt to understand the relation between his evocation of Sanskrit texts and a particular thematization of modernity. This relation—which indeed is no single link but an entire tissue of threads, resonances, and echoes—might best be understood precisely as a *link*, and not as a contradiction. I will suggest that Rakesh's interest in Sanskrit texts is intimately connected to his quest for modernity: indeed, it is precisely his sense of the power of Sanskrit texts and of the comparative weakness and degeneration of modern Indian theater that leads him to consider how modern theater might retain the linguistic and poetic complexity of Sanskrit drama while addressing and representing the concerns of its own time. Early traditions assume new significance for postcolonial modernity; what interests me more in this case is the conviction that underlies this phenomenon. This is the conviction that in order to be truly modern, the literary text must recognize and thus *appoint* its own predecessors; it has to establish a distinct and new relation to them. In effect, the modern writer rewrites literary history.

Alaka Is Now Forgotten: Kalidasa and Modern Hindi Writers

The question posed by Dvivedi in the dream essay—*Kalidasa kaun hai?* Who is Kalidasa?—is echoed in the work of other twentieth-century Hindi writers, including Dharmavir Bharati, Muktibodh, Srikant Verma, and Mohan Rakesh. In the short essay on the Kanchnar tree, Dvivedi asks this question in the context of comparing two figures: the artist and the Santhal girl. Who is Kalidasa, he asks, the one who "takes down" the Kanchnar flowers on paper, or the one who lifts them to the head? (Kalidasa kaun hai? Nīche kāgaz par utār lene vālā, yā ūpar sir par charhā lene vālā?).[3] The question is about Kalidasa's conception and practice of poetry, as well as about our understanding of Kalidasa. Dvivedi has no answer, but he is astonished that readers before him have not been troubled by such questions. If we call to mind some of the assumptions that have shaped critical writing on Kalidasa, perhaps we could also pose the question thus: Is Kalidasa a historian's poet, providing a faithful representation of fourth-century India, or is he someone else—an imperial poet, for example, delighting in the flowering of the Gupta empire, or an indulgent aesthete, culling blossoms of poetry for his own pleasure. Dvivedi's two figures, however, are not easily deciphered, and from another perspective we might read them very differently: the artist as the man of culture—the one who imitates nature because he already has a detached relation to it and a sense of its transience—and the Santhal girl as the unselfconscious one, linked to the landscape in a more immediate way.

Dvivedi's work, however, suggests yet another—a third—reading of these two figures. As Namwar Singh has argued in his thoughtful book *Dūsrī Paraṃparā Kī Khoj (In Search of Another Tradition)*, much of Dvivedi's work might be read in terms of his attempt to discover, within the Sanskrit tradition, significant signs of non-Aryan contributions. Namwar Singh argues that Dvivedi was the first Hindi scholar to reveal the layered memories buried beneath the flowers of Sanskrit poetry. He was the first to suggest that Kalidasa, until then celebrated as the great poet of Aryan culture, may instead have been the poet most indebted to non-Aryan tribes such as the Gandharvas, the Yakṣas, and the Kinnaras:

> For the first time, it was he [Dvivedi] who experienced that "each flower, each animal, each bird appears before us with the burden of countless memories . . . Do we know all of them? And have we been able to render clear the meaning of whatever we know?" . . . The pandits who love Kalidasa must surely have been jolted by the revelation that the poet whom they had until then considered as the great singer of Aryan culture, was the one most indebted to the beliefs and beauty-imaginings *[saundarya-kalpanāyen]* of non-Aryan tribes *[jātis]* such as the Gandharvas, Yakṣas, and Kinnaras.[4]

Keeping in mind this powerful strand in Dvivedi's work, the question about the Santhal girl and the presumably nontribal (possibly urban?) artist acquires another dimension, asking us to consider who might be more closely related to the genealogy of Kalidasa's own work. The question "Who is Kalidasa?" would thus lead us to wonder whether this monumental work, which in modern India became inextricably associated with the "golden age" of "Hindu" India—the Gupta empire of the fourth century—might have drawn inspiration from precisely those cultural groups that have been most marginalized in the popular vision of the modern nation. [5]

Namwar Singh proposes that though Dvivedi was drawn to a particular delineation of beauty in Kalidasa's work that he characterized as non-Aryan—a beauty conceived in terms of sweetness, grace, and suggestive power—he was equally concerned to distinguish this emphasis on the aesthetic from a decadent feudal culture. Singh quotes an extended passage from Dvivedi's commentary on Kalidasa's *Meghadūta,* where Dvivedi connects Kalidasa's ideal of beauty with the marks of labor, dwelling at length on an image of perspiring peasant women gathering flowers in the fields. Dvivedi evidently wishes to claim that the ideal of beauty valued by Kalidasa is closely linked with a celebration of the laboring human body. However, as Namwar Singh notes, the beauty of the flower-gathering women described in the passage may be indicative of Dvivedi's own ideal, not Kalidasa's: "This perspiration-bathed beauty of the flower-gatherers is not Kalidasa's; it is the beauty of Dvivedi's 'Kalidasa'—modernity bursting from the classical tradition!"[6] He goes on to suggest that Dvivedi's idealized figure of feminine beauty might be closer to a modern tradition of Hindi poetry, for example the work of Surya Kant Tripathi Nirala, who wrote the famous *Voh Torhtī Pathar (She Breaks Stones).* Dvivedi's desire to discover, in Kalidasa's work, a political consciousness that would satisfy his modern heirs thus leads him to make several startling claims—some more convincing than others.

Such a response, which manifests at once an unmistakable attachment to the work or the name of Kalidasa and a desire to recontextualize, reconfigure, or even disavow that work, may be traced in several Hindi texts of the mid-twentieth century. Going further than Dvivedi, Srikant Verma's well-known poem *Bhaṭkā Megh (The Cloud Astray),* first published in 1956), explicitly signals Verma's decision to break with a certain tradition of poetry, of which Kalidasa was still the most powerful symbol. Written in the voice of the cloud addressed by the Yakṣa in Kalidasa's *Meghadūta,* the poem expresses the cloud's decision not to go to the mythic city of Alaka but instead to remain connected to the impoverishment and despair it sees on the earth below. I translate a few lines here:

I have gone astray—
The first cloud of Aṣārh.
Unable even to touch the petals
Of the white flower of Alaka.

Cursed by some curse
I have sky-strayed.
In the gap of centuries I absorb; I wander.
Kalidasa! I have gone astray.
Forgotten the path to Alaka
—seated on lotuses of pearl.

[. . .] Alaka is forgotten; now I will
Quench the thirst of this earth;
Listen to the mute cry
Of withered trees and sprouts [. . .]

Forgive me, my poet!
Now I cannot go to Alaka [. . .]
I, the first cloud of Aṣārh,
Wandering in the gap of centuries
Kiss, over and over again,
The rough brow of dry earth.[7]

By identifying with the cloud, the poet expresses his decision not to carry the love message entrusted to him by the Yakṣa—and, by implication, by Kalidasa himself.[8] Instead of carrying a message of romantic love to a mythical city (Alaka), the cloud decides to turn toward the less lyrical reality of the earthly landscape of modern India, thus signaling a change in the very nature and subject of poetry. The poet's own voice ventriloquizing through the figure of the cloud seems to be markedly discernible in some verses:

How can I possibly forget
The earth that gave me birth? [. . .]
I am torn—forgive me, my poet!
I have seen more than what you showed me—
I have seen centuries washed in the eyes of man.

Much has happened since Kalidasa wrote, and the modern poet has "seen more than" what Kalidasa had shown him. At the same time, there seems to be a charge of irresponsibility leveled against Kalidasa, though it is not a charge that can be clearly stated, being itself articulated by way of substitutions and implicit contrasts. "How can I possibly forget," asks Verma, and in this context it is of course impossible not to be reminded of the one who did forget:

Dusyanta, the callous one from Kalidasa's play *Abhijñānaśākuntala.* Dusyanta forgot not only his love but also his responsibility—and of this the modern poet is acutely aware. It appears that Kalidasa is thus twice castigated: for writing romantic poetry and, even within the circuit of that poetry, for forgiving—and hence "forgetting"—Dusyanta's forgetting of Sakuntala. Although Kalidasa appears here as a name that best exemplifies the kind of poetry Verma now *refuses* to write, the modern poet nevertheless must link himself to this name by speaking in the voice of Kalidasa's cloud. Thus the "earth" that gives birth to the poet appears both as a parched landscape *and* as the poetic tradition in which the poet situates himself. In a related vein, Verma writes elsewhere that he can never perceive himself in separation from those who lived before him: "I always feel that I am a link in an endless chain . . . Nothing outside that chain."[9] To be a poet, to be a part of that chain, means establishing a relation, however nominal or even antagonistic, with Kalidasa. The very gesture of disavowal shows us that Kalidasa is still imagined as the one who has given modern poets the assignment to write, convey, or transmit poetic speech, so that a rejection of that specific assignment entails an appeal to him.

Dharamvir Bharati's *Yakṣa Kā Nivedan* (The Plea of the Yakṣa, published in *Ṭhaṇḍā Lohā* in 1952) is similarly ambivalent in its evocation of Kalidasa. Written in the voice of the Yakṣa from Meghduta, it presents a series of accusations against Kalidasa, who has condemned the Yakṣa to endless misery by imprisoning him within the frame of his poem. The Yakṣa suggests that Kalidasa has been liberated from his own sorrow by creating the Yakṣa but, by doing so, has left the Yakṣa to dwell forever in a strange and terrible existence:

> In what mysterious life have you dragged me?
> Forever and ever I have lost the human world.
> What game were you playing, O Prince of dreams,
> Will I never be liberated from this pain?
> Tell me how I may escape from these verses
> —-This strange womb, between god and ghost.[10]

Although the poem ends with a familiar consolation, where Kalidasa is imagined as telling the Yakṣa that every beauty in the world is consecrated *(abhiṣikt)* by his sorrow, that does not happen until the Yakṣa has expressed his desire to set fire to the poem that imprisons him: "If only I could acquire freedom from this prison / I myself would ignite all its verses." The poem suggests that

Kalidasa may, in fact, be responsible not only for the strange plight of the Yakṣa but for poetry itself—for the way it functions in the world and the images it creates. It is as though Kalidasa were the one to have first created or discovered this "strange womb" that produces something that defies classification. This odd object, poetry itself, may at times seem "divine"—capable of a perfection beyond ordinary human reach—and at other times ghostly—the sign or remainder of what once existed. Thus even as the poem questions the motivations and impulses that create poetry, it nevertheless turns the anguished Yakṣa into a devotee and a disciple of Kalidasa: after all, the Yakṣa too now expresses his own sorrow by way of poetry, and the case against meter *(chhand)* is itself articulated in meter. Kalidasa seems doomed to repeatedly appear in modern poetry as the progenitor who is at once accused and revered.

Mohan Rakesh and Modern Hindi Drama

Among modern Hindi writers, Mohan Rakesh's engagement with Sanskrit texts stands out because of its complexity and duration. His first play, *Āṣārh kā ek din* (A Day in the Month of Rain, 1958),[11] widely considered to be one of the most significant works of modern Hindi drama, presents an imagined narrative of Kalidasa's life, while his second play, *Lahron Ke Rājhans* (The Royal Swans of the Waves), is based on Ashvaghosha's first-century text *Saundarananda.* Rakesh also translated Sudraka's *Mricchakatikam* and Kalidasa's *Abhijñānaśākuntala* into Hindi and in his youth started his own literary career by writing poetry in Sanskrit. He obtained a Shastri (degree) in Sanskrit, a B.A. in English, and an M.A. in Hindi and Sanskrit—a trajectory that would be virtually unheard of today, given how sharp the divisions between the study of Hindi and English literature have become in India in recent decades.

Though Rakesh's work exhibits a deep familiarity and engagement with Sanskrit texts, his relation to these texts is quite different from Rabindranath Tagore's or Hazariprasad Dvivedi's. Instead of turning to them for forgotten or lost ideals that may be usefully revived for the education of the modern Indian, Rakesh evokes Sanskrit texts in order to explore with greater intensity a persistent concern with Indian modernity. This coupling of "Indian" with "modernity" *(ādhuniktā)* should be read in terms of modernity's own quest for the contemporary, the local, and the immediate—a quest frequently marked in Rakesh's writing. Though the desire for modernity is undoubtedly an ancient and perhaps universal desire, in literary texts the focus of this desire often seems to be on a kind of immediacy: the desire to capture the presence of the present. For Rakesh, the term "Indian" in "Indian modernity" would not have been the sign of a national aspiration; instead, it would have designated the temporal and linguistic specificity that he sought in his quest for modernity.

Certainly Rakesh is not alone among modern Indian dramatists in turning to earlier narratives. As the critic Jai Dev Taneja writes, "It is not accidental . . . that almost all significant plays in modern Indian dramatic literature are based on historical-mythic tales and characters."[12] Beginning with Jaishankar Prasad's *Skandagupta,* he goes on to name several such plays, including Jagdish Chandra Mathur's *Konārk,* Karnad's *Tughlaq,* Dharmavir Bharati's *Andhā Yuga,* and, of course, Mohan Rakesh's first two plays. Ten years earlier, in his introduction to Rakesh's second play, *Lahron ke Rājhans,* the drama critic Suresh Awasthi had made a similar remark: "In modern Hindi dramatic literature, there are a few excellent works—*Skandagupta, Konārk, Andhā Yuga,* and *Āṣārh kā ek din*—and they are all historical." He goes on to say that these works stand out because their writers did not merely reproduce a historical or traditional plot but rather presented these plots in a new environment and a modern context.[13] The list since that time has grown, particularly if we don't restrict it to Hindi drama. The works of Girish Karnad and Ratna Thiyam have become exemplary in this regard. A detailed analysis of this phenomenon may be found in Aparna Dharwadker's recent book *Theaters of Independence.* "The first significant thematic formation to appear in Indian theater after independence," she writes, "consists of a succession of major plays that invoke the nation's ancient, premodern, and precolonial past through the two principle modes of retrospective representation—myth and history."[14]

In an article written in 1972, the director Ebrahim Alkazi discusses in particular the evocation of Sanskrit texts in modern drama and offers an analytic response.[15] He proposes that for many dramatists the turn to Sanskrit texts was a way to escape from the challenge of creating new artistic symbols based on the resources of their own world—a world that many of them saw as hollow and fragmented. This argument corroborates some of Rakesh's own remarks, where he claims that the name Kalidasa provided him with a more powerful and effective symbol than any he could have created on his own.[16] In an interview with Carlo Coppola in 1968, Rakesh insists that, in spite of their apparent connection to early texts, both *Āṣārh kā ek din* and *Lahron Ke Rājhans* are modern plays that focus on dilemmas peculiar to modernity. The first, according to him, is about a man torn between the attractions of an institutionally successful life and some other less articulate, less definable desire to follow his own beliefs and inclinations. The second, he says, similarly illustrates the condition of a man who wants material or physical comfort on the one hand but, on the other, is in search of something intangible. He implies that such conflicts are integrally related to the conditions of contemporary life: "About myself, I can say with certainty that I have not written a single word which is not connected to the present . . . In my opinion, *Āṣārh kā ek Din* is not about Kalidasa . . . In the play, I wanted to portray the conflict of today's writer—the writer who is attracted by the benefits offered by governments or other institutions, and on the other hand, is also committed to himself in a way. And for this, I needlessly dragged poor Kalidasa into the play . . . But the play is about the contemporary human being."[17]

Such comments, though immensely significant, cannot be read as statements of fact. In my own analysis of Rakesh's play, I will attempt to demonstrate that Kalidasa is not merely a symbol for the modern writer, nor has he simply been dragged into a modern plot, as Rakesh suggests. Kalidasa's own work provides at least a suggestive frame for the play, so that the relation between the two deserves more scrutiny. And indeed Rakesh himself elsewhere claims that the play is connected to his own reading of Kalidasa's work: "However the character of Kalidasa appears in *Āṣārh kā ek Din,* it is not very removed from his personality as it is concentrated in his works; though yes, from the perspective of creating a modern symbol, some small changes have definitely been made."[18]

Such statements make us aware of the difficulties involved in assessing the relation between Rakesh's play and the work of Kalidasa. By allowing us to glimpse the presumptions that guide Rakesh's reading of Kalidasa, they show us that it may indeed have been impossible for Rakesh to read Kalidasa as other than a "modern" poet—that is to say, other than as sanctioned by a modern conception of the writer. When Rakesh suggests that Kalidasa's works provide a window to his personality, he assumes that the work reflects the author's life. As I will discuss in my reading of the ninth-century theoretician Anandavardhana in chapter 5, Sanskrit literary critics generally assumed that poets worked with the stories they were familiar with; they wrote about what other poets had already written about, not necessarily about their own lives and experiences. Thus the act of turning Kalidasa into the "author" of his work—the assumption that his personality might be condensed in his work, or that the themes in his work might be the expression of an inner, emotional story (rather than the expression, for instance, of cultural or conventional expectations)—may already be a significant aspect of the "modernization" of Kalidasa.

But Rakesh's reflections on modernity also indicate that his work was driven by larger historical imperatives. In several contexts, he expresses a commitment to being his own contemporary: to writing and thinking about the world he lived in, and about the singularity of his own time. In an essay called "The Real Creation-Dilemma of Today" he criticizes the attempt to perceive the social "explosion" of his time in relation to, or in comparison with, the changes that have occurred previously in history, and he claims that nothing in the past may be comparable to the occurrences of the past ten years. The scientific progress, technological revolution, and political instability that characterize this time, he writes, are entirely unprecedented and cannot be seen as the return, or the repetition, of any earlier moment of change in human history. The cultural beliefs and forms of interpersonal relations that guide human beings have now been shattered in a unique and singular way. That is why, he says, the crisis faced by the contemporary writer is also a new and unprecedented crisis.[19]

His response to this crisis is to call for greater reflection on the idea of modernity. The loneliness, estrangement, futility, and despair that have so far been associated with modernity have now become stale. He writes that such despair was itself a symptom of the fact that old values, though shattered, continued to exercise power over modern consciousness: "Somewhere, there remained the memory of being connected to these values, that is why the degradation of those values caused bitterness."[20] To be truly modern means to turn one's face away from the past, toward the future. To be connected to the present entails attempting to leave the threshold of the present (29).

These reflections on time must be taken seriously. They suggest that one of the tasks Rakesh assigned to himself as a writer—or one of the tasks he perceived as being necessary for his time—was to wrench the present away from the overarching grasp of the past and to orient it toward the future. That is why he asserts that the essence of the present lies in its anticipation of the future; that is to say, in what is potential, unknown, and imagined. The present exists as pure potential, and to be connected with it means to grasp this as its essential characteristic. Such concerns, which appear repeatedly in Rakesh's discussions about literary language, are intertwined with concerns that today we may call postcolonial. Questions regarding language and form, as well as those regarding a community's relation to its past, are all inflected by the sense that there is something unprecedented about the postcolonial situation, which has to be met with neither nativism nor a rush toward westernization.[21] There are no easy paths here, and Rakesh's representation of early texts and of times preceding his own document some recurring conflicts and confusions. At several moments in his work the past becomes a figure for a time when things were *in their place*—locatable by language. For example, the very concept of "alienation," which surfaces frequently in Rakesh's writing, signals such a figure of the past, since alienation itself designates, or one could even say *produces*, the proper or lost relation, in deviance from which it announces the alienation of the subject.[22] But at other moments, and especially in the two plays I will discuss here, it seems that the past itself has been injected retrospectively with some of the dilemmas Rakesh perceives in his own time, so that it becomes vividly manifest as the past "of" modernity.

These often conflicting representations of the past correspondingly inform Rakesh's perception of tradition. An essay by Susan Friedman, "Definitional Excursions: The Meanings of Modern/Modernity/Modernism," lucidly describes the symbiotic relation between modernity and tradition: "Relationally speaking, modernity is the insistence upon the Now—the present and its future as resistance to the past, especially the immediate past. It establishes a cult of the new that constructs retrospectively a sense of tradition from which it declares independence. Paradoxically, such a tradition—or, the awareness of it as 'tradition'—might come into existence only at the moment of rebellion against it."[23] Friedman proposes that the declaration of modernity needs nothing so much as the canonization of the tradition against which the modern may emerge. While this is true of much self-consciously new or modern writing in India, a postcolonial consciousness also makes the terrain more complex, since here the turn *toward* a tradition that has been devalued by the colonial encounter may also become an act of declaring "independence." We are well aware of this dynamic.

In my remarks about Rakesh's work, I will suggest that his interest in Sanskrit literature is inseparable from his deep commitment to writing about his own time—a commitment that is apparent not just in the themes of his works but also in his role as one of the initiators of the *nayī kahānī* (the New Story) movement in Hindi and, most of all, in his lasting preoccupation with finding a contemporary idiom of theatrical language. His evocation of Sanskrit texts must be read in terms of this commitment. It suggests an implicit recognition that in order for the present of postcoloniality to be open toward the future, such a present has to seize the opportunity to reconsider, and in a sense rewrite, the tradition bequeathed to it. There is an unavoidable element of narcissistic identification here. Rakesh's early work, for instance, seems to mine Sanskrit texts for moments and figures that may be recast in ways that resonate with his own concerns. He applies pressure on certain points to facilitate their transformation into a shape with which the modern reader might identify. Yet in rendering Sanskrit texts more familiar to the modern reader, the plays also draw attention to their own work of innovation. The more they echo, the more evident becomes the difference in the echo. "Tradition" then appears as the necessary but inaccessible or unreadable surface against which modernity can be staged. The fact that it only becomes accessible through its necessarily transformed inscriptions underwrites for us its essential solitude—a solitude that appears most striking in the postcolonial context of a double rupture, both temporal and "cultural," for lack of a better term.

Rakesh's early plays start from this point of departure; they stage the modernity of the protagonists by placing them in an apparently anachronistic setting. Likewise, his reflections on language, while exhibiting an intense search for a contemporary idiom, also exhibit the conviction that such an idiom can only be heard aganist its history and the associations it carries. A truly "modern" language would perhaps be as incomprehensible and meaningless as a representation of modernity that had severed all connections with the literary tradition.

Āṣārh kā ek Din (A Day in the Month of Rain)

In its very choice of subject and language, *Āṣārh kā ek din* testifies to the larger questions that occupied Rakesh and his contemporaries. On one level, the play presents a reading of Kalidasa's work, but on another, its central concern is nothing less than the very possibility of a modern Hindi theater. Highlighting the relation between the content and the impulse of the play, the theater critic Nemichandra Jain has rightly remarked:

> *Āṣārh kā ek Din* is, in a fundamental way, different from the many so-called historical dramas in Hindi because one finds in it neither a so-called description of the past, nor a revivalist anthem to the past, nor the attempt to create sentimental melodramatic situations. Its perspective is much more modern and subtle and that is why it is truly the sign of the beginning of modern Hindi drama.[24]

The central character in the play is Mallika, the companion and friend of Kalidasa. Mallika and Kalidasa live in a beautiful mountain village in the Gupta empire. When the play opens, Kalidasa has already composed his early work *Ṛtusaṃhāra,* and Mallika is already the object of public censure because of her association with Kalidasa, who is generally derided in the village as a good-for-nothing. In an obvious reversal of Dusyanta's entry as a hunter in *Abhijñānaśākuntalam,* Kalidasa first appears on stage in Rakesh's play carrying a baby deer wounded by a hunter's arrow and attempting to soothe and nurse it. It turns out that the deer has been wounded by one of the king's men who has come to the village to inform Kalidasa about his appointment as the court poet. Thus the association between aggression and courtly life is established early in the play, and the hostility between the village and the court is underscored when Mallika's mother, Ambika, remarks that whenever she sees the king's men in the village, she senses that some disaster is imminent.

In spite of his initial hesitation, Kalidasa is persuaded by Mallika to accept the royal honor and go to Ujjayini. Once he departs, Mallika does not hear from him, though occasionally she hears reports about him. He marries Priyangumanjari, a princess who is renowned for her scholarship and beauty, and he becomes involved in political affairs, so that eventually he is appointed as the ruler of Kashmir.[25] In the meantime, he also composes some of his most renowned works, including *Meghadūta, Abhijñānaśākuntala,* and *Raghuvaṃśa.* He does not send Mallika any of his works, but she is able to procure manuscripts from traders coming through the village. Kalidasa, along with his wife and various attendants, in fact passes through the village on his way to Kashmir, but even then he does not come to see Mallika. However, his wife visits Mallika at home and, in a particularly demeaning conversation, offers to take her to Kashmir as her companion and even to arrange a marriage for her to one of their male attendants. The royal visit also becomes an occasion for Rakesh to mock the urban visitors' hunt for the exotic: their avid search for "local" color, language, costume. The court's relation to the village, marked in every way by imperial arrogance, becomes also an implicit comment on modernity's relation to antiquity, its often imbecilic and clumsy tabulation of artifacts, languages, customs.

Mallika's mother has believed all along that Kalidasa is a self-absorbed and selfish man, incapable of reciprocating Mallika's love, but Mallika's faith in him remains unshaken, even after the death of her mother and her own relationship with Vilom, a man she has despised all her life. Vilom (whose name literally means 'against the hair or grain,' 'opposing') is clearly the antithesis to Kalidasa: in one dialogue, he calls himself "an unsuccessful Kalidasa." Indeed, the play sustains a fundamental ambiguity in its portrayal of Kalidasa. His actions repeatedly confirm Ambika's and Vilom's judgment of him, and yet Mallika is throughout presented as the one who knows and understands him best.

The bond between Kalidasa and Mallika is doubtless central to the play. In a soliloquy toward the end of the play, Mallika says to an absent Kalidasa, "Even if I did not remain in your life, you always remained in mine. I never let you wander from my side. You continued to create and I believed that I too am meaningful, that my life is also productive."[26] At the conclusion of the play, Kalidasa arrives briefly to see Mallika, having now abandoned both his marriage and his political status. Describing his loneliness and alienation in the court, he says,

> People think that I have written a great deal in that life and atmosphere. But I know that I have written nothing there. Whatever I have written has been gathered from this life. The landscape of *Kumārasambhava* is this Himalaya, and you are the ascetic Uma. The Yakṣa's torment in *Meghadūta* is my own torment, and you are the Yakṣini crushed by longing. In *Abhijñānaśākuntalam,* it was you whom I saw in the form of Śakuntalā. Whenever I tried to write, I reiterated the history of your and my life.[27]

Although his words suggest that Mallika too has occupied a singular and central place in his life, they paradoxically also confirm the impression that her mother had of him. In Kalidasa's entire oeuvre, it is this one story, the story of love and separation, of Kalidasa and Mallika, that is written over and over again. But whose story is it, really, and what are the limits of Kalidasa's imagination? The play ensures that we ask such questions. Kalidasa is taken aback at all the changes he sees in Mallika's home and repeatedly expresses how estranged he now feels: "How this house has changed too. And I had hoped that everything would be the same, just as it used to be, in its old place . . . but nothing is in its place anymore."[28]

It seems that Kalidasa had never fully realized that others, besides him, live in a temporal world subject to the inexorable force of time. For him, Mallika and her world had remained enclosed in an ideal space of inspiration, outside the sphere of life. The play suggests that Kalidasa has been able to cast

Mallika as the ascetic Uma of *Kumārasaṃbhava,* the tormented Yakṣini of *Meghadūta,* the forsaken Śakuntalā of *Abhijñānaśākuntala* in part because he was never entirely conscious of the real Mallika; he could not afford to maintain too vivid a sense of her own troubled life. It is only at the end of the play, after he realizes that Mallika now has a daughter of her own, that Kalidasa seems to understand how time affects others.

When the play first appeared in 1958, this portrayal of Kalidasa offended many of Rakesh's contemporaries. Kalidasa is the great Indian poet of love, and his work is usually read as depicting the movement from mere passion to true love via a period of separation—*viyoga.* The Kalidasa of Rakesh's play was held to be too narcissistic and weak, too distant from this ideal of fidelity. Sometimes Rakesh was accused of being un-Indian in his concerns, partly because of his portrayal of Kalidasa. For instance, in 1989 the critic Ramesh Gautam wrote that the play is more influenced by European modernism than by Sanskrit literature, and that Mohan Rakesh, the so-called founder of modern Hindi drama, was in fact speaking the language of Europe—of Sartre, Neitzsche, Freud, and Eliot—under the deceptive mask of presenting Indian tradition.[29]

Such criticism is not unfounded. But it wrongly assumes that the play takes as its task the presentation of "Indian tradition."[30] Against both Mohan Rakesh and Ramesh Gautam I would argue that the play provides us with neither a representation of Kalidasa the fourth-century poet nor a commentary on modern poets using Kalidasa as a mere symbol. Instead, it presents Kalidasa *as* a modern poet, and that is precisely its fantasy. That fantasy enables it both to imagine a closer relation to the figure of Kalidasa *and* to imagine a modern poet whose work would be as monumental and as enduring as Kalidasa's. The pay-off, we may notice, is considerable. On the one hand, despite all the criticism implicit in Rakesh's play, Kalidasa "gains" in this play the qualities of conflict, uncertainty, and ambivalence that had become the sign of a sensitive or thoughtful modern interiority; and on the other, the modern poet gains the stature and the linguistic sophistication that seemed to be the provenance of the ancients.

At the same time, the play establishes its distance from Kalidasa's work by offering, in its plot and language, a critical reading of this work and, in effect, by "teaching" Kalidasa how to be a reader of his own work. In some obvious ways, the plot of the play refers to the plot of *Abhijñānaśākuntala.* Like Dusyanta, Kalidasa himself leaves the woman who loves him to go to the city and apparently forgets about her. This "forgetting," which turns out to be both a commemoration (of an idealized Mallika) and a forgetting (of the real woman), implicitly questions and undermines the curses—the opaque external exigencies—that sometimes guide the plots of Kalidasa's works and save the male protagonists from responsibility. In Rakesh's play, such forgetting cannot be erased and the play does not end happily. Indeed it marks its distance from all of Kalidasa's work by refusing to incorporate the period of *viyoga* (separation) into the trajectory of a "true"—and ultimately rewarding— love story. In this play, the period of separation never comes to an end; rather than being one necessary element in the dialectical movement of love, it remains at the center of a fundamentally unequal relationship. The character Kalidasa's reflections on time in the last lines of Rakesh's play may be read as a critical commentary on the work of the historical Kalidasa. He had returned to Mallika with the illusion that it may be possible to begin again, to begin from the beginning, but now he realizes that time is more powerful because it "does not wait" (111). Kalidasa the character finally understands what the writer didn't: that time cannot be recuperated, that *viyoga* cannot be simply erased in the movement toward reunion.

While Kalidasa marries the princess, Mallika seems to have contracted a relationship with Vilom under duress. Indeed, the Mallika whom we see announcing her independence at the beginning of the play seems to be, at the end, a woman painfully trapped by the constraints of her life. In the first act, when her mother mentions marriage to her, she claims she does not want to marry, going on to say defiantly that no one has the right to criticize her choices: "Mallika's life is her own property. If she wants to destroy it, what right does anyone have to cast aspersions on her?"[31] By the last act, however, the Mallika (lit. 'mistress') who considered her life her own property has receded. Speaking to an absent Kalidasa, she describes her daughter as the child of her "lack," and herself as no longer having even a name: "Do you know that having lost my name, I have acquired an adjective, and now I am, in my own view, not a name, but a mere adjective."[32] There is no substantive sense to her life anymore.

In the meanwhile, Kalidasa has made a name for himself: indeed, he has acquired yet another name, Matrigupta, as the ruler of Kashmir and an associate of the Gupta rulers. Visually, the play highlights the contrast between the two characters: Mallika remains in the same hamlet and the same home, which shows increasing signs of decay and neglect as the play progresses. Kalidasa's life is more dynamic: he arrives and departs, acquires fame and fortune, and at the end, makes a choice to give up his life at the court and go elsewhere. However, the most vivid contrast that emerges in the play is not between Mallika and Kalidasa as characters but rather between the deprivation, sorrow, and slow decay of Mallika's life on the one hand—evoked by several elements of the play and constantly present to the audience—and on the other, the fine skill and extravagant beauty of Kalidasa's poetry, which, silently resonating behind the scene, accompanies the entire play. Whether in reading or watching the play, one is powerfully struck by the sense that its guiding impulse is to reveal, by exposure, the ground beneath this poetry.

Perhaps this contrast becomes most obvious when Kalidasa, on returning to the village at the end of the play, notices the now worn and smudged bundle of handmade pages that Mallika had woven for him, expecting that she would have an opportunity to present them to him. The pages are now marked with the imprint of fallen tears, nail marks, pressed flower petals. "How are these pages still blank, Mallika?" asks Kalidasa. "An epic has already been written on them: an epic of endless chapters."[33] We are thus presented with a new proposition: not that the separation of lovers is redeemed by reunion, as in Kalidasa's own work, but rather that Mallika's despair might have produced its own epic. This epic has been displaced by Kalidasa's renowned and familiar poetry but it can never be redeemed by it. Instead of an economy of compensation or "poetic" justice, we are thus faced with an incommensurability that cannot be redressed.

By now we know that in Rakesh's play the name "Kalidasa" designates at once several figures. It is the name by which the author of certain canonical Sanskrit works is known, but because of the symbolic weight of these works it also designates the great poet in general: the poet who stands close to the origin of a tradition, so closely connected to its movement that his success itself appears to have determined the measure of his skill. Through the figure of Mallika, Kalidasa's most ardent reader and admirer, the play certainly attests to the power of Kalidasa's poetry, but this very figure also renders the play skeptical of everything Kalidasa represents. In effect, the play appears to ask whether poetry that repeatedly aestheticizes pain must not also have inscribed within it a hazy but unmistakable treachery—a subtle treachery that renders unhappy experience lyrical. This is an old question, but it is given a new twist, for in a more pragmatic vein, the play asks whether Kalidasa, like Rakesh's own contemporaries, did not make political compromises in order to ensure the success of his work. Indeed, not only are we are presented with two diverging assessments of Kalidasa within the play itself—Mallika's and Ambika/Vilom's—but at the end we are left with the sense that judging between the two is less important than allowing for their possible simultaneity. The play suggests that Kaldasa may be at once the sensitive, emotional, impressionable poet of love and the self-absorbed and self-serving man of success; that the one need not exclude the other, and, worse, that the two might be deeply connected. In each case, an inescapably instrumental relation, to both one's experience and the public world, is highlighted.

The question of the artist's integrity was one that repeatedly drew Rakesh's attention. It is a theme to which he returns in his novel *Andhere Band Kamre* (Dark Closed Rooms, 1961). Set in Delhi, the novel focuses on the relationship between Harbans, a professor and an aspiring writer, and his wife Nilima, a dancer. In one section, Harbans accompanies his wife and her dance troupe on a tour of Europe and is disgusted by all the petty monetary troubles and quarrels that are part of the troupe's life. Their ambitions and preoccupations do not conform to his ideal image of the artist: "Are these the people who describe themselves as devotees of art? Are such petty objectives hidden behind the whole worship of art? Doesn't devotion to art make the human mind radiant and large? Is this the vision called the artist's aesthetic vision? How petty is the selfishness of each of them. Can't these people arise from the swamp of such selfishness and perceive the reality of their situation?"[34]

The narrative voice never entirely endorses Harbans's point of view, repeatedly fluctuating between different perspectives and assessments, as in *Āṣārh kā ek Din*. Nevertheless, the theme of political constraints or monetary gains affecting the writer/artist emerges strongly in the narrative. While the artist's response to these seductions is not always criticized in the same tone of naive idealism that we notice in Harbans's voice, it is nonetheless clear that "art" as an independent and conceptually coherent category—with all its attendant qualifications (real art, true art, and so on)—never ceases to function as a strong player in the conceptual frame of the narrative. By the end, the novel becomes a bitter comment on the hold that government institutions—and indeed, foreign sponsors—have on Indian writers and artists.

These resonances between the novel and the play enable us to see how, in *Āṣārh kā ek Din*, Kalidasa plays in his "own" life and his own historical period, so to speak, the role of a modern writer. Sanskrit drama becomes the stage, as it were, for the performance of modern dilemmas and tragedies. It is in this way that the play produces a sense of alienation. By presenting its characters as living in a time and a space in which they seem to be interlopers, it dramatizes the modern condition that Rakesh wanted to represent in his work. We notice elsewhere in Rakesh's writing that when he attempts to represent his own age, the modern age, he represents it as a strange and catastrophic burden: as that which powerfully affects but does not integrally mold those who find themselves alive in that era. Thus Rakesh writes:

> In order to portray the reality of today accurately, we will have to map the chaos and stench of our life, while living in the very midst of it, and will have to portray that human consciousness which is restless in the midst of this stench and anxious to push it away . . . We must keep faith that even in the midst of this chaotic atmosphere, human strength and vitality have not disappeared.[35]

The human consciousness that is restless in the midst of stench and chaos thus seems to be a consciousness unused to chaos, one that finds life around it an oppressive anomaly and the reality of "today" a deviation from some norm that guides its expectations. Much of Rakesh's work may be read in terms of such a perception. His protagonists seem to be human beings living in a world that appears repulsive to them in many ways—a world in which others, ordinary people, may survive by making endless compromises—but in which these more thoughtful or sensitive protagonists feel oppressed and paralyzed. Thus modernity is most pointedly represented as resistance against modernity. If characters from Sanskrit texts seem to Rakesh to be the most compelling symbols for illustrating crises that, he insists, are peculiar to modernity, it is perhaps because those crises are perceived in relation to human beings who, like these characters, appear to have suddenly found themselves in a world from which they are estranged and to which they do not belong.

Rakesh's second play, *Lahron ke Rājhans* (The Royal Swans of the Waves) is, in this regard, similar to *Āṣārh kā ek Din.* Based on Ashvaghosha's *Saundarananda,* the play focuses on the confusion of Nanda, the Buddha's half-brother, and his inability to choose between the life of a householder and the life of a monk. While this indecision is already dramatized in a powerful way by Ashvaghosha's text, it acquires new dimensions in Rakesh's play, which ends not with the education of Nanda and his full acceptance of renunciation but instead with a heightening of the tension. Thus the two plays that Rakesh wrote in response to Sanskrit texts both focus on characters who seem suspended in some fundamental indecision. Neither Kalidasa in *Āṣārh kā ek Din* nor Nanda in *Lahron Ke Rājhans* can decide on a satisfying course of action. They are susceptible to persuasion but prone to uncertainty. When Kalidasa or Ashvaghosha represent the conflict between love and duty, they do so in order to finally celebrate the "victory" of one term over the other, or at any rate, in order to end the conflict. In Rakesh's work this conflict is transformed into a fundamental tension that remains unresolved even at the end of the play.

Indecision and the Modern Protagonist

Ashvaghosha's *Saundarananda* is based on a Buddhist parable concerning the initiation and education of the Buddha's half-brother, Nanda. The story records Nanda's conflict about leaving his wife and home in two registers. First, in the most obvious manner, it is a story that depicts Nanda's personal anguish and uncertainty, which will eventually be cured by his education by the Buddhist monks and by the Buddha himself. Second, at a more insistent level, the text's representation of Nanda and Sundari indicates its *own* "seduction" by the erotic story that it must overcome and renounce, in the interest of its professed didactic ends.

At the beginning of the narrative, Nanda appears to be happily married to the beautiful Sundari. She and Nanda are entirely engrossed in one another, though Nanda's devotion to his wife is also presented as a sign of his weakness. One day, while he is helping her adorn herself, they hear that Gautama Buddha himself came to their palace, asking for alms, but had to leave without receiving anything. All the serving women were busy in beauty preparations: perfuming clothes, preparing baths, and making flower necklaces. Immersed in these frivolous activities, none of them noticed the Buddha. When Nanda hears that the Buddha has left the palace without alms, he is shaken and ashamed. He wishes to convince his brother to return and be welcomed, as is his due. Here, as in Kalidasa's *Śakuntalā,* love becomes the bad enclosure that renders its inhabitants blind to duty, and particularly to the duty of hospitality. At the same time, hospitality calls in its most severe form; it is asceticism itself, the "enemy" of love, that demands hospitality.

Nanda's wife Sundari agrees to let him go but asks that he return soon—before the beauty marks she has just applied turn dry. Although Nanda's departure at this point should not be terribly momentous—we are told that he is simply going for a short while, to bring his elder brother back to the palace and give him alms—the scene is already dense with all the pathos of Nanda's uncertainty and Sundari's sorrow. The narrator already perceives what is to follow and this anticipation causes him to dwell long on this parting scene:

> She, with dancing eyes now still and sad, considered her departing
> beloved,

> Like a doe, leaving aside young blades of grass, with ears erect, and
> head turned,
> Looks at the departing deer turned toward her.[36]

Bhrāntaṃ mṛgaṃ bhrāntamukhī mṛgīva, writes Ashvaghosha, "Like a turned-face doe [looking at] a turning deer," and the word that recurs, not accidentally, is *bhrāntiḥ:* turning around or revolving, but also moving or wandering, and often used in the sense of wandering from the right path; wandering in error or delusion. Thus the movement that dramatizes the mutual attraction of the couple is at the same time represented as a movement of simultaneous delusion and error. But in spite of this *coup de mot,* it seems that the very force of the conventional simile has diverted Ashvaghosha from his didactic mission. In describing Nanda and Sundari as deer and doe, and in superimposing upon the image of the coquettish, proud Sundari the figure of the doe with its erect ears and large, still eyes, the verse renders entirely innocent and spontaneous the bond between the two lovers. They become creatures of the forest who have wandered by mistake into a difficult parable. The later references to predatory, fickle women and hapless men will seek to question and shake not only Nanda's preoccupation but also this image and the aesthetic sphere to which it belongs.

The verses that follow focus on Nanda's conflict, again prefiguring a tension that will assume sharper dimensions later in the text. A series of similes depict him as being pulled by two opposing forces: regard for the Buddha and love for his wife. These are the verses that seem to have provided the initial inspiration for Mohan Rakesh's play *Lahron Ke Rājhans.* Rakesh's epigraph for the play is the second line of the following couplet:

> He was pulled by regard for the Buddha, and pulled again, by
> passion for his wife;
> From indecision, he could neither go nor stay, like a royal swan
> caught among the waves.[37]

Nanda finally leaves to follow the Buddha and, in a state of confusion and apprehension, he is initiated against his will. In Ashvaghosha's text, the initiation *(dīkṣā)* is presented as a moment of cruel coercion, and Nanda weeps as his hair is shorn—a detail apparently introduced by Ashvaghosha himself: "When his hair was being taken away, his face, bent low and covered with tears, glistened like a lotus on a bent stalk, wet with rain water."[38] After the initiation, he continues to pine for his wife, and it is only at the end of the story, after a series of crucial moments of education, that he becomes a perfect renouncer. At first he is persuaded that the divine nymphs *(apsarās)* who await him in heaven offer rewards more enticing than any his mortal wife can bestow, but by the end he learns that it is desire itself that must be renounced in order to attain peace. During the course of his conversion, he is presented with several conventional images describing the perils of associating with, and savoring, women: contact with women is as dangerous as the proximity of poisonous vines, venomous snakes, and unsheathed swords; women are depicted as tireless predators, ready to attack any man they find. Women can never be trusted: several verses represent them as being incapable of true friendship and, furthermore, as presenting obstacles to any male friendships a man may form.

Thus in Ashvaghosha's work women at one level appear only as temptations that must be resisted on the path toward salvation. In many ways, the work is predictably and blatantly misogynist: its tirades against the impurity, fickleness, and sexual voracity of women find no counterpart in Kalidasa's exuberant—if equally troubling—philogyny. Both *Saundarananda* and *Buddhacarita* revolve around a male figure whose education entails the renunciation of desire. In both works, though more obviously in *Saundarananda,* women are the most prominent symbol of the desired object that appears attractive and enticing but is in reality unreliable and impure. Needless to say, the "human being"—the one susceptible to both temptation and education—is always assumed to be male; women are part of the series of objects available for his sensual gratification. Both texts agree that the pleasure women promise is transient and subject to the ravages of time; in the long run, such apparent pleasure brings more pain than happiness. *Rāga* (sensual desire) is recurrently figured as a tormenting fire. It is noteworthy that later Sanskrit poets adopt the same image but radically change its implications: in Sanskrit love poetry the torment caused by this fire is quenched not by asceticism *(tyāga)* but by consummation.

But as other readers have noted, Ashvaghosha's work is not all about the evils and the dangers represented by women. Writing about the erotic quality of *Saundarananda,* the twentieth-century Bengali scholar Buddhadeva Bose attributes this quality partly to the influence of other writers, notably Valmiki, the traditionally recognized author of the *Rāmāyaṇa.* "Even the ascetic Ashvaghosha," he writes, "was disturbed by the picture of Ravana's household in *Sundara-kanda.*"[39] That is why, Bose suggests, his own work is also capable of "disturbing"—that is to say, arousing—its readers. Though its susceptibility to the erotic does not render the work any less misogynist, it is nonetheless striking that the verses describing Nanda's indecision, together with Sundari's and Nanda's laments in books 6 and 7, would be so eloquent in their representation of the very passion that the poem, as a whole, deems delusional and mistaken. Such passages appear thus to exceed their assigned function within the trajectory of the narrative. Perhaps Ashvaghosha himself was troubled by such a possibility, for in the penultimate verse of the poem he claims that the poem was written to instruct listeners on the path toward salvation *(muktiḥ)*, not to give pleasure. Whatever in it exists besides, or exceeds, the purpose of education, exists because of the laws of poetry *(kāvyadharmāt)*; it exists in order to sweeten the message, as honey sweetens bitter medicine (18.63). But whether or not the honey serves only to sweeten the medicine remains a question, especially when we see how later writers have read Ashvaghosha's work. As I suggested in the previous chapter, the images of ambivalence that stand out in book 4 of *Saundarananda* seem to be taken over by Kalidasa and subtly transformed, so that in the latter's work the medicine may exist only to deepen, by contrast, the sweetness of the honey.

It seems quite clear that Mohan Rakesh's prolonged engagement with *Saundarananda* is a testament to his own changing relation to the text. In 1946–47, he wrote a short story about Nanda and Sundari but never published it. A year or two later he reworked the story as a radio play titled *Sundari,* which was broadcast in Bombay. But he was not happy with the play, and in 1956–57 wrote it yet again as the one-act play *Rāt Bītne Tak* (Till the Passing of Night); it was broadcast in Jullundhar and later published. In 1965 he published a much-changed and developed version—a three-act play called *Lahron ke Rājhans.* But obviously this too was not entirely satisfying, for in 1966, working in concert with the director Shyamanand Jalan and actors of the Anamika theater group in Calcutta, he rewrote the third act and made some changes in the earlier acts as well. This version was published in 1968.[40]

The versions readily available today are the one-act play *Rāt Bītne Tak* and the 1965 version of *Lahron ke Rājhans.* The two are different in several aspects. *Rāt Bītne Tak* seems to be a moral parable about renouncing sensual pleasure; it shows us most clearly that Rakesh first responded to Ashvaghosha's text not by questioning its terms but instead by being persuaded of their validity and power. It is basically a play about the education of Sundari rather than Nanda. Initially, both are presented as being immersed in sensual gratification, but Sundari is the one who openly mocks the Buddha. Nanda's conflict is dramatized in the space of a few moments and manifests itself as an inner voice that mocks his lowly desires. At daybreak, he leaves his palace to give alms to the group of monks who have departed, unwelcomed, from the palace, and he returns a little while later as a member of that group. In the last lines of the play, Sundari goes to fill their bowls and is startled to find her husband among the group. "Will I give alms to you today?" she asks. "What alms can I give you?" In response, Nanda delivers a mini-sermon:

> You can give a lot, Sundari. You are proud of your beauty, aren't you? Place that pride in this begging bowl. Doesn't your greatest desire appear to you to be the desire for happiness? Today, give me that desire as alms. The night has passed, Sundari. I have placed my inner darkness in the begging bowl of Gautama Buddha. You should place your inner darkness in mine.[41]

The play ends with Sundari uncertainly joining in the chorus of the group: "I go to the refuge of the Dharma. I go to the refuge of the Buddha. I go to the refuge of the Sangha."

The later play is considerably more nuanced. At the center of the play is Nanda and his indecision. As in Ashvaghosha's story, he is initiated against his will, and after his hair is shorn, he leaves the Buddha with tears in his eyes. He even returns to the palace later, and Sundari, half-waking from sleep, momentarily sees him as a monk. She screams, and he instantly leaves her. At the end, all we know is that he has returned to the Buddha, ostensibly in search of his hair. This search is evidently a metaphor for several other quests. The play concludes on an unmistakable note of despair and anxiety.

Thus the later play makes a break with Ashvaghosha's text, and even more with the Buddhist parable that provided the basic plot for Ashvaghosha. The parable unequivocally presents Nanda's desire for domestic life as a delusory desire; it presents Nanda being taken away by the Buddha on his wedding day and subsequently being haunted by the memory of his beautiful wife, who, on his departure, had beseeched him to return soon. His attachment to her is explained simply in terms of lust, and the Buddha initially makes use of this very lust to "entice" Nanda on to the path of meditation by granting him a vision of the heavenly nymphs who await him.

As I have suggested, Ashvaghosha's *Saundarananda* is considerably more complex, though it does not depart dramatically from the plot of the Buddhist parable. In spite of its complexity, however, it, like the parable, presents

Nanda's indecision as a sign of weakness; the purpose of the story is to show how this weakness was overcome. Rakesh's later play, *Lahron ke Rājhans,* fundamentally alters this. Here, it is Nanda's indecision—rather than his conquest of it—that makes him the protagonist. His very indecision seems most attractive to the text; it renders him the prototype of the man who is not weak but perhaps too thoughtful and sensitive to accept the limited choices before him. Among the characters added in this version are two workers at the palace, Svetanga and Syamanga. At the very beginning of the play, Syamanga is presented as someone who thinks too much, questions too much, and is consequently unable to keep his mind on the mundane tasks before him. All through the play, he seems to be Nanda's partner in distress: together, they represent that part of the town population that, in spite of being drawn to the Buddha's message, cannot embrace it wholeheartedly. The last voice we hear as the curtain falls is Syamanga's: "One ray of light . . . just one ray . . . "

Rakesh saw the two plays *(Āṣārh kā ek Din* and *Lahron ke Rājhans)* as illustrating a similar dilemma. In comparing them, he seems to align all the so-called worldly pleasures together: fame, success, domestic life, and erotic satisfaction. In *Lahron ke Rājhans,* Sundari comes to represent this aspect of life, just as Gautama Buddha comes to represent the search for peace in some other realm. But let us follow the mapping of gender here. In both plays, a male character conveys the particular quality of conflict or indecision that Rakesh associates with modern consciousness.[42] In *Āṣārh kā ek Din,* the two conflicting pursuits that tempt the male protagonist are symbolized by two women: Mallika and Kalidasa's wife Priyangumanjari. In *Lahron ke Rājhans,* they are symbolized by Gautama Buddha on the one hand and Nanda's wife Sundari on the other. Indeed, in this play, Sundari is from the very beginning positioned as the antagonist of the Buddha. In defiance of the entire town, she has organized a *kāmotsava*—a festival of pleasure—the night before the Buddha's wife Yashodhara is to be initiated. Speaking to her friend and maid, Alka (who is also Syamanga's friend), Sundari holds Yashodhara responsible for the Buddha's own quest for salvation: "If Lady Yashodhara's beauty had been able to keep Prince Siddhartha captive, would he not still be the Prince Siddhartha? Would he be Gautama Buddha, giving sermons to people on the riverbank? It is a very simple matter, Alka. If the attraction of a woman makes a man a man, her degeneration makes him into a Gautama Buddha."[43]

It is tempting to read Sundari's words as recognizing, obliquely, the misogyny of renunciation; to say that she positions herself as the Buddha's opponent in response to the Buddhist parables that have already positioned her as the enemy to be conquered. But unfortunately she is not a very compelling opponent. Indeed, by entirely accepting the terms laid out by the renouncer's discourse, she confirms all the tiresome divisions that support this discourse. She accepts the fundamental assessment of women as being primarily—and singularly—objects of sexual attraction, even if she seeks to give this assessment a different valence. There is something terribly predictable about her, just as there is about Priyangumanjari in *Āṣārh kā ek Din*. The politically astute and educated princess can only appear in Rakesh's play as an arrogant and calculating woman; though Kalidasa is married to her for several years, the text never presents any evidence of his emotional attachment to her. Here, she can represent only the avenue toward success. Thus both women appear in these plays only to illustrate more vividly a choice or confusion experienced by the male protagonists.

In the case of *Lahron ke Rājhans* this is especially clear. Earlier fragments of the play, now published in *Ekatra*, reveal that only in the later version was Sundari presented as the obstinate advocate of the pleasure festival *(kāmotsava)*. In a scene from the radio play *Rāt Bītne Tak*, it is Nanda who organizes the pleasure festival and insists that it be held that very night—the night when Gautama Buddha had returned to his birthplace, Kapilavastu. Talking to his friend Maitreya, Nanda says: "The pleasure festival is a festival of desire. And how can today's desire wait till tomorrow? Tonight the pleasure festival will certainly be celebrated in Nanda's palace."[44] In the later version, it is Sundari who organizes the pleasure festival and exactly the same words are now spoken by her. There could hardly be a clearer indication that Sundari, as a character, developed simply as a representation of one aspect of Nanda, an aspect that had to be externalized in order for Nanda to emerge as the sensitive and conflict-ridden character of the later play.

Alka and Sundari are obviously in contrast in the play, just as Mallika and Priyangumanjari are in *Āṣārh kā ek Din*. Whereas Alka is sympathetic to the troubled dilemma of the man she loves, Syamanga, Sundari is unyielding in her attitude toward Nanda and, more generally, toward the power exercised by the Buddha. These seem to be the two positions to which women are assigned in some other works by Rakesh as well, most notably in the novel *Andhere Band Kamre*, where the sisters Nilima and Shukla occupy opposing positions. It thus seems that the male in these texts remains the "subject" of modernity, just as the male was the subject of salvation or renunciation in the Buddhist texts; he is the one whose quest is divided and who is himself divided. Rakesh's own focus on the divided male subject as the emblem of modernity took shape gradually, as is attested by the differences between *Rāt Bītne Tak* and the later version *Lahron ke Rājhans.* A story about the education of Sundari or about Nanda's definitive "defeat" of Sundari and everything she represents eventually became a story about Nanda's continual and unresolved conflict. The development of the story between 1957 and 1965 thus represents, in fact, the development of Nanda. But Nanda is able to develop in the way most valued by Rakesh—he is able to become a character who reveals something particular and distinctive about the modern Indian condition—only at a certain cost. His emergence as a modern character demands that both Gautama Buddha and Sundari (to use Rakesh's own code) remain comparatively static. The dramatization of Nanda's conflict requires that these two poles remain untroubled themselves, as though left untouched by the currents that have shaken Nanda. Rakesh's work can only represent modern consciousness by placing it in relation to other elements that themselves remain unhistoricized. The two plays together suggest that although male *responses* to the choices before them may have changed from antiquity to modernity, the choices themselves have remained relatively equivalent through the centuries.[45] In spite of the complexity of his work, Rakesh thus participates in a broad movement that represents modern consciousness as constitutively male, and implicitly presents modernity itself as the surpassing or overcoming of features that have been coded "feminine."

The Language of Theater

Dipesh Chakrabarty's influential book *Provincializing Europe* is in large part concerned with the predicament of modern historical consciousness and its apprehension of the world. In the epilogue, Chakrabarty discusses the objectification of the past produced by the desire for "the true present." The phrase is Paul de Man's, who is cited by Chakrabarty via Marshall Berman. Chakrabarty writes:

> If the rise of the modern historical consciousness speaks of the coming of a certain modern and political way of inhabiting the world, I suggest that it also speaks of a very particular relation to the past. This is the desire on the part of the subject of political modernity both to create the past as amenable to objectification and to be at the same time free of this object called "history." In fact, one can argue that the attempt to objectify the past is an expression of the

> desire to be free of the past, the desire to create what Paul de Man once called "the true present." What is the "true present"? The "full power of the idea of modernity,'" writes Marshall Berman quoting de Man, "lay in a 'desire to wipe out whatever came earlier,' so as to achieve 'a radically new departure, a point that could be a true present.'" The true present is what is produced when we act as if we could reduce the past to a nullity. It is a kind of a zero point in history—the pastless time, for example, of a *tabula rasa*, the *terra nullius*, or the blueprint.[46]

In the essay titled "Literary History and Literary Modernity" (published in 1971 in *Blindness and Insight*) from which this quote is taken, de Man does indeed discuss Nietzsche's emphasis on deliberate forgetting in these terms. But in a characteristic move, he does not stop here. The paragraph that Chakrabarty cites ends with the following sentence, "Yet the shrill grandiloquence of the tone [Nietzsche's] may make one suspect that the issue is not as simple as it may at first appear."[47] As we read on, we gather that via the apparent antagonism of the figures of history and modernity, what de Man is most concerned with exploring is the nature of language as such and of the human as linguistic being. The desire for modernity, the essay suggests, is nothing but the desire for immediacy: the desire for the ability to act in an unmediated way. It is thus the desire to forget representation itself or to imagine that representation can be, in Baudelaire's paradoxical diction, "the representation of the present." When de Man writes that "the appeal of modernity haunts all literature,"[48] he means that no writing would ever take place if it were not conceived of *as an act*—as something capable of exerting its own singular force, in freedom from the past. And yet it turns out that history and modernity, which appear to be conceptually opposed (endless mediation on the one hand and an absolute impatience with mediation on the other), are integrally related and perhaps indispensable to one another. History and modernity thus become figures for illustrating the conflict between language *as it functions* (as abstract, allegorical, and historical) and language as writers would *like* it to function (as unmediated, original, and concrete). They become figures whose very opposition plays out and dramatizes a tension that is inherent in, and constitutive of, language as such.

The concept of modernity is for de Man essentially a temporal concept, one that depends on the primacy and privilege of the present. When considered in terms of literature, it thus poses a fundamental question regarding the relation between language and temporality. Since, according to de Man, linguistic events necessarily render temporal structures complex, the essay concentrates on how writing is both engendered by and unable to sustain such a privileging of "modernity": "The ambivalence of writing is such that it can be considered both an act and an interpretative process that follows after an act with which it cannot coincide" (152). Immediacy and reflection are not sequential here, despite the movement of the sentence. Instead, it is their very simultaneity and interdependence that constitutes writing as the paradigmatic act of language, and literature as the arena where "modernity" and "history" antagonistically sustain one another:

> The continuous appeal of modernity, the desire to break out of literature toward the reality of the moment, prevails, and in its turn, folding back upon itself, engenders the repetition and the continuation of literature. Thus modernity, which is fundamentally a falling away from literature and a rejection of history, also acts as the principle that gives literature duration and historical existence. (162)

What is gained by locating the desire for modernity as a moment, a necessary temptation that is built into language? It seems to me that only by acknowledging this moment as a *structural* condition for literary modernity can we gain some understanding of the particular complexities that ensue when we read literary texts in terms of the idea of modernity. Enumerating thematic or even formal elements that bear some relationship (however profound) to an economic, political, historical, or philosophical idea of the modern still leaves us standing at a distance, as it were, from the predicament of the writer who is concerned with "re-presenting" the present. Only the turn to language can bring us closer.

Paul de Man's analysis of the problem specific to literary modernity helps us to theoretically contextualize Mohan Rakesh's quest for a contemporary language that would be able to represent what he strongly perceived as the specificity of his time. Rakesh's early interest in Sanskrit texts is closely related to his attempt to build a Hindi theater strong enough to be the contemporary heir of Sanskrit drama. Involved in this project was both an emphatic rejection of Parsi theater[49] and the search for a theater that would fulfill the "cultural aspirations" of the Hindi-speaking region.[50] Sanskrit drama may have provided a model here because of its focus on poetry and linguistic nuance; indeed, it is traditionally classified as *driśya kāvya* (visual poetry).

But precisely this attention to language—to its own potential for thought or beauty—later became a source of dissatisfaction for Rakesh. In an interview with Mohan Maharshi, he expresses his disappointment with the language of all his plays:

> My first two plays were appreciated because of their literary beauty. And I felt that for this very reason they were not able to express the environment and pace that surrounded me . . . In my third play I really struggled to grasp the environment around myself, and searched for a language that would be the language of everyday conversation. But even that did not really succeed. For the past three years I am in search of a contemporary idea of the word that belongs only to the theater.[51]

Such frustration with "literary" language is evident in Rakesh's later work. Like several of his contemporaries, he believed that one of the tasks of the postcolonial generation was to discover or fashion a new language for the nation. The search for a "contemporary idea of the word that belongs only to the theater" arose from his conviction that theater—the public space for the public experience of language—would be the ideal space where such an unliterary, yet immensely powerful, language would evolve:

> I want to go closer to that language which is the language of being, not the language of living. Many people will find this unmodern *(anādhunik)*, but I strongly feel that fragments of analytical articles or scholarly prose are literary infiltrators that have no place in theater . . . The fragmented language of theater should be the language of our being which should tell us something about our time. (112)

Theatrical language is to represent and hence reveal historical existence in its concreteness and specificity. But in order to do that, it first has to establish a true relation *(vāstavik sambandh)* to its own time (110). Most plays, says Rakesh, even when they are otherwise good, "are not the experience of today" (110). Literary language will not suffice now: "Till now the dramatist has been fundamentally a literary person, very attracted by the literary potential of language" (111). But he insists that this has been a trap, for himself as well as others. Elsewhere, in an interview with Carlo Copolla, he says that writers seem to be turning away from poetry to the short story because of a pervasive restlessness, a desire to "capture the color of our time."[52]

However, this desire to somehow make one's language coincide with one's time seems doomed to frustration. Time moves so fast, everything changes so rapidly that the writer has no opportunity to "capture" the present: "Every morning on waking up one feels belated" (*Ekatra* 113). The present is where one is not. The present is elsewhere, always on the move; promising immanence, it paradoxically remains within the heart of ideality. If "literary" language is to be cast off, it is presumably because it cannot but belong to other times; its very power lies in its suggestive and allusive nature, which allows it to gesture beyond the present moment. But what kind of a language would be able to evoke nothing but the present?

This is not a matter merely of vocabulary, though vocabulary is doubtless a part of this search. A more fundamental idea of sound and rhythm, most clearly articulated in the essay "Word and Sound" *(Śabd aur Dhvani)*, poses the problem most succinctly. Rakesh proposes here that in its fundamental form the word is born from sound and is the fruition of sound. What is most significant in language is not the meaning of individual words but rather the way certain word clusters convey a rhythm, since this rhythm is indeed the sign of mental emotions. There is an attempt here to provide a theory of language that would not begin with the word but instead with sequences of words, sound clusters that gather resonance in terms of their associations. Such a theory implies a necessary dependence on the past, and hence Rakesh writes unequivocally that language can only be meaningful, in the simplest sense, insofar as it does not belong only to the present:

> *A word that has no historical associations can only be a sequence of meaningless sounds, not a meaningful part of language* . . . Even a newly chiseled word is never completely free from historical associations. Roots, prefixes, endings—all these in themselves are the associations available to us from history or tradition. Any new word is the repetition of those associations. The word is able to convey meaning only to the extent that those associations grant meaning to it.[53]

If language as a structure resonates or becomes meaningful only because of its history and tradition, then the search for a language that can capture the present will always have to run up against the inherently mediated and allusive nature of language. A consciousness of this predicament pervades Rakesh's entire work and lends a particular density to his thinking of modernity. This does not mean that he gives up on the search for a contemporary idiom but that this search itself is constantly reframed and understood in different ways:

> In order to communicate any emotion, it is not words that are created, but rather a few sounds in a particular rhythm. In their long historical context, these sounds can be recognized in the form of separate words. To use words creatively means to search for ever-new rhythms in the rhythm of these contexts. That is why no word-sequence becomes alive without an interior rhythm and the graph of this rhythm or sound is its actual meaningfulness.[54]

Here the phonic rather than meaningful aspect of language is emphasized. Language communicates—or rather, makes an impact—by virtue of sound and rhythm. However, rhythm is also a signifying element. The task of the writer is to awaken new rhythms, consonant with his own time, in word clusters, but at the same time, the new rhythm only becomes audible in the context of an old one: "To use words creatively means to search for ever new rhythms in the rhythm of [their historical] contexts." His persistent search for a new language, a contemporary idiom, or a cadence attuned to a particular historical moment has to be read in conjunction with such reflections. They provide some insight into Rakesh's early plays and his attempt to pose the question of the modern by evoking early texts and recasting familiar names, tropes, and narratives.

However, we should also note a technological and political context for Rakesh's attention to theatrical language. His concerns about theater are often articulated in response to two new media: radio and film. The advent of film seems particularly important: Rakesh perceived film as a rival and a threat and felt that theater must define its force by distinguishing itself from film. This discussion is conducted in some detail in the course of a conversation with the Russian dramatist Alexie Aburzov. Responding to Aburzov's contention that theater is essentially a visual rather than an auditory medium, Rakesh argues that the phenomenon of film has forced new distinctions to emerge:

> In our literary theory drama has been given the denomination of visual poetry. But since we may compare two different media of drama [film and theater] today, therefore the question of fundamental elements *(mūl-tatva)* can only be raised today. The fundamental difference between the two media is only that in one, words are

> born in terms of the scene, and in the other, the scene in terms of words . . . Until today, the necessity of raising such a question was not experienced, because until the beginning of this century, theater was the only dramatic medium. We received from it alone a full satisfaction in the manifestation of the visual. But it was precisely the incompleteness of the visual element in theater that allowed a new visual medium to progress so quickly, to the extent that in just a few decades, doubt has arisen regarding the very survival of the theater.[55]

Film comes into being because theater has never been a complete visual medium. In responding to this lack, it also highlights the essential feature of theater: its fundamental relationship to sound. Rakesh's response to the challenge posed by film thus took the form of emphasizing and deepening the linguistic element in theater. He believed that to neglect the primacy of language in theater would create a situation in which theater ultimately would be unable to compete with film. To this end, he wrote at some length about the role of the playwright in theater and the advantages of the playwright being part of the production process whenever possible. He consistently conceived of theater in terms of the impact of words and sound elements on the consciousness of the audience. The popularity of radio plays during his lifetime gave further impetus to this conception. Rakesh wrote several short plays specifically for the radio; it may not be unreasonable to say that the radio play, which presented drama as an entirely auditory medium, might have conformed to his ideal conception of drama.

Running through these conversations and writings is the question of postcoloniality. This comes up, for example, when the significance of technical innovation in theater is dismissed on the grounds of the economic conditions of third world countries.[56] Unlike some of his contemporaries, Rakesh thought that conceiving of the development of theater in terms of technical innovations would only create more economic dependence on national or international organizations and thus limit the independence of the dramatic enterprise. His attention to the language of theater also allows him to shift the focus away from aspirations that would ultimately depend on economic factors. Here, as elsewhere, his aim is to suggest that postcolonial writing must break away from Western criteria of excellence. Writing not about theater but about the short story, Rakesh notes that those who consider Chekhov's, Maupassant's, and O'Henry's stories as ideal and always wish to compare new (Hindi) writers with these figures give evidence of their own imitative characteristic: "Worse or better, the works of many of our new writers are nevertheless different from those of these 'all time greats'—and to the same extent, are different also from the work of contemporary (great) foreign writers. For now, it would be better if we let it remain at this difference of the New Story, its 'identity' . . . The New Story writers do not yet want an eternal [ahistorical] analysis *[śāśvat mūlyānkan]* from the perspective of eternal values *[śāśvat mūlya]*."[57] I cite this passage because it signals a discontent with the idea of "eternal" values that clearly acquires a political dimension here: insofar as such values are linked to power, they are also linked to the West and will manifest the force of the Western tradition. A different perspective is needed even to perceive, let alone appreciate, the work of new Indian writers.

I have dwelt on Rakesh's reflections on language in order to suggest that the search for modern forms of expression was, in his work, always conducted in relation to, and in negotiation with, a consciousness of history. In some measure, it was the very depth of that historical consciousness that made this search both necessary and significant. I've suggested in this chapter that though his focus on the present was deeply connected to his experience of his own time as an enigma—a particularly fraught historical moment—it was also connected to his consciousness of a tension within language itself, which repeatedly aspires toward a presence it can only present as ideality. "Literariness" became for Rakesh a sign of this ideality, which he repeatedly strove to overcome, especially in his later work. His relation to Sanskrit texts, and in particular to the work of Kalidasa, must be read in this context. In a sense it was the artifice of Kalidasa's work—its *absolute* literariness—with which Rakesh had to contend, in various ways and with various strategies. Undeniably he was in some measure captivated precisely by that literariness when he attempted to rewrite Sanskrit texts by introducing or amplifying in them those cadences that would resonate with the urban, educated, post-colonial generation of readers. Poetic language, which gains its strength by the slow and dense infusion of historical associations, at times functions as a defense against the degeneration and alienation of the modern world, but at other times it obstructs a true apprehension of the present. However, as Rakesh discovered, it was not an easy task to turn against that language, for to forfeit it entirely in the quest of contemporaneity would yield nothing but silence. Sanskrit poetry—and its most powerful symbol, Kalidasa—thus comes to represent the historical dimension of language itself. The strong current of Sanskrit in Rakesh's work provokes, as though from within, an intense and antagonistic encounter with this dimension of language.

Today, we may be critical of some of the assumptions and predilections that shaped Rakesh's adaptations of Sanskrit works, in particular when we consider his representation of gender. Nevertheless, these adaptations remain significant for us as examples of a far-reaching attempt to engage the concept of tradition: an attempt to connect tradition in a fundamental manner to reading, writing, and language. Once again, his remarks on the development of the short story are pertinent. The new short story certainly represents the development of a tradition, he writes, but this development is not like the growth of a plant. Instead, this development is best understood as the *transformation* of a thought or a culture. "Confusion often arises," he writes in a characteristically biting note, "because people apply the rules of botanical science to the development of a literary tradition."[58] The insight that tradition can neither be abandoned nor conceived as an organic form sustains all of Rakesh's work. It is an insight whose significance and value we often seem to forget.

3

Allegory and Violence: Gandhi's Reading of the *Bhagavad Gītā*

> *It was through Gandhi that the Gita came closest to being a canonical text in Hindu consciousness.*
>
> —Ashis Nandy, *Traditions, Tyranny and Utopias*

Two armies stand facing each other on the battlefield. On both sides, legions of heroes, broad shouldered, courageous, and serene—but also filled with the desire to fight, eager for blood, ready to pit their strength against each other. Suddenly the most skilled among them all, the archer with the surest aim, is struck with paralyzing despair. What are we fighting for, he asks in dread. How can we slay our enemies who are also our kinsmen and teachers, those to whom we are bound by the bonds of familiarity, family, and friendship? Is victory worth this cost? For what, for whom, do we go into battle? And then a guide emerges. Not a mortal like the rest but a divine lover and destroyer of creation. He arrives to give counsel, to lay anxiety to rest, and to inspire. In response to mortal queries, he sings a celestial song. What does the song say? The one who speaks from knowledge, from absolute and transcendent knowledge, what does he teach? The words of the song have been recorded, commented on, translated in many tongues. But what is their secret meaning? In reading or listening to them, who is touched, and where? And is it possible to speak only of that touch—which is neither communicated nor transferred, but simply registered—or do we not, in speaking of those words, also try to steal from them some of their authority, their claim to truth, their knowledge of the sanctioned way of being?

Perhaps it is sheer madness to write today about the *Bhagavad Gītā*. Has not everything been said about it already? What else is left to say about a text that has already inspired countless commentaries, readings, historical and critical analyses? And yet, if we still read the *Bhagavad Gītā*, we should still write about it—even if it is only to repeat what others have already said. Since what the god said will always remain uncertain—even more profoundly uncertain than who the god was, or why he spoke in Sanskrit, or why he appeared then, at that moment of battle—perhaps it is important that we try to articulate *what* we read when we read the *Bhagavad Gītā.*

Assuming enormous significance during the nationalist period in India, the *Bhagavad Gītā* (The Song of the Lord, usually simply called the *Gītā*) gave rise to a sort of nationalist seminar, providing a frame for wide-ranging debates about violence, resistance, duty, caste, and indeed the very activity of reading traditional religious texts. It became pivotal and provocative not only because of its popularity as a religious text but also because of the political charge of its plot and themes. A part of the Sanskrit epic the *Mahābhārata,* the *Gītā* stages a dialogue between the warrior Arjuna and the divine figure Krishna. The *Mahābhārata,* often considered the longest poem in the world, is believed to have been composed over a period of several hundred years.[1] Though authorship is traditionally ascribed to the poet Vyasa, most scholars believe that it was composed by several generations of bards. The *Gītā* is a very small part of the *Mahābhārata,*[2] and we may take 200 BCE as an approximate date for its composition, relying on the authority of the Sanskrit scholar J. A. B. van Buitenen. The dialogue between Arjuna and Krishna occurs just before the epic battle; it is prompted by Arjuna's reluctance to engage in war with his kinsmen over inheritance and kingship, and Krishna's long and multifaceted response convinces Arjuna that his duty, as a warrior and a prince, lies in fighting.

When Krishna urges Arjuna to fulfill his duty as a warrior (a Ksatriya) and not to shrink from battle, he also provides a larger ground for his argument, presenting a picture of the ideal disciple and the ideal life. Are all his arguments integrally connected, and is it indeed the same Krishna who speaks all through the text? When does the singer sing in his own voice, and when does his voice become an echo of local prejudice or a tissue of citations? What belongs to the heart of the song, and which sign will guide us to that heart? While readings of the *Gītā* often struggle with such questions—and the questions often remain similar, even in their more secular guise—they emerge with particular intensity in the comments of M. K. Gandhi. Indeed, among modern readings of the *Gītā,* Gandhi's is perhaps the most astonishing. The *Gītā* remained for Gandhi a most inspiring text, one to which he frequently turned for support and guidance. Unlike most of his contemporaries, he was convinced that the text was ultimately not an advocate of violence—even of necessary and just violence—but that on the contrary it presented a sound and reliable guide to a life of nonviolence, *ahimsa.* In other words, he was convinced that the text must be read in such a way as to draw out and accentuate its real concerns and to discard as accidental noise whatever interfered with this reading. While his remarks about the *Gītā* are of interest to us for many reasons, the most remarkable task performed by this reading is to foreground a rift in the text and to put that rift to work. Thus the god's song becomes in Gandhi's reading a mortal song, riven by the division of body and soul. Following the *Gītā*'s own injunction to regard the body as transient and insignificant, Gandhi attempts to follow instead the soul or the spirit of the song. Keeping my focus on the question of violence, as it is addressed in the *Gītā* and in Gandhi's remarks about the *Gītā*, I will discuss here how Gandhi radically reorients the ancient text in the name of preserving its authority. He is committed, not to a historically or even philosophically accurate reading but to the interests of the present. Though he would not have phrased it in this way, his reading seems to respond to the following question: How can the *Gītā* be read as a politically useful text today? This should not be understood as an instrumental question—one that focuses only on strategy—since, as we know, the political was for Gandhi inseparable from the ethical (or from the "religious," which was often his way of talking about the ethical). Such an approach is at odds with the usual scholarly approach. The scholarly approach, even when concerned with contemporary questions, is nevertheless constrained by its commitment to *understanding*, rather than refashioning, the past. In this chapter, I attempt to juxtapose these two approaches and think about the differing imperatives and desires that guide them. My aim is to think about them in relation to one another and to gauge the limits of each enterprise: limits that only become visible through the exercise of juxtaposition.

The consciousness of modernity is perhaps always connected with the question of one's relation to the past: at the moment when that relation becomes a question, a threshold has been crossed. Nietzsche's essay "On the Uses and Disadvantages of History for Life," to which I referred in the last chapter, is a paradigmatic text in this regard. Let me briefly explain why I find that essay helpful in thinking about modern Indian approaches to the *Gītā* and to Sanskrit texts in general. The essay presents a passionate indictment of modernity for having lost the capacity to connect knowledge with practice:

> In the end, modern man drags around with him a huge quantity of indigestible stones of knowledge, which then, as in the fairy tale, can sometimes be heard rumbling about inside him. And in this rumbling there is betrayed the most characteristic quality of modern man: the remarkable antithesis between an interior which fails to correspond

> to any exterior and an exterior which fails to correspond to any interior—an antithesis unknown to the peoples of earlier times. Knowledge, consumed for the greater part without hunger for it and even counter to one's needs, now no longer acts as an agent for transforming the outside world but remains concealed within a chaotic inner world which modern man describes with a curious pride as his uniquely characteristic "subjectivity."[3]

The target of Nietzsche's polemic is a specific kind of knowledge, which he calls "scientific." This knowledge belongs to the surveyor of the past who wishes to master the past instead of incorporating and using its resources. Against history as science, which wishes to resolve all phenomena into knowledge so as to liberate itself from the power of phenomena,[4] Nietzsche distinguishes three other modes in which history pertains to the "living man" and, correspondingly, three different "species" of history: the monumental, the antiquarian, and the critical. The first allows us to imitate the greatness of the past, the second to revere and be content with our origins, and the third to perceive the injustice of the past and condemn it. All three are necessary, in different measure, for history to serve life.

In the last chapter I noted that Paul de Man reads "life" in this essay as a figure for action, and history, correspondingly, as a figure for mediation. These two, despite their apparent opposition, remain intimately connected. Here, I will briefly pursue the distinction Nietzsche proposes between the "historical" and the "unhistorical." Just as the historical designates, for Nietzsche, a knowledge of finitude, distinction, and measure, the unhistorical designates passion—being seized from without. Such a realm of the "unhistorical" remains associated with both "life" and "action":

> What deed would man be capable of if he had not first entered into that vaporous region of the unhistorical? Or, to desert this imagery and illustrate by example: imagine a man seized by a vehement passion for a woman or a great idea: how different the world has become to him! (64)

Keeping in mind the necessity of the "unhistorical," Nietzsche attempts to think about ways in which history may "serve" rather than paralyze life. In doing so, it seems that his desire is for an alternative, conscious memory, that would liberate his contemporaries from the weight of both unconscious, inhibiting memories and the historical knowledge of finitude and mortality.

As the essay progresses, however, it also becomes increasingly clear that a specific political question, that of modern German identity, is at stake. Nietzsche's engagement with history and the capacity for action is also an attempt to answer the question, How are modern Germans to be the true heirs of the Greeks?[5] The imitability of the Greeks lies in the fact that when faced with "the danger of being overwhelmed by what was past and foreign," the Greeks were able to reassert their own identity. This is a story about how the Greeks, instead of succumbing to the "entire" Orient and remaining its "overburdened heirs and epigones," "organized" and "augmented" their knowledge so as to become, instead, the origin of the Occident.[6] The threat of the past emerges now as the threat of cultural difference, and the "past" can thus be read here as a figure for the force of an imperial foreignness. However, the central structuring terms in this passage are not "foreign" and "native," but "chaos" and "organization." The Greeks, according to Nietzsche, responded selectively to their past: they took what they needed and discarded the rest. This is of course the argument Nietzsche has been making all through the essay. Historical knowledge must be valued only to the extent that it is useful for the present. History as science is now clearly framed as a modern *mistake:* a mistake that, while promising sovereignty, in fact fails to deliver it, because it is not selective, "subjective," and finally, egoistic enough in its engagement with the past.

The attractions of such a polemic for postcolonial subjects are obvious, though we should also be wary of some of the currents running through it, and especially of its desire for a sovereign cultural identity. Nevertheless, the essay poses the question of the use of historical knowledge in a manner that remains remarkably relevant and thought provoking. In thinking about the differences between my own reading of the *Gītā* and Gandhi's reading of it in light of Nietzsche's work, it seemed to me that it may be most productive to consider these differences symptoms of two divergent approaches, both to the past and to the activity of reading itself. Rather than simply applying to this situation the modes of relating to history that Nietzsche proposes (the critical and the monumental mode), I here demarcate them in ways that seem more precise in this context. Keeping the emphasis on ways of *reading* the texts of the past, I provisionally identify one as a history reader's approach, and the second as an activist reader's approach. Not a traditional historian, the history reader believes that historical sense is always predicated on acts of reading and not on empirical knowledge. Though she recognizes the fundamental precariousness of the enterprise, she nevertheless confronts the text as a web of *intelligible* (if indeterminate) signs that refer to a bygone world. She knows that her own access to the material that would help her to "make sense" of these signs is limited, so she also relies on the work of other history readers. Most significantly for our discussion, she seems impelled—by the formal demands of narrative, by aesthetic imperatives, or by an unexamined faith in structure—to bring disparate and contradictory elements of the texts she reads in relation to one another. Faced with apparent gaps or contradictions in a text, she attempts to construct a latent logic that would explain such contradictions. She tries not to ignore details that do not fit with her narrative but to change her narrative to account for the details. Though she is aware that the words of the text, even if she reads them in the "original" language, have acquired different resonances for her, she attempts to understand them as coming from afar. She may be like the historian Nietzsche disparages in that she reads mainly to understand the past and not to be instructed, except in an indirect way. It is not that she perceives the text only as an archival object that has no relation to the present. But she thinks that the text's relation to the present can only be interrupted and redirected, if you will, by reading it in terms of its context and reception.

The activist reader proceeds along a different path. He assumes that the text may in fact be radically disjointed and polyphonous and therefore does not expect it to be coherent. Because of this, he feels no compulsion to accord equal significance to all that he hears in the text but instead listens carefully only to the voice that speaks to him and amplifies it at the expense of the others. He wishes to bring to the present a sense of the past that will open, as it were, a breach and allow the present to turn in a different direction: in this, he may not be unlike the history reader. However, his method is quite different. He is less interested in exposing the injustices of the past or in turning people away from their ignorant reverence of the past than in turning the past into his ally. He therefore tries to gather from it an authoritative resource in order to radically question the habits and desires of the present. Although he is certainly not a classicist, he seems to be in accord with Nietzsche when Nietzsche states, "I do not know what meaning classical studies could have for our time if they were not untimely—that is to say, acting counter to our time and thereby acting on our time and, let us hope, for the benefit of a time to come" (60).

The first two sections of this chapter are written from my own perspective—that is to say, the perspective of a history reader. In the third section, I attempt to give an account of Gandhi's—an activist reader's—reading of the

Gītā. Finally, I try to gauge both the distance and the proximity between the two readings and to think about the limits of each reading in the context of contemporary India.

Arjuna's Despair

The *Mahābhārata* recounts the story of a dispute over sovereignty between two sets of cousins, the five Pandavas and the hundred Kauravas. Threatened by the imperial success of the Pandavas, the eldest of the Kauravas, Duryodhana, decides that his cousins must be defeated, not in the battlefield but in some other arena. On the advice of his maternal uncle, he invites Yudhisthira, the eldest Pandava, to a game of dice. Twice defeated and bitterly humiliated, Yudhisthira and his brothers, along with their common wife Draupadi, are forced to forsake their kingdom and go into exile for twelve years. According to the terms of the challenge, they must then spend a thirteenth year in disguise before they can regain their land and wealth. Of course at the end of the thirteen years, Duryodhana has no desire to return any part of the kingdom to his cousins. A relay of embassies fails to persuade Duryodhana to keep his part of the initial contract, and finally the Pandavas decide that their only recourse is war. Various kinsmen as well as rulers of neighboring kingdoms and tribes align themselves with one or the other of the warring groups, though, as one might imagine in a case like this, loyalties often remain divided and uncertain. Several elders feel that the Pandavas have been wronged and privately support their claim to part of the kingdom, but nevertheless in the end they fight for the Kauravas on whose patronage they depend.

As the battle is about to begin, it is Yudhisthira, the eldest of the Pandavas, who first becomes discouraged. Seeing the army of the Kauravas, larger and more impressive than his own, he wonders how the Pandavas can possibly win against an army led by the great Bhishma himself. Arjuna, his younger brother, at this time reassures him. He argues that victory comes not to those who are strong but to those who are truthful and lawful. As though anticipating the argument Krishna will later make, Arjuna remarks that the path to victory lies in abandoning greed and delusion, and that the Pandavas should fight without focusing on the conceit of the self:

> tyaktvādharmaṃ ca lobhaṃ ca mohaṃ codyamam āsthitāḥ
> yudhyadhvam anahaṃkārā yato dharmas tato jayaḥ (6.21.11)[7]

Besides, he adds, Krishna himself is with the Pandavas and will ensure their success. Just a few passages later, however, it is Arjuna who is assailed by doubts, though of a different kind. Consumed by fear of winning, rather than losing, he asks: what would this victory be worth? Shaken to the core, he experiences that which a warrior must never experience: compassion for his enemy and a deep sense of kinship with those on the other side.

At the commencement of the battle, he stands in the middle of the battlefield with his friend and charioteer Krishna. Krishna is a somewhat ambiguous figure in the epic. He is, on one level, a tribal warlord, a prince of the Yadava clan, and related to Arjuna through marriage. On another level, he is an incarnation of the Hindu god Vishnu, the lord of the universe who periodically takes human form to deliver the earth of evil. Surveying the army facing him, Arjuna experiences a deep crisis. How can he fight his own kinsmen, his elders, teachers, and friends, for the sake of a kingdom? Would that not be a sin, and would not his victory destroy precisely the community that would make success meaningful?

In response to his anxieties, Krishna delivers the sermon that we know as the *Bhagavad Gītā,* the Song of the Lord. It is a fairly long section of eighteen chapters; Arjuna frequently interrupts with doubts and questions, and Krishna responds each time with detailed explanations regarding human action, duty, desire, and devotion. Much of the argument draws on an ideal of detachment: a stoic ideal of performing one's duty without hope or fear. Arjuna must not let his attachment to his kinsmen delude and confuse him; he must perform his duty as a warrior (a Ksatriya), engaging in actions that are prescribed for him and dedicating them to Krishna himself, the lord of the universe and recipient of all actions undertaken in the spirit of sacrifice:

> Without hatred of any creature, friendly and compassionate
> without possessiveness and self-pride, equable in happiness and
> unhappiness . . . such a devotee of mine is beloved of me [. . .]
> A man who remains the same toward friend or foe, in honor or
> dishonor, in heat or cold, in happiness or misery . . . firm of mind,
> and devoted—such a man is dear to me. (6.34.13–20)[8]

It is on the basis of this foundational frame that Krishna urges Arjuna to perform his duty without desire for the fruits of his actions. The distinction between friend and enemy, analogous to the distinction Arjuna evokes between one's "own" people *(svajanaḥ)* and one's enemies, is presented as one among other superficial, sensible, or otherwise misleading distinctions, and thus Krishna can disassociate the act of killing from this distinction. Arjuna's duty as a warrior involves neither making such judgments (about friends and enemies) nor, indeed, taking responsibility for his own act. In the course of his explanation, Krishna reveals himself as the supreme deity in the monstrous figure of devouring Time, thereby divesting the warrior of the delusion that he himself might cause the death of his kinsmen. "I am Time grown old to destroy the world," says Krishna, "Embarked on the course of world annihilation. . . Therefore raise yourself now and reap rich fame, Rule the plentiful realm by defeating your foes! I myself have doomed them ages ago: Be merely my hand [*nimitta:* lit. instrument] in this, Left-handed Archer!" (6.33.32–33).[9] By the end of the discourse, Arjuna's doubts have been allayed, and the battle begins.

Let us examine what Arjuna's despair signifies in the context of the epic. Watching all his relatives assembled before him—fathers, grandfathers, teachers, brothers, sons, and friends in both armies—Arjuna is *kṛpayā parayāviṣṭo,* "overcome by compassion" (6.23.28). He suffers debilitating anxiety: his limbs give way, his mouth is dry, his skin burns.

> Having killed my kinsmen in battle, I do not foresee anything beneficial. I have no desire, Krishna, for either victory or the comforts of kingship. What is the kingdom to us, Govinda [Krishna], or what indeed are the pleasures of life? Those for whose sake we would desire kingdom, pleasure and comforts, they themselves stand in battle, relinquishing their precious [lit: hard to relinquish] lives. (6.23.32–33)

Arjuna conceives of the battle as a means of gaining kingship and its pleasures; he is in despair because he thinks that the means, while making the end available, will render it undesirable. His words indicate, first, that Arjuna believes his actions to be impelled by desire. The verb *kāṅkṣ* (to desire or want), repeated twice in the verses cited above, is etymologically connected to *kāma:* love, desire, or passion; and precisely the opposition between *kāma* and *karma* (deed, action, work) will inform the trajectory of Krishna's discourse. Second, these words indicate that the ends of war—territorial conquest, wealth, and power—have value for Arjuna *only insofar as he is connected to others.* The phrase *yeṣām arthe* (for the sake of whom) carries a dense weight in the line "Those for the sake of whom we would desire kingdom, pleasure and comforts," unequivocally declaring that pleasure and power are desired for the sake of others, for the family, and not solely for the self. And third, they tell us that Arjuna is acutely conscious here of the value of life; he is overcome by compassion *(kṛpayā parayāviṣṭo)* because he perceives that the men standing before him have staked their "hard to relinquish" lives for this familial dispute. In Arjuna's *kṛpā* (tenderness, compassion), may we not also detect all the resonances of the related verb *kṛp* (to mourn, lament, grieve, pity) as a buried strain, binding a consciousness of the other's mortality to the more usual sense of compassion or pity?

All three elements together frame a concept of human life that understands precisely *mortal* life as infinitely desirable and understands men as anchored to this desire both by objects of ambition (whether material or ideal: wealth or fame) and by their relation to the community, which makes ambition meaningful. War, as Arjuna understands it, is a phenomenon generated by, and woven into, this concept of life. It is a means to secure the goods of life for oneself and those to whom one is attached. However ideologically determined this idea of war may be, it is what allows Arjuna to make sense of war. We can only glimpse the significance of Arjuna's questions if we understand that this idea of war has now been shaken. His question indicates that what faces him is not war as he has hitherto understood it to be; it is something else.

We arrive at this reading of the question partly because of how the question is answered. The question and the answer shape one another; the one is read by way of the other. Krishna's response, focused on providing a new justification for war, suggests that available justifications are no longer sufficient—either because prevalent ideals of life have been decisively challenged or because war itself has come to be perceived as unbearable violence. Israel Selvanagayam and Nick Sutton, among others, have argued that the historical figure of the emperor Asoka, whose revulsion toward war must have had a far-reaching impact, must be recognized as decisively significant in this context.[10] A new justification of war will therefore attempt to galvanize new ideals of duty, action, and community. Partly appropriating the ideals of Buddhism, the *Gītā* will valorize the figure of a man unattached both to friends and to mortal life itself; one whose actions are impelled only by duty and not by desire. Detachment becomes the privileged means for the salvation of the soul. Indeed, insofar as Krishna's law constitutes its subject as an individual concerned solely about his own destiny, it bears a curious resemblance to some strains in modern liberal law. From this perspective, we could read the *Gītā* as performing some very specific tasks, among which is the task of preserving the formal and hierarchical structure of social community, while at the same time negating the individual's affective connection to this community. Arjuna's questions may now be read as resisting the ideal of a community founded on detachment.

But perhaps we should not unduly valorize Arjuna's concern for his kinsmen. As the dialogue progresses, the question "How can we be happy, Madhava [Krishna], having killed our own people *[svajanam]*" acquires a more technical meaning in Arjuna's discourse. Killing kinsmen, teachers, and elders is a sin, and he dreads the consequences of committing such a sin. This violation would destroy the eternal family laws *(kuladharma sanātanāḥ),* which in turn would lead to the corruption of women, and thus to the transgression of caste laws and the terrifying eventuality of miscegenation. Those responsible for this catastrophe, Arjuna says, are surely destined for hell, and even their ancestors will lose their place in heaven, bereft of the traditional offerings to ancestral souls. Having first drawn attention to Arjuna's love for his kin, the text now stages his fear of committing a sin. Does the latter mitigate the former, and take away from its initial power? Or may the two in fact be elements of the same quandary?

This movement from compassion to fear of sin often draws the attention of readers. In his review of Humboldt's *Gītā* lectures, written in 1827, Hegel takes this question as an occasion to explore deficiencies in the "Indian" concept of morality. Since Arjuna's reluctance to fight is not explained only in terms of his attachment to kin, the text seems to aver that such attachment alone cannot form the basis of a lawful moral stance. From Hegel's perspective, Arjuna's fear of transgression thus makes evident the weakness of the text. Instead of appealing to love alone, Arjuna now appeals to religious beliefs that are already debased as superstition in Hegel's account. I will quote at some length to make the argument clear:

> Whether this doubt [regarding killing relatives] involves a *moral* quality, as it seems to do at first, must be dependent on the nature of that value which in the Indian Arjuna's mentality is attached to family-ties. To the moral understanding of the European the sense of this tie is the moral in itself so that the love for one's family is as such the completion, and morality consists only in the fact that all friendship etc. as well as actions and duties related to family-relationship, have that love as their foundation and as a self-sufficient starting point. We see, however, that it is not this moral

> sentiment which in the hero causes the reluctance to lead his relatives to the slaughter . . . Great importance is attached to the conversion of this tie into a superstitious context, into an immoral belief in the dependence of the soul's fate after death on the cake and water-libations of the relatives, that is to say of those who have remained true to the caste-distinctions.[11]

What troubles Hegel is that love for the family is not *in itself* considered sufficient basis for articulating a moral principle; that love is not itself the foundation of morality. Instead this love must be explained by way of a "superstitious" narrative about the interdependence of generations and the significance of caste. Hegel's may be a paradigmatic "modern" reading, insofar as it presents itself as rationality steadily forging ahead to uncover the obfuscations of myth. I'd like to dwell on this reading for a moment, less because it is Hegel's and more because it is a reading that, in one form or another, would probably seem quite persuasive today.

Let us, then, for a moment, juxtapose these remarks against Hegel's famous reading of Sophocles' *Antigone,* where a related anxiety about the laws of kinship emerges. Here Hegel aligns family piety with "the law of the woman; the law of the inward life, a life which has not yet attained its full actualization."[12] The law of the "inward" life remains, for Hegel, incomplete; it cannot be sustained but must give way to the fuller, more developed law of the state. As Judith Butler writes, Antigone is read by Hegel "not as a political figure, one whose defiant speech has political implications, but rather as one who articulates a prepolitical opposition to politics, representing *kinship as the sphere that conditions the possibility of politics without ever entering into it.*"[13] In the interpretation of the play authorized by Hegel, "Antigone comes to represent kinship and its dissolution, and Creon comes to represent an emergent ethical order and state authority based on principles of universality" (3). For Butler, this reading raises the larger question of the separability of kinship and state. Questioning the assumption of their separability, she examines how the two, Antigone and Creon, but also kinship and the state, become in Sophocles' text "implicated in the idiom of the other" (10). For us what is most of interest in Butler's reading is her insistence that the state, as envisaged by Hegel, crucially depends on kinship, and yet "demands a partial repudiation" of kinship and the family (12). This repudiation stems from the state's commitment to war (we recall that in *Antigone,* the brother whom Antigone dares to bury, in defiance of Creon's decree, has fought against Thebes and is hence declared a traitor). In Hegel's remarks, war produces, as it were, the boundary of the state, both literally and conceptually, and by so doing, it sets the state in opposition to the family, to the love of kin or "womankind," which represents this love. In Butler's own words, "The state receives its army from the family, and the family meets its dissolution in the state" (36).

In his comments on the *Gītā,* Hegel remains conscious—all too conscious perhaps—of the differences separating European and Indian sensibility.[14] This separation may be just as necessary for the Hegelian system as is the one between the state and the family noted by Butler. However, what also leaps out for us today is in fact a shared similarity between Krishna's discourse in the *Gītā* and Hegel's text: precisely the necessity of negating and disavowing the community of kin, both in Hegel's response to Antigone, and in Krishna's response to Arjuna.[15] In both cases a familial love that threatens the work of kingship and more precisely, of war as the enabling condition of kingship is at stake. Kinship presents an affective excess that the state must master, subdue, or sublimate. So powerful is this excess that perhaps it cannot even be articulated persuasively within the terms of these texts—that would be one way of reading the apparent incoherence of both Antigone's and Arjuna's arguments. In Arjuna's case, the move from bewildering compassion to the familiar logic of caste laws may then be read as a symptom of the "lawlessness" to which such compassion has been relegated; it must be swiftly channeled into other arguments as soon as it dares to surface. How strong would be the threat of a compassion that can scarcely appear before being hustled away! We may then surmise that compassion for kin appears in the *Gītā* only in order to be decisively negated: to make room for a new war that would no longer be related to the idea of protecting the community of kin or of providing for them. A new kind of warrior has to be produced who would fight because he perceives war as his supreme duty and those he kills as faceless and nameless.

Indian readers have also not found it easy to accommodate Arjuna's compassion, which has often been understood as stemming from false attachment—an attachment that must be overcome on the path toward moral awakening. Indeed, if the problem for Hegel is not enough love, or rather not love enough, for several Indian readers, the problem is too much love. This might be because they read Arjuna's despair from the perspective of Krishna's response, which places the blame squarely on Arjuna's misplaced conception of attachment. Focusing on this, they sometimes ignore his fear of breaking the law, though, as I will suggest, these two aspects of Arjuna's despair are closely related.

In an article published in *Young India* in 1930, Gandhi writes: "We have to experience such distress as Arjuna experienced. Knowledge cannot be obtained without spiritual anguish and thirst for knowledge . . . The true Kurukshetra[16] is our body . . . In this battlefield lies one battle or another always before us, and most of such battles arise out of the ideas, 'this is mine, this is thine.' Such battles arise out the difference between 'my people and thy people.' Hence the Lord will later on tell Arjuna that the root of all irreligion is attachment and aversion. Believe a thing to be 'mine' and attachment is created for it. Believe a thing to be 'not mine' and aversion is created—enmity is created."[17]

A decade later he writes in *Harijan* (1940) that the question before Arjuna was not of nonviolence "but whether he should slay his nearest and dearest."[18] Gandhi is not alone in reading Arjuna's resistance to war in these terms. The earliest extant commentary on the *Gītā,* that of Sankara (ninth century), says that Arjuna's grief and delusion were caused by his attachment to his kinsmen and friends, by the notion that "I am theirs and they are mine."[19] Among Gandhi's own contemporaries, the Bengali writer Aurobindo Ghose in one instance describes Arjuna's compassion as "an impotence full of a weak self-pity"; according to him, Arjuna shrinks from killing his opponents "because they are 'one's own people' and without them life will be empty."[20]

In understanding Arjuna's concerns only in terms of emotional or familial attachment, these readings accept the premises persuasively structured by Krishna's response. Certainly attachment seems to be a strong force in Arjuna's remarks here, as in several speeches later in the epic when he laments the deaths of those he loved. But though attachment may account for much of Arjuna's despair, it would not account for the depths of his anxiety. Keeping in mind his wrenching and debilitating anxiety about violating the law—an anxiety dramatized powerfully by the text—I would argue that the distinction between "mine" and "thine" becomes significant not only because of proprietary affection but more significantly because of the basic ethos of the law of the Ksatriya, the warrior, as Arjuna understands that ethos. Insofar as the law of the warrior is to protect his own and to injure the other, and insofar as the duty of war crucially depends on this distinction, the warrior is the one for whom this limit constitutes, as it were, the very basis of law. Indeed, we could say that the warrior's position within the social structure is unique, because it allows him to perceive the communal boundary of duty: *his duty is to act towards others in exactly the ways he may not act towards his own.*[21] The warrior thus cannot function without this basic distinction between "mine" and "thine" and the law of the Ksatriya would be a meaningless law without this distinction.

In this context, let us recall that this is the same Arjuna who, when enraged, shows himself quite ready to kill one or more of his own brothers.[22] And in other instances, he has also faced an army of relatives in war with no such compunction. Indeed, we should perhaps not read Arjuna's dilemma too literally—as D. D. Kosambi does, for example, when he writes that "the history of India always shows not only brothers but even father and son fighting to the death over the throne, without the slightest hesitation or need for divine guidance."[23] If the question arises with such intensity in a cultural text, it is perhaps because a political system based on valorizing kinship is no longer tenable and has to be surpassed. The historian Romila Thapar's conclusions about the historical context of the Sanskrit epics affirm this reading: "The earlier sections of both texts [the *Rāmāyaṇa* and the *Mahābhārata*] depict a society which is closer in spirit to the lineage system . . . The later additions would date to a period when the lineage system had declined and the state had emerged."[24] Surely an epic that recounts, in enormous detail, a familial dispute resulting in a calamitous war must bear some relation to this historical passage.

Hence, we may surmise that the *Gītā* belongs to a period when a new justification for war must now be presented, as well as a new ethos for the warrior. Although war may still be waged for gaining the goods of life, that can no longer be acknowledged as its aim. Instead it has to be presented as a moral duty, and moreover, as a duty on which individual salvation depends. Thus the *Gītā* aims at once to persuade Arjuna to wage war in the name of dharma (moral law, righteousness) *and* to act with a view to *mokṣa* (liberation). Early sections of the *Gītā* reveal that this is not an easy task and that the two may not be immediately reconcilable. They suggest that a possible conflict may arise between dharma as a normative *social* order and *mokṣa* as the pursuit of individual salvation. As the ninth-century commentator Sankara notes, even dharma can be a "sin" for the one who seeks liberation, inasmuch as it causes bondage.[25]

Such conflict is dramatized when a character is no longer clear about which law to follow, if following one prescribed law will *necessarily* lead to the transgression of another. Indeed, the entire epic dramatizes a foundational crisis by drawing our attention to a series of attempts to find a ground for dharma. We could understand this historically—in terms of changing conceptions of dharma, the necessity of responding to or otherwise subsuming the challenge posed by Buddhism and Jainism—or structurally, in terms of a constitutive problem governing the relation between law and justice. In any case, it is clear that the problem, as it emerges in the text of the epic, has to do with a particular *function* of dharma: to dharma is entrusted the task of moving seamlessly between the language of political expedience and the language of ethics, and the epic recurrently draws our attention to the gaps between these two. The *Gītā,* read from a distance, appears to affirm that only the transformation of one of the players into a divine figure can accomplish this task.

It is no less significant that this transformation must be staged as an eruptive and powerful moment of epiphany, when Krishna abandons his "disguise" as Arjuna's friend and charioteer and emerges in his divine form. In spite of Krishna's many arguments about the unreliability of the senses, his discourse must be sealed by the blaze of epiphany. Arjuna desires to *see* this form: draṣṭum icchāmi te rūpam aiśvaraṃ puruṣottama (I wish to see your sovereign form, O foremost among men! 6.33.3),[26] returning to the very touchstone of sense certainty from which the discourse had wished to wean him. The confusion generated by the conflicting interests of various social laws can end only by making room for a transcendent law, which would appear to discard the language of social duty for the language of pure morality. Most simply put, this law presents an ideal of nonattachment to the world and attachment only to the divine. But should we not also note that "nonattachment"—and indeed, unconcern for the self and its desires—is valorized precisely because it leads to "personal" liberation—the liberation of one's own soul from the cycle of rebirth? Is it not ironic that the concept of "selfless" duty comes to the fore exactly at the moment when the community of kin is being implicitly negated, and concern for the individual destiny of the self gathers force? To be selfless is perhaps to be concerned solely about the transcendent and otherworldly self.

Krishna's Skill

Krishna's response to Arjuna presents an elaborate metaphysical system. My interest here is less in the details of the theological system and more in the arguments presented to convince Arjuna to put aside his fears and engage in battle. While the rhetorical dexterity of the response is unmistakable, it also draws its force from the very figure of Krishna. A heroic god in the role of a guide and an intimate friend is an inherently seductive figure—and how much more so when that god has also accrued, through the ages, the attributes of a divine lover. Today, it is this Krishna whom we read addressing Arjuna in the *Gītā:*

> kutas tvā kaśmalam idaṃ viṣame samupasthitam
> anāryajuṣṭam asvargyam akīrtikaram Arjuna
> klaibyaṃ mā sma gamaḥ Pārtha naitat tvayy upapadyate
> kṣudraṃ hṛdayadaurabalyaṃ tyaktvottiṣṭha paraṃtapa (6.24.2–3)[27]

> Whence this dejection, Arjuna, in this place of peril:
> Unworthy of an Arya, and leading neither to heaven nor fame.
> Do not go to impotence, Partha, it does not become you,
> Renouce this petty weakness of the heart, and rise, O tormentor of foes.

From the very beginning, Krishna presents Arjuna's doubts in terms of weakness; his dejection as a sign of unmanliness and impotence. The power of manliness as an uncontested value will continue to structure subsequent readings of the *Gītā,* including Gandhi's own reading—radically idiosyncratic in so many other ways. Needless to say, the specific context for the assertion of manliness had changed by Gandhi's time, but the extent to which the same constellation of terms—war, renunciation, weakness, manliness—continues to structure political discourse is remarkable.

As I read the text, it seems that Krishna's argument as a whole is indeed an extended response to the question What ideal of war and of the warrior would justify the killing of one's own people? Krishna responds, first, by enunciating what indeed appears to be a universally applicable law: of the mortality of the body and the immortality of the soul. Thus he presents a foundation that would render irrelevant the distinction between mine and thine, or friend and foe, by establishing a universality, a common ground, on which all men must base their actions. Nothing that truly exists can be killed, says Krishna; the indestructible, immeasurable Being that pervades all beings is beyond death, and the transience of the body does not affect it. Here then is a law that applies equally to all beings; not only does it render insignificant the relationships between warring enemies and the specific context of different battles; it also appears to posit a prior equality: anterior, and perhaps superior, to the law of caste.

But let us pause to ask why the doctrine of the immortality of the soul is enunciated on the battlefield, and how it might be connected to the anxieties specific to the warrior. This doctrine is summoned not to assuage the warrior's fear of (his own) death but rather to counter the double paralysis of guilt and mourning; in other words, it is presented as a response to the anxiety produced by "lawful" killing. Though ostensibly addressed to all, the warrior is the privileged and particular addressee of a discourse that connects the soul's immortality to an injunction against mourning. In effect, Krishna's words seek to free Arjuna of his compassion.

Though the idea of the immortal soul may appear to signify the equality of all beings, it in fact paves the way for an argument about the justification of caste divisions. Because the embodied being (the soul) in the body is never slayable, Arjuna should not let his sorrow about others obstruct his duty as a Ksatriya.

> dehī nityaṃ avadhyo 'yam dehe sarvasya Bhārata,
> tasmāt sarvāṇi bhūtāni na tvaṃ śocitum arhasi
> svadharmam api cāvekṣya na vikampitum arhasi
> dharmyād dhi yuddhāc chreyo 'nyat kṣatriyasya na vidyate
> (6.24.30–31).

> In all beings the embodied one in the body is forever unslayable,
> Bharata
> Therefore it is not worthy of you to sorrow over all creatures.
> Or, having perceived your own dharma, to tremble and waver.
> For a Ksatriya, nothing is known to be better than a lawful war.

Krishna's second argument builds on this one, by again reminding Arjuna that nothing is better for a Ksatriya than fighting a lawful war, and nothing worse than refusing such an opportunity. Evading a crucial question, Krishna does not explain why the war is lawful, only indicating that Arjuna's assumption regarding the ends of war (kingship and comforts) might in fact form the core of the problem. At this point, Krishna arrives at the famous line "your right is only to the action, never to the results" (karmāṇy evādhikāras te, mā phalesu kadācana 6.24.47). From this we might assume that the war becomes lawful if it is fought in a certain spirit—without concern for the advantages of victory. This is of a piece with Krishna's entire discourse, which addresses the question of justice or ethics only in terms of the individual's *orientation* toward action, and not in terms of the action itself. In this case, however, there is an added ambiguity. Actions are declared to be lawful if they are in conformity with caste duties, but war presents us with a particularly striking example of a duty that itself needs qualification (it must be lawful in its own right) in order to be considered legitimate. It is not enough for the warrior to fight; his war must also be lawful.

Commenting on the ambiguity of the term *dharmayuddha* (usually translated as "just war") in the epic, the philosopher Bimal K. Matilal asks how we might understand this war as lawful or just. He writes that he finds it "impossible to agree with those who wish to interpret the battle in the epic as an allegory of the battle between good and evil," since the epic narrative so consciously draws attention to the uncertainty of that distinction. He believes the battle was called *dharmayuddha* in a "technical sense"—because both sides agreed, at the beginning, to observe the rules of battle; they "agreed to fight a war on the basis of fairness by observing a number of familiar rules and practices on humanitarian grounds."[28] However, Matilal, along with many other readers, readily admits that in fact the battle turns into an arena where most of these rules—so piously enunciated earlier—are successively transgressed. In that case, we might perhaps say that the text, despite itself, draws us not to the available sense but rather to the *irony* of the term *dharmayuddha* as used by Krishna. Since the text does not allow for any stable meaning to be attached to the term, it strikes us as part of the rhetorical strategy employed by Krishna in his effort to persuade Arjuna to fight. The repetition of the term *dharmayuddha* in Krishna's discourse appears now as a *substitute* for a substantive argument regarding the bases for a just war.

Thus we may conclude that the text of the *Gītā,* as well as numerous passages scattered through the voluminous text of the *Mahābhārata,* attest to a historical anxiety about the political and social structures predicated on the potential of war. It seems that the position of the warrior (the Ksatriya) had become a nodal point for various uncertainties; that somehow—possibly through an articulation of the horrors of war—the virtues of compassion and forgiveness were already in powerful tension with those of bravery and military skill. This is of course not a new argument. David Gitomer has noted that the "primary discourse of the emerging epic text (which includes all its 'versions' and retellings in other genres)" may be read as "a series of attempts to come to terms with the inherently problematic and self-destructive nature of social institutions—in this case of course ksatriya institutions."[29] In his thoughtful introduction to the *Gītā,* J. A. B. van Buitenen also reads this conflict historically: "At the time when all the materials that were to go into the final redactorial version of the great epic . . . were collected, materials that hailed from many milieus and many centuries, a change of sensitivity away from the war books had taken place, a change from the martial spirit toward a more reflective and in certain ways more quietist mood."[30] It was now considered essential to justify war in accordance with a new affirmation of sacrifice; to present the warrior not as a figure in quest of mortal goods but instead as a figure in quest of salvation. In a similar vein, Israel Selvanayagam suggests that in response to the challenge posed by diverse Śramaṇa groups who opposed the sacrifice-centered Vedic society and sought to interiorize the very idea of sacrifice, the epic provides a renewed affirmation of Vedic sacrifice and indeed "tries to interpet the duty of the ksatriyas on the battlefield as their distinctive sacrifice."[31]

Historically oriented readings have thus repeatedly drawn attention to the latent impact of renunciatory ideas and practices on the epic's representation of war and, in particular, on the dialogue dramatized by the *Gītā.* In such readings Arjuna becomes, as it were, the spokesperson for resistance, and Krishna the advocate of Brahminical and Ksatriya orthodoxy. Thus, discussing Arjuna's "trauma" in the *Bhagavad Gītā,* Patrick Olivelle writes: "Renunciatory ideals such as not injuring any living creature and the assertion of the individual as the ultimate moral agent were no doubt at the root of such moral dilemmas that underlie the inner conflict of tradition."[32] I have drawn on these readings but also suggested that Arjuna's remarks should perhaps be read as indicative not of a commitment to nonviolence as such but of a commitment to a different concept of war predicated on the warrior's loyalty to kin. Such a commitment, perhaps infused with the resistant discourse of the renunciants, enables Arjuna's anxiety to be articulated. Krishna's response counters this challenge by selectively rewriting the concept of renunciation for the ends of war. A strain in the idea and practice of renunciation—which may potentially challenge the very basis of temporal power based on force—is instead brilliantly deployed in the service of defending the warrior's duty and reiterating the legitimacy of the *varna* system.

For it is obvious that the very concept of kingship is fundamentally in question and that the king is perceived as a figure that must redefine its relation to dharma. In the *Udyogaparvan,* the section immediately preceding the war books of the *Mahābhārata,* we read an exchange between Yudhisthira, Sanjaya, and Krishna, that enables us to link debates regarding kingship with the concerns of the *Gītā.* Sanjaya, the charioteer of King Dhritrashtra, has come to counsel Yuddhisthira against going to war. He has been sent by the aged king, whose blindness is clearly symbolic of his prevailing weakness: his love for his son Duryodhana, which renders the son's vices invisible in the father's eyes. As Sanjaya urges Yudhisthira to refrain from fighting with his cousins, his speech prefigures some of Arjuna's queries in the *Gītā*, questioning the value of a victory obtained through the death of kinsmen. In one verse, Sanjaya criticizes the law of Ksatriyas: "That law which prevails among you / To injure those who don't injure you, is not commendable" (5.24.3). Even though he is referring here to Duryodhana's act of denying Yudhisthira his patrimony, the pronoun *yuṣmākam* (of you, plural) seems to include Yudhisthira as well among the followers of this law.[33]

In his response to Sanjaya, Yudhisthira claims that Dhritrashtra's desire for empire, for unrivalled sovereignty over the earth, lies at the root of the conflict. Peace is not possible, he says, because of Dhritrashtra's aversion to sharing wealth: "Dhritrashtra, with his sons, wishes indeed for unrivalled rule over the earth"(5.26.19). Were he not faced with such imperial avarice, Yudhisthira would not be driven to war: "Why would a man go to war? Who indeed is so cursed by the gods as to choose war?" (5.26.3) He insists that he wants nothing that is not his due, and only seeks the restoration of his livelihood. Finally he asks for Krishna's advice, and Krishna's response is in many ways a prologue to his sermon in the *Gītā*. He begins by asserting the significance of the path of work, thus laying the ground for his main argument: Yudhisthira can only perform the work assigned to him—the work of kingship—by regaining his kingdom, and therefore he is entitled to fight for his inheritance. Yet some doubts evidently remain regarding the justification of violence, because at the conclusion of this part of his speech, Krishna again reminds Sanjaya that war is among the duties of kings: "Since you think better of peace, I wish to hear your response to this question: Does the duty of kings lie in fighting or in not fighting?" (5.29.19). Krishna thus presents a circular argument: Yudhisthira must fight in order to become a king, and he also must fight because he is (already) a king.

The passage that follows reveals that not only does the text recognize a structural relation between kingship, property, and violence, but it also registers how this relation can always threaten to turn the king into his double, the robber. In an extended section, Krishna explains that war comes into being when a king desires the wealth of others and becomes a robber. Such robbers must be killed—indeed, it is virtuous to kill them—since no one would want to be robbed of their property: "Then again the share of Pandu's sons is fixed. Why should it be taken away from us by others? At this stage, to be killed while fighting would be praise-worthy for us. Ancestral wealth is superior to the kingdom of another" (5.29.29). If we read such passages in conjunction with the early parts of the epic, where Krishna himself advises Yudhisthira to perform the Rajasuya sacrifice to establish his dominion over all the Ksatriyas *(Sabhapārvan)*, it becomes evident that the Kauravas are not the only ones who dream of empire. Indeed, the robber analogy is indicative of a larger contradiction informing the concept of kingship: on the one hand, it is a king's duty to extend his dominion (according to the *Manusmṛti*, "What has not been acquired is to be desired by the king"),[34] and on the other, his attempt to do so may be condemned as robbery, and incite violence. The distinction "mine/thine" is essential to Krishna's argument here, even though it applies to property rather than people. Indeed, it seems that it would be impossible to frame any concept of territorial kingship without recourse to this distinction. However, to read Krishna's various statements as "contradictory," as though these ideas were manifestations of a single thought, is no doubt a mistake. It may be more productive to read the repeated emphasis on the distinction "mine/thine" as indicative of something unresolved; an underlying tension that marks the contiguous discourses of kingship, kinship, property, propriety, belonging, and ownership.

In the sections I have discussed, Krishna wishes to maintain class/caste divisions, giving them a divine as well as a "natural" foundation, but he simultaneously wishes to "liberate" Arjuna from affiliative connections. The community of caste is subordinated even as caste identity is privileged. But attachment as such is not to be abandoned. Indeed, by presenting himself as the *sole legitimate object* of Arjuna's desire, by redirecting all attachment toward himself, Krishna allows us to glimpse the dream of every transcendent law: to counter the threat of any affiliation, any affective connection, that does not pass through its own circuit. Thus the famous lines at the end of the text: manmana bhava madbhakto madyaji mam namaskuru . . . sarvadharman partityajya mam ekam saranam vraja: Focus your mind on me, be my devotee, my sacrificer, and bow to me . . . Abandon all laws and seek refuge with me alone (6.40.65–66). All tensions, all legal and religious dilemmas can thus be rendered insignificant. Most important of all, the arid doctrine of renunciation can thus be infused with the warmth of passion, now directed toward the divine Krishna himself. As Madeleine Biardeau has noted, "It is impossible to explain the teaching of the *Gītā* on activity without desire without this precondition of a transfer of man's whole capacity for desire onto God."[35]

It is clear by now that the history reader's reading is a secular reading. From the beginning, I have approached the *Gītā* as a historical, not a divine, text, and my aim has been to "account for" many of the apparently spiritual elements of the *Gītā.* Such elements—which would include the element of Bhakti (devotion), which presents Krishna as the sole object of the devotee's love; the discourse of renunciation, which reminds the devotee of the transience of worldly things and commands him to focus on the performance of his duty and not on its results; and most significantly, the body/soul division, which presents the soul as immortal and essential and the body correspondingly as temporal and inessential—have all been read as inextricably connected with a political project. As I have speculated, this project may involve the consolidation of territorial kingship, the devaluation of kinship and lineage structures, the affirmation of caste distinctions and duties, and, finally, the production of a new political subject. Such a subject would be persuaded to perceive its actions increasingly in relation to the destiny of its soul and less in relation to an affective community, which, like all intermediary communities, presents a potential threat to the state.

This reading has also brought its own political concerns to the text, since it is crucially concerned with the *Gītā's* representation of war. It sees the text as a threat, insofar as the text presents war as an apolitical and spiritual duty. It perceives the *Gītā* as part of that variegated and multilingual series of texts that presents war as a higher duty, leading to the salvation of the soul. It is guided by the idea that in order to be sustained, the violence of war must periodically be presented as *nonviolence:* that is to say, as something that maintains, rather than violates or threatens, a desired cosmic order. This idea will be discussed in greater detail in the following chapter. For now, suffice to say that according to this reading, the renouncer, who might otherwise have appeared as the king's double, adversary, and antagonist, is incorporated by the text within the project of kingship. Finally, I have read the *Gītā* here as the sign of an admission that the confusion generated by conflicting perceptions of dharma can no longer be settled without recourse to an external and transcendent voice: a voice whose origin is more decisive than the content of its utterance. A crucial and remarkable aspect of the text of the *Mahābhārata:* its repeated, almost compulsive staging of argument and counterargument, of harsh and bitter dialogues that occur not only among enemies but also among friends and brothers, goes into retreat at this instance. Giving sanctity to the duty of war now requires the emergence of a figure both divine and seductive: the handsome god, the divine friend, Krishna of the mocking face and terrible mouth.

Let me pause for a moment to consider the premises of my reading. I assumed that the spiritual elements of the text function *merely* as the means for articulating these political ends and should be treated as strategy or appearance. I proceeded as though the task of the reader were to distinguish between the persuasive strategy (the rhetoric) of the text, and its "true" aim or theme. However, if that were the case, then reading the text would simply entail an exposure of its strategy, whether in terms of authorial intention, narrative desire, or, more broadly, as cultural false consciousness. In other words, reading would entail recovering, assigning, and naming a site of duplicity, however complex or mediated that site might be. This is where Gandhi's reading makes me pause. For it lucidly demonstrates that the spiritual elements may *exceed* their deployment as mere means. The subordination of means to ends, which the *Gītā* calls into question on moral grounds when it asks the devotee not to focus on the fruit of action, also seems theoretically flawed when it comes to understanding how a text works or what effects it is capable of generating. Indeed, if what we have so far considered the means (in this case, the rhetoric of spirituality and renunciation) are instead read as the *ends* of the text, the text can acquire an altogether different significance. Which model of language and of literariness would enable us to draw a clear distinction between the rhetoric and the theme, or the rhetoric and the argument of a text, and on what grounds would we subscribe to such a model? Does not language instead constantly present us with instances where the thematic center or persuasive force of narratives only emerges as an effect of their rhetorical excess? Is there not something incommensurable and immeasurable about the relation between rhetoric and theme, which constitutes the enduring enigma of the text? Gandhi's reading, which overturns many of the premises of my secular reading, also provokes us to pose such questions.

Allegory

If, as we have seen, the duties of the warrior had already become open to questioning during the time of the *Mahābhārata*, by the time of the nationalist period many centuries later this ambivalence had not disappeared but had instead acquired new meaning, content, and complexity. The *Gītā*'s call to arms, its oft repeated injunction *yudhyasva* (Fight!), its ability to present violence as a sacred duty had a strong appeal, particularly among young Hindu men eager to find a spiritual sanction for armed resistance against British rule. Gandhi's intervention in this scene was remarkable in many ways, for while consistently upholding the authority of the *Gītā*, he continued to advocate nonviolence as not only a moral but also a strategic means to win *swaraj*.

How did Gandhi reconcile his belief in nonviolence with the injunctions of the *Gītā*, and how did he continue to find inspiration in that text? One clue is provided in a line from *Hind Swaraj*: "A nation that is desirous of securing Home Rule *cannot afford to* despise its ancestors."[36] Although spoken in a different context, the sentence captures well some of the pressures of the moment. Gandhi was no different from many nationalists of his time in believing that it was important to awaken in a colonized people a sense of pride in their past and their inherited texts. Indeed, as we know, Gandhi went further than most others in his valorization of the ancient world. Yet the trope of penury must also be noted. If a nation cannot "afford" to despise its ancestors, should it then be constrained to revere them? These are, as we know, rather misplaced alternatives. A depth of engagement with the past may be more valuable than the judgment it yields. Indeed, the act of reading assumes significance only when immediate judgment—and particularly the judgment most easily available to a modernizing public (the judgment of contempt)—has been, in principle, placed in question.

In all his comments on the *Gītā*, Gandhi seems, above all, to be aware that at hand is a text: that is to say, an entity that may not conform to a single law. He seems to believe that the task of the reader likewise is not to relate all elements of the text into a single thread or to search for a unifying logic that would account for everything that appears in the text. Confronted by the co-appearance of two aspects of the *Gītā*, its focus on renunciation and its support for war, Gandhi thus responds quite unlike the history reader, who, as we have seen, attempts to find a political reason for the coappearance of these two elements and proceeds by asking what the *function* of such coappearance might be. The history reader asks what this co-appearance might *enable* the text to do and arrives at a historically and politically plausible answer, namely, that the doctrine and rhetoric of renunciation in the text serve to legitimize war. Gandhi proceeds quite differently. Like the history reader, he notes the disjunction between these two aspects of the text, but unlike her, he does not ask if a latent political logic connects them. Instead, he decides that since renunciation is fundamentally at odds with war, the two cannot be reconciled. This seems to be a radically different approach, depending on an altogether different set of premises and aims. Even the history reader, who prides herself on her irreverence, is forced to acknowledge that it demonstrates irreverence of another order, in the sense that it decides from the outset, as it were, that its primary allegiance is to something else besides the text. The text, if one may put it in this way, becomes *almost* accidental. Gandhi's remarks about the *Gītā* are thus engaged in accounting for this accidental text, and consequently, the trope on which he often depends is allegory. In 1925, Gandhi wrote in *Young India:*

> My Krishna has nothing to do with any historical person.[37] I would refuse to bow my head to the Krishna who would kill because his pride is hurt, or the Krishna whom non-Hindus portray as a dissolute youth. I believe in Krishna of my imagination as a perfect incarnation . . . But if it was proved to me that the *Mahābhārata* is history in the same sense that modern historical books are, that every word of the *Mahābhārata* is authentic and that the Krishna of the *Mahābhārata* actually did some of the acts attributed to him, even at the risk of being banished from the Hindu fold, I should not hesitate to reject that Krishna as God incarnate. But to me, the *Mahābhārata* is a profoundly religious book, largely allegorical, in no way meant to be a historical record. It is the description of the eternal duel going on within ourselves . . . Nor do I regard the *Mahābhārata* as we have it now as a faultless copy of the original. On the contrary I consider that it has undergone many emendations.[38]

The passage suggests that a "historical" person would be one to whom access would be available through his or her textual representation. Modern historical books, which describe people as they were and the acts they "actually" performed, are thus presented here as examples of texts that may be read literally. The *Mahābhārata,* however, is a different kind of text, one that Gandhi calls allegorical. By this he does not mean that it presents us with a series of signifiers bearing a formal and conventional (rather than natural or imitative) relation to a set of signified terms. Instead, what Gandhi takes from the usual sense of allegory is the idea of the radical insufficiency and poverty of the signifier. The *Mahābhārata* is allegorical because its appearance—the language we read—is an inadequate indicator of its meaning, quite apart from the fact that the text we read today may be a flawed text to begin with. What thus faces us is a text that is at once fallen and unreliable and, at the same time, "profoundly religious" and capable of indicating the perfection of Krishna. Walter Benjamin's remarks on the antinomies of the allegorical are helpful here:

> Any person, any object, any relationship can mean absolutely anything else. With this possibility a destructive, but just verdict is passed on the profane world: it is characterized as a world in which the detail is of no great importance. But it will be unmistakably apparent, especially to anyone who is familiar with allegorical textual exegesis, that all of the things which are used to signify derive, from the very fact of their pointing to something else, a power which makes them appear no longer commensurable with profane things, which raises them onto a higher plane, and which can, indeed, sanctify them. Considered in allegorical terms, then, the profane world is both elevated and devalued.[39]

The text of the *Mahābhārata,* which becomes, in Gandhi's reading, an instance of the "profane world," is clearly, for him, a text in which the detail is not important. As a text, it is both elevated and devalued, exactly in the manner described by Benjamin. The words that signify derive their power not just from pointing to something else but primarily from pointing to a divine significance. That such "significance" is constitutively "divine" is implicit in Benjamin's remarks, which we may read in conjunction with Derrida's assertion that "the age of the sign is essentially theological."[40] As soon as the distinction between the sensible and the intelligible comes into play, we are in the realm of the profane and the sacred. Allegory enacts, as it were, this melodrama of the sign. This accounts for its wide appeal, even as it presents a rather curious paradox. Gandhi's reading of the *Mahābhārata* is symptomatic in this regard. The recourse to allegory enables him to retain the *Mahābhārata*—and in particular the *Gītā*—as a profoundly religious and important text, even as it is read as an imperfect indicator of its real meaning.

Because the text is contradictory, imperfect, and flawed, the reader must read it critically and selectively: not everything belongs on the same plane, some parts are more persuasive or more significant than others.[41]

> I am not a literalist. Therefore I try to understand the spirit of the various scriptures of the world. I apply the test of Truth and Ahimsa laid down by these very scriptures for interpretation. I reject what is inconsistent with that test, and I appropriate all that is consistent with it. The story of a shudra having been punished by Ramachandra for daring to learn the Vedas, I reject as an interpolation. And in any event, I worship Rama, the perfect being of my conception, not a

> historical person facts about whose life may vary with the progress of new historical discoveries and researches. Tulsidas had nothing to do with the Rama of history. Judged by historical test, his Ramayana would be fit for the scrap heap. As a spiritual experience, his book is almost unrivalled at least for me. And then, too, I do not swear by every word that is to be found in so many editions published as the Ramayana of Tulsidas. It is the spirit running through the book that holds me spellbound.[42]

A literalist thus becomes a gullible consumer of texts who approaches them without a critical faculty of judgment. Unlike such a reader, Gandhi attempts to understand the spirit of the work, and, at one level, he does so in the most rigorous way: by using internal criteria to determine inconsistencies and contradictions. These criteria do not confuse him, because he begins from the standpoint of belief; from a prior conviction that Rama (or in the case of the *Gītā,* Krishna) is a perfect being.

Gandhi's approach to the *Gītā* may seem to be curiously analogous to the *Gītā's* own approach to earlier canonical texts in that both present themselves as continuing traditions of thought that they in fact oppose or transform. Many readers of the *Gītā* have commented on its complex response to the antagonistic theological doctrines of its time: a response characterized by both assimilation and reorientation. The historian D. D. Kosambi writes thus about the remarkable synthetic ability of the *Gītā:* "No violence is done to any preceding doctrine except vedic *yajna.* The essential is taken from each by a remarkably keen mind capable of deep and sympathetic study: all are fitted together with consummate skill and literary ability, and cemented by *bhakti* without developing their contradictions."[43] Van Buitenen similarly reads the *Gītā* as a text that addresses itself to various irreconcilable traditions and attempts to define "the right kind of action against, on the one hand, the overzealous advocates of Vedic ritualism and, on the other, the proponents of the doctrine that all acts should be given up."[44] From a different perspective, Alf Hiltebeitel has argued that "the epic narrative itself has been structured in part to bridge the gap between Vedic and Puranic mythologies."[45] Though Gandhi never uses such distinctions, it seems quite clear that he too read the *Gītā* as a text that placed itself within the very tradition that it wanted to question or to reorient. Once again, Gandhi has discussed this in linguistic terms:

> Because a poet puts a particular truth before the world, it does not necessarily follow that he has known or worked out all its great

> consequences, or that having done so, he is able always to express them fully. In this perhaps lies the greatness of the poem and the poet. A poet's meaning is limitless. Like man, the meaning of great writings suffers evolution. On examining the history of languages, we notice that the meaning of important words has changed or expanded. This is true of the *Gitā*. The author has himself extended the meanings of some of the current words . . . It is possible, that in the age prior to that of the *Gitā*, offering of animals in sacrifice was permissible. But there is not a trace of it in the sacrifice in the *Gitā* sense . . . Similarly has the meaning of the word *sannyasa* [renunciation] undergone, in the *Gitā*, a transformation. The *sannyasa* of the *Gitā* will not tolerate complete cessation of all activity . . . Thus the author of the *Gitā* by extending meanings of words has taught us to imitate him. Let it be granted, that according to the letter of the *Gitā* it is possible to say that warfare is consistent with renunciation of fruit. But after 40 years' unremitting endeavour fully to enforce the teaching of the *Gitā* in my own life, I have, in all humility, felt that perfect renunciation is impossible without perfect observance of ahimsa in every shape and form.[46]

The argument again hinges on the insufficiency of the "letter" of the text. Because the *Gītā* itself "extends" the meanings of words, it shows us that the letter of the text is not transparent; its significance is subject to temporal change. The terms used in a work must be read in relation to the new arguments they produce. But Gandhi now takes this a step further. If the reader finds a contradiction in the text, he or she may similarly decide to disregard the letter of the text in deciding its true import. This import does not pretend to correspond to the letter of the text but to something else, which Gandhi calls spirit, following a common convention. As Philip Lutgendorf has remarked in the context of a discussion of the *Rāmcaritamānas*, Gandhi "reserved the right to interpret the spirit of the text in his own fashion and (in the metaphor of the couplet he was so fond of citing) to strain out the 'milk' and discard the 'water.'"[47] If we pay closer attention to the function of this spirit, we find that once established as the animating principle of the text, it indeed allows the text to "live"; to transcend its own historical limits and become a guide for future generations. Gandhi knows very well that the *Gītā* is not an advocate of nonviolence, but he argues that if put into practice, its proclaimed ideal of renunciation would inevitably lead to nonviolence. In

1936 he writes in the *Harijan,* "I have admitted in my introduction to the Gita known as *Anasakti Yoga* that it is not a treatise on non-violence, nor was it written to condemn war. Hinduism, as it is practiced today or has even been known to have ever been practiced, has certainly not condemned war as I do."[48] However, just as the *Gītā* itself "breathed new life into Hinduism," Gandhi too wishes to give an "extended but in no way strained meaning" to the text and to Hinduism itself.[49]

If we were to follow Gandhi in "extending" the meaning of words, we could perhaps say that in the age of capitalism, renunciation of desire may also acquire a different significance. Instead of signaling moral puritanism and a dread of sensory pleasure, as is often thought, it may signal a radical questioning of desire itself as that which is enmeshed in and produced by ideology. Thus it may entail a recognition that desires are already part of a hegemonic realm, already in the service of socioeconomic ends that the subject blindly appropriates as its own, in the name of desire. Correspondingly, Gandhi's *liberation* of the discourse of renunciation from the ends of war may restore and heighten a skeptical impulse that has perhaps always coursed through this discourse in some measure. In other words, by engaging renunciation as *practice,* Gandhi enables us to perceive in it anew a profound interrogation of the authority of the king and the hegemonic structures of sociopolitical life.

Gandhi's enterprise is thus quite different from that of the history reader. The latter assigns herself the task of understanding the text as a historical object, while Gandhi, the activist reader, reads in order to selectively incorporate elements of the text into his life. He has no use for historical knowledge but only for that which inspires or helps him to act. He is looking for a conduct book, and the *Gītā* appears to him in this light. In a remarkable passage in his autobiography, he describes how this book became his "dictionary of daily reference": "Just as I turned to the English dictionary for the meaning of English words that I did not understand, I turned to this dictionary for conduct for a ready solution of all my troubles and trials. Words like aparigraha (non-possession) and samabhava (equability) gripped me."[50] What grips him through the *Gītā* is perhaps what had *already* gripped him but now becomes strikingly powerful because it shines forth as a Sanskrit word, at once familiar yet distant, resonant yet authoritative, giving Gandhi the sanction to follow his convictions. The text becomes sacred to the extent that it may correspond to, or strengthen, the convictions of the activist reader. Already in 1922 Gandhi wrote: "Though my views on *Ahimsa* are a result of my study of most of the faiths of the world, they are now no longer dependent upon the authority of these works. They are a part of my life and if I suddenly discovered that the religious books read by me bore a different interpretation from the one I had learnt to give them, I should still hold the view of *ahimsa* as I am about to set forth here."[51] Such an approach, which seems distinctly modern in its premises,[52] is succinctly reiterated elsewhere: "I cannot let a scriptural text supercede my reason."[53]

This approach allows Gandhi to read the *Gītā* as a text that may be of present use to its readers. Once divorced from the imperative to conduct war, the idea of renunciation of desire may be aligned instead with *ahimsa* and play a critical role in redefining the terms of contemporary politics. He thus took from the text only what he found most compelling for his own work. Of course his idiosyncratic reading, supported neither by the traditional commentaries nor by the letter of the text, has drawn criticism. Responding to two such critics, Agehananda Bharati and D. M. Datta, Ashis Nandy claims that it was precisely Gandhi's disregard (and ignorance) of Brahminical thought that allowed him to affirm "the non-canonical and the folk" and hence to reinterpret Hinduism in his own manner. "He had acquired the right to 'distort' authoritatively."[54] By this Nandy presumably means that he had demonstrated that his primary concern was for the living Hindus around him, and that this concern allowed him to interpret Hinduism in his own way. But perhaps he also means that Gandhi was equally guided by a concern for *Hinduism*—not for its textual traditions but for a set of cultural practices that, while deserving of change (or, in some cases "distortion"), were not, according to Gandhi, deserving of abandonment. His articulation of this concern has perhaps posed the most provocative and difficult questions for those who read Gandhi's work. If I gave him every benefit of the doubt, I'd say that his concern may not have been for specific traditions, but rather for *tradition itself,* whose gradual erosion seemed catastrophic to him. For at times it seems evident that his loyalty lay less with particular aspects of a tradition and more with the idea that modernity needs tradition: that is to say, a less violent and less dismissive relation to the past. And yet we must also note that at other times this loyalty appears as a disturbing commitment to orthodoxy.

Caste

The question of violence/nonviolence is not the only political question addressed by the *Gītā:* as we have seen, its response to violence is predicated on the idea of disinterested duty, crucially linked to the structure of caste. While a selective reading of early Sanskrit texts makes it possible to present nonviolence as a "Hindu" ideal in its own right, the question of caste poses a more difficult dilemma. An opposition to the very institution of caste would inevitably be read as an attack on Hinduism itself: an attack that would have seemed both misguided and meaningless to Gandhi. Therefore, in spite of all his attempts to argue against "the monster of untouchability,"[55] Gandhi remains committed to a certain conception of the classic *varna* system, which he distinguishes from the modern caste system. *Varna* literally means color, but may also mean a category or a genre. It designates the four-fold division of Hindu society into Brahmin, Ksatriya, Vaishya, and Shudra (priest, warrior/king, cultivator or trader, and servant); thus it is different from the manifold *jati* (subcaste) system, which has traditionally categorized on the basis of specific professions.

As is typical of Gandhi's response to traditional institutions, he attempts to rearticulate *varna* in a way that appears to endorse the premises of the system while also reorienting it toward something quite different: his own ideal of an economically noncompetitive society. Read in the best possible light, such an attempt may signal an ambition to reframe inequality in such a way as to make it the basis for a (different) kind of equality, in a changed context. However, by neither advocating the abolition of *varna* nor supporting its orthodox and traditional structure, Gandhi managed to offend people on both sides of the political spectrum. His refusal to acknowledge that hierarchy is endemic to caste seemed as perverse to his contemporaries as it does to us today. Thus he writes: "The moment untouchability goes, the caste-system itself will be purified, that is to say, according to my dream, it will resolve itself into the true Varna Dharma, the four divisions of society, each complementary of the others, and none inferior or superior to any other, each as necessary for the whole body of Hinduism as any other."[56] He understands *varna* to mean "pre-determination of the choice of man's profession"—a system in which each (male) child follows the profession of his ancestors. He advocates this system for the whole world, insisting that "it is not a human institution, but an immutable law of Nature,"[57] and in one instance he goes so far as to say that "a shudra has as much right to knowledge as a brahmana, *but he falls from his estate if he tries to gain his livelihood through teaching.*"[58] None of this makes much sense except from a perspective that considers the very condition of choice as an inevitable conduit to self-indulgence, competition, and ambition. Indeed, a terror of choice runs through so many of Gandhi's texts (for example, in his valorization of vows as a regular practice) that one wonders how strongly his "utopian" vision was determined by his singularly bleak perception of human propensities.

His writings about caste reveal again an attempt to represent the *varna* system as a system whose meaning is yet to be determined, and indeed, may be determined anew from the modern reader's perspective. By framing *varna* as a system that prescribes division of labor without hierarchy, he suggests that it may become a powerful means of resisting the competitive materialism of industrial capitalist societies. Thus Gandhi envisions a society where interdining and intermarriage are permitted, where each profession is considered equal, so that there is no competition for more lucrative jobs and all work is granted the same dignity: "I consider that it is unmanly for any person to claim superiority over a fellow-being." This doctrine of *varna* he claims to derive not from the Hindu shastras but from the *Bhagavad Gītā*.[59]

Let us quickly compare these ideas with those of some of his contemporaries in order to grasp their particular valence. In an address given at Tokyo University in 1944, Subhas Chandra Bose said,

> With regard to caste, that is now no problem for us, because caste, as it existed in the old times, does not exist today. Now, what is the caste system? The caste system means that a community is divided into certain groups on a professional or vocational basis and marriage takes place within each group. In modern India there is no such caste distinction. A member of one caste is free to take up any other profession . . . For Free India, therefore caste is no problem at all.[60]

Even allowing for the possibility that Bose might be eager to dispel some prevailing myths about Indian society for a foreign audience, this is an astonishingly sanguine statement. But we see here the fundamental difference between Bose's and Gandhi's visions: the freedom that Bose idealizes—the freedom to "take up" any profession—is precisely the value of which Gandhi is most suspicious.

Needless to say, Bose's optimistic views about the virtual disappearance of caste in modern India were not shared by many of his contemporaries. Gandhi's most articulate critic on this matter was B. R. Ambedkar, himself a member of an "untouchable" caste. In his searing indictment of Gandhian politics *(What Congress and Gandhi Have Done to the Untouchables)* Ambedkar writes: "By its very genius Hinduism believes in social separation which is another name for social disunity and even creates social separation. If the Hindus wish to be one they will have to discard Hinduism . . . Hinduism is the greatest obstacle to Hindu unity."[61] Like Gandhi, Ambedkar believed that caste was intrinsic to the structure of Hinduism, but unlike Gandhi, he perceived it as an essentially corrosive and divisive rather than a cohesive force. While Ambedkar disagreed with many of Gandhi's opinions and found many of his policies offensive, his sharpest critique, in most cases, was directed against Gandhi's unwillingness to recognize the untouchables as a political group and to encourage independent political organization and action among them. As we know, Gandhi followed a similar approach in his responses to peasant and worker groups: the case of Champaran has been particularly well documented.[62]

In his writings on caste, Gandhi makes an argument similar to the one he makes about violence in the *Gītā*. The canonical texts are rendered radically open to interpretation, and their meaning becomes an effect of the interpretive act. The authority of the text is thus now vested in the interpreter, who is led by his own heart and not by the words on the page. In 1941, in a manifesto-like statement, Gandhi writes again that the "interpretation of accepted texts is capable of indefinite evolution, even as the human intellect and heart are," but in the very next statement, he asserts that "nothing in the *shastras* which is manifestly contrary to universal truths and morals can stand."[63] The idea of evolution—which we may read as the textual capacity for (re)signification—seems to reach a certain limit in the "universality" of truth. And yet, what may appear as a limit to us is precisely the enabling factor for Gandhi. That is to say, precisely because of his belief in truth, he felt authorized to read the sacred texts in a willful and often idiosyncratic manner: "That interpretation is not true which conflicts with Truth. To one who doubts even Truth, the scriptures have no meaning."[64] "Truth"— something ahistorical and constant that transcends the letter of the text—is to decide the meaning of the scriptures. We will presently return to question the function of this truth.

Ambedkar's arguments about canonical Hindu texts proceed quite differently. But in spite of his sharp disagreement with Gandhi, at a certain juncture there may be a methodological congruence between the two. I base my observation on a well-known speech Ambedkar wrote for the 1936 annual conference of the Jat Pat Todak Mandal of Lahore ("The Society for Dismantling/Breaking Caste").[65] Here, Ambedkar characterizes caste as not only a discriminatory and hierarchical system but, more fundamentally, as a system that presents a barrier to the formation of a broader community, whether "Hindu" or Indian. Caste, he writes, inculcates a "tribal morality" (*Annihilation,* 64). It demands an unthinking and instinctive allegiance that cannot but be an obstacle to democracy. He argues that urging people to interdine and intermarry is not adequate for dismantling caste, for the reluctance of Hindus to mix with other castes is simply a symptom of the problem. The true cause of caste discrimination, he asserts, is the religiosity of the Hindus, their belief in the Hindu shastras. Since the shastras themselves uphold the principle of caste—indeed, since they define it as a crucial feature of Hinduism—it is necessary to destroy Hindu belief in the sanctity of the shastras (*Annihilation,* 83). This is what leads Ambedkar to take the radical step of demanding that contemporary reformers must become revolutionaries: "You must not only discard the Shastras, you must deny their authority, as did Buddha and Nanak. You must have the courage to tell the Hindus that what is wrong with them is their religion" (84). Following his own conviction, Ambedkar ends the speech by announcing his intention of leaving the Hindu community and converting to Buddhism.

In Gandhi's short response to the piece, originally published in *Harijan* (July 1936), he agrees with Ambedkar that a belief in the shastras is necessary to remain a Hindu: "How can a Muslim remain one if he rejects the Quran, or a Christian remain Christian if he rejects the Bible?" (*Annihilation,* 112). But as we may expect, he disagrees with Ambedkar's interpretation of the shastras, and indeed, with his entire approach to the scripture, arguing that the Hindu texts comprise a vast corpus that has grown over the centuries and therefore must be read selectively. Not every text that is considered a "shastra" carries the same moral authority. The Hindu scriptures that Gandhi believes in do not endorse the practice of caste but instead subscribe to the institution of varna. This institution, according to Gandhi, "teaches us that we have each one of us to earn bread by following the ancestral calling" (*Annihilation,* 108). It considers all professions equal and does not forbid social intercourse. The texts Ambedkar cites in his argument—texts that advocate discrimination on the basis of caste—must not be considered true scriptures: "Thus, many of the texts that Dr. Ambedkar quotes from the Smritis cannot be accepted as authentic. The scriptures, properly so called, can only be concerned with eternal verities and must appeal to any conscience, i.e. any heart whose eyes of understanding have been opened" (*Annihilation,* 108).

According to Gandhi, a text can only be regarded as scripture when it is concerned with eternal verities and when it appeals to a being for whom perception and vision have merged entirely with "understanding." Insofar as the scriptures must appeal to "any conscience," they must have universal appeal and validity—indeed, that is their test. At the same time, it seems that the scriptures Gandhi evokes here can exist only in an extratextual and ahistorical space for no existent texts can fulfill such criteria. This is a move we have also noted in Gandhi's treatment of the *Gītā*. By consistently appealing to the material degradation of the scriptures, to their true existence in a transcendent realm, he in fact attests to the poverty of the available scriptures. The dual function of allegory then becomes clear: on the one hand, allegory preserves the value of the existent, historical, and unreliable text of the scriptures by maintaining the connection between this text and its transcendent (and finally, indeterminable) meaning. On the other hand, this transcendent meaning, and the very consistency of the appeal to such a meaning, also functions as a way of silently critiquing the available texts and pointing to their insufficiencies.

It is here that a momentary convergence between Ambedkar's and Gandhi's moves becomes perceptible. Ambedkar also states that spiritual principles should be universal in their appeal, and he finds the Hindu texts lacking in this regard. But instead of attributing this lack to the inauthenticity of certain texts or the limitations of certain readers, he attributes it to Hinduism itself. In criticizing Hinduism, he emphasizes that he is not criticizing religion as such. Toward the end of the essay, he approvingly cites Burke's assertion that "true religion is the foundation of society" (*Annihilation,* 97). The idea of a "true" religion as Ambedkar describes it, and especially its relation to law and democracy, deserves a more extensive commentary. Here, I only wish to draw attention to the distinction that Ambedkar makes between principle and rule—a distinction that is crucial to his argument. True religion, he writes, must be a matter only of principles, not of rules; principles guide one's general conduct, providing one with the conceptual ability to judge in different situations, but they do not prescribe specific acts. The problem with Hinduism is that it prescribes only rules and does not inculcate principles:

> What is this Hindu religion? Is it a set of principles or is it a code of rules? Now the Hindu Religion, as contained in the Vedas and the Smritis, is nothing but a mass of sacrificial, societal, political

> and sanitary rules and regulations, all mixed up. What is called Religion by the Hindu is nothing but a multitude of commands and prohibitions. Religion, in the sense of spiritual principles, truly universal, applicable to all races, to all countries, to all times, is not to be found in them, and if it is, it does not form the governing part of a Hindu's life. (*Annihilation*, 95–96)

Ambedkar's "principles" are not so different from Gandhi's "eternal verities." Only in the name of these principles can a critique of specific texts and acts be articulated. Both Gandhi and Ambedkar judge Hindu texts on the basis of "universal" principles, and perhaps both find them wanting—even if in Gandhi's case such a judgment is never explicitly made. But their response to this "lack" is different: Gandhi calls, in effect, for a different and more selective reading, while Ambedkar calls for a radical and complete rejection. If Gandhi does not follow the course advocated by Ambedkar, it may be because of commitments that today appear naive, mistaken, or even fundamentally reactionary. Indeed, his approach can easily seem populist or politically expedient, while I suspect Ambedkar's arguments will be more persuasive for many of us now. But it is striking that for all their differences, both remain committed to the idea that modernity must be sustained by tradition. Let us remember that in rejecting the caste-driven Hindu texts, Ambedkar turned to Buddhism. It would be interesting to investigate, in another project, whether in his writings about Buddhist texts Ambedkar was forced to turn to allegory, as Gandhi was, in defending the Hindu shastras.

For it seems quite clear that the turn to allegory in Gandhi's writings should thus be read as indicative of a tension. Though apparently deployed in defense of Hindu texts, allegory also becomes a means to indict them. Allegory is needed because the letter of the text does not suffice and therefore one must have recourse to the text's invisible "spirit" in order to defend it.

The History Reader and the Activist Reader

Let me return to the distinction with which I began: the history reader and the activist reader. I am aware of some disingenuousness in juxtaposing these two approaches, since I clearly identify with one rather than the other, and yet both can only be presented here from my perspective. But in juxtaposing them, I have also attempted to see how closely they may be linked. Both highlight certain aspects of the texts they read and critique or neglect others; both are in some ways political as well as allegorical, but there are also differences between them. Nor is it a matter of choosing between the two, making a conscious decision to follow one or the other approach. In the end, the history reader perhaps cannot take the activist reader as her model, however strong her affective relation to early texts may be or however urgent her concerns for the present may be. Her primary interest remains in *reading:* an exercise in which the text can never be accidental. At the same time, she perceives that other readers, who maintain, as it were, a relation to kinship to these texts (Gandhi often spoke of the *Gītā* as a mother), are also able to treat them as kin: with an instinctive intimacy, irreverence, and, of course, violence. Because of this violence, which enables them to disregard the letter of the text in the pursuit of action and truth, they can also be dangerous. Gandhi is remarkable precisely because he remains an anomaly among activist readers of the *Gītā.* More numerous are those of whom Rabindranath Tagore has provided an example in the figure of Amulya in his novel *The Home and the World.* Recruited into violence and thievery under the sway of lofty nationalist ideals, Amulya explains himself to Bimala: "The Gita tells us . . . that no one can kill the soul. Killing is a mere word. So also is the taking away of money. Whose is the money? No one has created it."[66]

In more recent times, the *Gītā* has often been "practiced" and used as an inspiration by Hindu nationalists. Several days before the demolition of the Babri mosque in Ayodhya in December 1992, recitation from the *Gītā* began on the disputed site. At the conclusion of the recital on December 5, leaders of Hindu nationalist parties announced that the battle of Kurukshetra was about to begin.[67] The mosque was demolished on December 6, and in the days of hatred and madness that followed, thousands of Muslims were killed in various parts of India. I do not mean to conflate such appropriations of the *Gītā* with Gandhi's appropriation, for the two are evidently in opposition. I only wish to emphasize what may be a fairly obvious point: that reading ancient texts as an allegorical guide to practice is usually a risky and dangerous affair.

In the end, what can the history reader learn from an activist reader such as Gandhi? In thinking about this question I have realized that proceeding in the manner I have charted in this chapter may be a sign of my profession, but it is also a mark of privilege. Though in a broad sense history readers are always "political," yet they are also shielded from the imperative of making immediate political interventions. Activist readings force us to ask what the stakes of reading are: for what ends is a particular reading pursued at a particular time and which premises are reinstated by doing so? The question of the *ends* of reading, to which Nietzsche drew our attention, may also have become an unavoidable question today. This is certainly true of the context of contemporary India, where the fate of the present seems to be inescapably linked to available readings of early texts.

4

The Lure of Violence: Dharamvir Bharati's *Andhā Yug* (The Blind Age)

> Andhā Yug *represents an extremely valuable and important endeavor by the new literary generation—an endeavor that calls for extensive argument.*
>
> —Muktibodh, *Racnāvali*

While the *Gītā* received enormous attention during the nationalist period, the story of the *Mahābhārata* as a whole, which had inspired poets, dramatists, and dancers for centuries, gained new relevance in India following the two world wars and the violence of the partition. The complex representation of violence, power, and law in the epic acquired new contemporary significance at a time when the young nation's triumph appeared to many as a terrifying disaster. It is not surprising that the *Mahābhārata*, perhaps more than any other Sanskrit text, has drawn the attention of modern writers and artists, since the range of political questions addressed by the epic is indeed astounding. In a thoughtful response to the "question of tragedy" in Sanskrit literature, David Gitomer has proposed that in Sanskrit literature the *Mahābhārata*, rather than dramatic texts, might perform the function of tragedy, not because of its "tragic vision," as some critics have suggested, but rather because of the kinds of questions it poses:

> Tragedy is also very clearly the locus of the problematic of the polity, the locus of the problematic of the individual responsible for the realization of the ideal of the rightly ordered society . . . One may look on the *Mahābhārata* as a genre, an institution even, where the crises of polity in all their human and cosmological significance are continually brought to the test. Just as the *continual* writing, production, and experiencing of tragedies was vital to the life of the Athenian polis, so too the *Mahābhārata* never wants to resolve itself.[1]

If we perceive the *Mahābhārata* as an institution of this kind, as Gitomer proposes, we can see why it would appear newly resonant whenever the consciousness of political crises became pervasive.

In the last chapter, I briefly discussed the historical context of the *Mahābhārata* and speculations regarding the specific tensions reflected in the epic. I mentioned the historian Romila Thapar's persuasive claim that the epic reflects a transition between two different kinds of society: an earlier lineage-based system and a monarchical state. Thapar suggests that if the epic presents the battle at Kurukshetra as the end of an epoch, that may be because the war indeed dramatizes the end of the era of Ksatriya chiefships and the inauguration of a monarchical state in the Ganges Valley. She speculates that "the intrinsic sorrow of the battle at Kurukshetra is not merely at the death of kinsmen but also at the dying of a society, a style, a political form."[2] Other scholars, including James Fitzgerald, have suggested that the emergence of the Mauryan empire and Emperor Ashoka's commitment to a rethinking of dharma presented a strong challenge to orthodox authority and that the epic as a whole may be read as a response to this challenge. Such reflections about the historical context of the epic are complicated by a consideration of its form. In a different discussion, Thapar suggests that "unlike myth, epic does not attempt to explain the universe or society. It is sufficient that the problems of society are laid bare, and even solutions are not sought since the ultimate solution is the dissolution of the system."[3]

The impulse that animates the form we recognize as "myth" is perhaps inherently pedantic and, in a way, conservative. Myth explains the way things are in order to caution and teach, and above all to teach the repeatability of things. Thapar suggests that the epic is different as a genre, and that it is different because it is a reflection of transition rather than permanence. It seeks the "ultimate dissolution" of the system in order to make room for a new kind of society. This may be why death and violence remain at the center of most narratives that we recognize as epic. Keeping the *Mahābhārata* as our model, we could assert that its distinction lies, above all, in being an *extended* and *collective* reflection on power and violence. While it may be true that the bards who composed the text represented only a small section of their societies and could articulate only a limited range of views, the very fact that they came from different periods and generations ensures that what is recorded in the text of the epic is a plurality of voices: a vast and often contradictory discussion concerning the warriors and kings whose actions are to be extolled by the poets.

Questions of authorial intention or desire, or of textual coherence, are thus rendered marginal and perhaps irrelevant in a text manifestly revised, rewritten, and expanded by several generations of poets. In this context, it is all the more remarkable that certain broad concerns run quite consistently through its verses. I would argue that the most salient of these concerns—the one that leaps out over and over again—has to do with the representation of war. In confronting the question "How are acts of war to be represented?" the poets encounter a series of enmeshed questions that persistently foreground the relation between language, violence, and law. If the epic testifies to a moment of crisis and change, that is also a moment when war began to be perceived as *violence,* properly speaking: as violating laws and norms that were crucial to the community's definition of itself. Thus the *Mahābhārata* exposes the persistently conflictual connection between war and violence: violence is precisely that which war wishes to master and suppress, but such mastery entails an appropriation of violence. Repeatedly, the epic strives to represent a violence without violence—a lawful war, a dharma yuddha, in order to exhibit the assimilation of violence within the right natural order—and repeatedly it finds this to be an impossible endeavor.[4]

If the epic becomes so resonant for modern readers, it is perhaps because the role of violence in political life has presented itself as an enigma for these readers as well. Thus modern readings, translations, and adaptations of the epic often become an index of contemporary anxieties and desires with respect to the politics of violence. In this chapter, I will focus on the work of Dharamvir Bharati (1926–97), one of the best known among the poets associated with *Nayī Kavitā,* "New Poetry,"[5] in Hindi. Part of a cosmopolitan generation of Hindi writers that was familiar with both Sanskrit texts and modern European writers, Bharati often wrote about modern India in a language strewn with references to a motley canon, fashioning a landscape where Freud, Dante, and Yeats casually encounter Arjuna, Yudhisthira, and Kalidasa's *yakṣa.* Besides poetry, he wrote essays, novels, and short stories and was editor of the weekly *Dharmayug* (a *Times of India* publication) from 1960 to 1989. In that role, he was also responsible for publishing the work of several young poets and fiction writers. His own work gained both critical acclaim and institutional recognition: he was awarded the Padma Shri in 1972 and the Sangeet Natak Akademi Award for playwriting in 1988.

Paying close attention to Bharati's evocation of themes and incidents from the *Mahābhārata,* I will discuss how the Sanskrit text becomes significant in terms of foregrounding a cluster of crises that Bharati specifically associates with modernity. His play *Andhā Yug* (The Blind Age) was written in 1953, less than a decade after India became independent. *Andhā Yug* is probably the best known of Bharati's works; it has been widely performed on the Hindi stage since two monumental productions of the 1960s: Satyadev Dubey's for Theater Unit, Bombay, in 1962, and Ebrahim Alkazi's for the National School of Drama in 1963. Written in free verse, the play is based on events following the last—eighteenth—day of the great war of the *Mahābhārata.* I am specifically interested in each text's representation of violence. In the *Mahābhārata,* though we notice an ongoing endeavor to present violence as lawful, in accord with either social or natural law, and moreover, as beautiful, we also notice a deep anxiety about it. Violence is described here not primarily as the external manifestation of political passion. It is framed either in terms of heroism and skill or as a harsh duty that even hardened warriors questioned at times. Bharati's play at one level presents a rather clear condemnation of violence as it associates violence with barbarity and animality. However, precisely such an association also renders violence attractive. Especially when the play is read alongside some of Bharati's other writings, it becomes clear that his moral condemnation of violence—which I read as representative of a modern liberal stance—remains entirely at the service of the (Hindu) state. Though Bharati's work critiques civil violence, it ultimately glorifies war as the arena where political passion is best displayed.

Andhā Yug: The Story

The Kauravas, sons of the blind king Dhritrashtra, have been decisively defeated by their cousins, the Pandavas, aided by the divine Krishna. But though decisive, the victory of the Pandavas is by no means unambivalent. During the course of a battle fought in the name of dharma (law, righteousness), dharma itself—in this context also encompassing the accepted code of war—has been repeatedly violated. Worse, it has often been violated by the "legitimate" heirs, the Pandavas, at the instigation of Krishna himself. In focusing on this confusion, Bharati's play stays close to questions raised by the *Mahābhārata* itself.

In the play, we see the return of the defeated Kaurava soldiers to their capital, the desolation of the king Dhritrashtra, and the bitterness and sorrow of his wife Gandhari, who has lost all her hundred sons in the war. Among the soldiers who return is Yuyutsu—Dhritrashtra's but not Gandhari's son. He is the only Kaurava to have survived the war, because he joined the Pandavas and fought against his brothers. Though initially he followed his conscience, he is unable to face the contempt of everyone after he returns, and toward the end of the play he attempts to kill himself. Along with Sanjaya (Dhritrashtra's charioteer, who was granted divine vision so he could observe and relate the events of the war to the blind king), and Asvatthama, the Brahmin warrior, son of the revered teacher Drona, Yuyutsu seems to represent an idealism that is gradually eroded. The play presents these three characters in relation to one another—a trio that by the end of the play comes to stand for moral paralysis—but Asvatthama, with his towering rage, is clearly at the center of the trio and, indeed, of the entire play. Like his father, Drona, Asvatthama fought on the side of the Kauravas. Drona had been the martial arts instructor for the Kaurava as well as the Pandava princes and is respected by both armies. The scene of Drona's death is particularly significant in the epic. Knowing that their victory depends on his death but finding him invincible, the Pandavas devise a plan to tell him that his son has died, guessing correctly that the news will render him incapable of fighting. Having killed an elephant conveniently named Asvatthama, they tell him that "Asvatthama" is dead. The incident forms one of the many deceptions that enable the Pandavas to win the war; this one is especially memorable because it is Yudhisthira himself, the eldest and most virtuous of the Pandavas, indeed, the embodiment of dharma, who is persuaded by Krishna to lie to Drona, so as to convince Drona of his son's death.

In the *Mahābhārata,* when Yudhisthira tells Drona that Asvatthama is dead, he quibbles; he plays, as it were, with the truth, by adding indistinctly that he means Asvatthama the elephant, not Asvatthama the man: "Avyaktamabravīdrājanhantaḥ kunjara ityuta" (Indistinctly the king said that it was the elephant who had been killed; Droṇaparvan, 7.164, 106). This trickery continues to haunt Yudhisthira through his life; in the Santi Parvan, this episode becomes one of the great sins confessed by him.[6] In Bharati's play, Drona's son Asvatthama repeatedly exploits this liminal space to which Yudhisthira's half-truth has relegated him—the space of confusion between man and beast—as he defiantly justifies his savagery: "Dharmarāja hokar ve bole/ 'nara yā kunjara' / mānava ko paśu se / unhon ne prithak nahīn kiyā / usa dina se main hoon / paśumātra, andh barbar paśu" (Dharma incarnate, he spoke, "man or beast" / He did not distinguish between the two. Since that day, I am a mere beast; a blind, savage beast.)[7] Thus Bharati uses the logic of performative speech to account for Asvatthama's actions. Asvatthama is one of only three Kaurava allies who have survived the war; he thirsts for revenge not only because the Kauravas have been defeated but also because he believes the Kauravas have been unfairly defeated. Diabolically inspired by the sight of an owl attacking and ravaging a host of sleeping crows, he carries out a gruesome nighttime massacre of the victorious Pandava army, in violation of the most common rules of war. With the reluctant help of the other two survivors, he slaughters not only his father's killer, Dhristadyumna, but also all the other heroes of the Pandava army except the five Pandava brothers who are not sleeping in the camp that night. Later, fearful of the Pandavas' wrath, he sends his most powerful weapon—a magic missile—against them. Somehow he is persuaded by Vyasa—believed to be the "author" of the *Mahābhārata*—to deflect the missile, which he then aims against the womb of the Pandava women, thereby killing the unborn children of the Pandavas. For this he is hunted by the Pandavas and Krishna, deprived of his treasure, and sentenced to an eternal life of bodily pain and exile. At the conclusion of the play, he recognizes the compassion of Krishna and acknowledges him as a savior, for Krishna, before his own death, takes on himself the suffering of Asvatthama.

Meanwhile, Yudhisthira has at last assumed his position as the ruler of the kingdom, but finds no sweetness in his success. The final verse of the chorus begins thus: "Us din jo Andhā Yug avatarit huā jag par / bītatā nahīn rah-rah kar dohrātā hai" (The blind age which descended then on the world / ends not, but is repeated time and again; GV 3, 455). However, in spite of the darkness, the paralysis of the warriors, and the slavishness of the masses, there remains, the verse says, a kernel of freedom and courage in the mind, which still manifests itself occasionally in responsible and free action ("dāyitvayukt, maryādit, mukt ācaraṇa men") and which is our only hope against doubt, slavery, and defeat.

When we compare Bharati's play to the Sanskrit epic, we notice that it makes several significant changes in its treatment of these events, but nevertheless the events and characters are clearly recognizable to those who have any familiarity with the story of the *Mahābhārata*. It is not hard to see why Bharati was so forcefully struck by the concluding sections of the epic, which foreground fundamental concerns about violence, law, and polity. The Second World War had just reincarnated epic violence for the modern world, its constitutions and treatises notwithstanding. But perhaps more significantly for South Asia, the 1950s was also a period of disillusionment for many who had anticipated that freedom from colonial rule would usher in a radically new era. Freedom, of course, when it arrived, was already scarred by the appalling violence of the partition of the country—a "familial" war in which victory and defeat were bound to be indistinguishable at some level. What followed, for Bharati and others like him, was disenchantment with the Congress and Nehru's policies. One of Bharati's poems, "Parājit Pīdhī Kā Gīt" (The Song of a Defeated Generation), written during the same period, begins thus: "Ham sab ke dāman par dāg, ham sab kī ātmā men jhūṭh, ham sab ke māthe par śarm, ham sab ke hāthon men ṭūṭī talvāron kī mūṭh" (A stain on all our garments / Lies in all our souls / Shame on all our brows / In all our hands, the hilts / Of broken swords; GV 3, 137).

Keeping in mind this wider context, we may begin our analysis by paying attention to the title of Bharati's play. What is it that renders this age "blind"? What is this age incapable of seeing? And why does Bharati present a question clearly meant for his own time in the shape of figures and events from the *Mahābhārata?* Obviously he does not simply repeat a story with which most of his audience is familiar—he changes the story; adding, emphasizing, deleting, and recasting events and characters. These changes render his play more relevant for his own time; they sharpen, highlight, or throw into relief particular strands in the original story. By focusing on the question of violence, Bharati in effect asks his audience to reflect on the *repetition* of violence: to make a connection between the scenes of violence portrayed in the epic and the violence they witness in their own landscape. The text thus asks us to consider the recurring, historical connection between political life and violence and, by commenting at once on the *Mahābhārata* and on twentieth-century India, offers as well a diagnosis of political violence.

The most legible explanation offered by the play for the recurrence of "epic" violence is one that locates the causes of violence in human weakness and transgression. It does this by connecting two phenomena: the transgression or breaking of *maryādā* and the death of Krishna. It suggests that violence—that is to say, the exercise of excessive or unlawful force—results from the transgression of certain limits, or more specifically, *from loss of the knowledge of limits.* The death of Krishna represents this loss, and correspondingly, divinity itself becomes a name for that which preserves the limit.

Maryādā, which in Hindi may signify dignity, honor, or propriety of conduct but also ethical self-restraint or limit, functions as a pivotal term both here and elsewhere in Bharati's work. But while on the one hand the play suggests that blindness/darkness results from the transgression of *maryādā,* at the same time it follows traditional narratives that associate the *kali yug,* the dark age, with the death of Krishna. Thus, like Gandhi, Bharati too has recourse to an allegorical reading that enables him to subsume the theological explanation within the fold of the more or less secular one. Krishna himself becomes, by the end of the play, a figure for ethical action, the causes of whose "death" may be located in human action. Such a connection collapses the sacred into the ethical in a manner that both preserves and negates the sacred, thus providing a way for modern India to remain both modern and "Indian" (traditional Hindu) at the same time.

In this way, the play on one level presents an indictment of political violence, which it frames as a symptom of ethical degeneration. In the sections that follow, I will pay attention to how it represents the relation between *maryādā* and violence, as well as the corresponding relation between Krishna and Asvatthama. However, despite its didactic tone, I will argue that finally it is not able to disavow an enduring fascination with violent action. Perhaps it is precisely the association of violence with animality and barbarity that also enables it to be associated with unrepressed passion. Ultimately, Bharati's work cannot relinquish its faith in such passion.

Maryādā and Violence

At the beginning of the play, the prologue first draws attention to the word *maryādā:*

> After the war
> This blind age descended:
> Situations, dispositions, and souls are all deformed
> A very narrow thread of *maryādā* remains
> But that too is tangled among both sides
> Only Krishna has the courage to untangle it
> He is protector of the future; he is unattached.
> The rest are mostly blind,
> Depraved, defeated, corrupt
> Inhabitants of dark inner caves.

The war has deformed souls to such an extent that everyone has become blind; unable to recognize *maryādā.* The term then recurs at many crucial junctures in the play. In the first act, Vidura (the wise one), half-brother to the blind king Dhritrashtra, reminds him of all those who had advised the king and his sons to refrain from fighting. Here, it seems that the very act of engaging in war was already a transgression of *maryādā.*

> Bhisma said this,
> The Guru Drona said it,
> In this very inner sanctum
> Krishna himself said:

Don't transgress [lit: 'break'] *maryādā*,
Maryādā transgressed
Like a crushed python
Will wrap itself around the Kuru clan
Snapping it like a piece of dry wood. (GV 3, 366)

Later in the play, the status and meaning of *maryādā* comes under closer scrutiny. Queen Gandhari judges it to be no more than an outer covering, a pretense, that inevitably falls away at crucial moments of action and decision, while the two gatekeepers, who play a role analogous to the role of the chorus in Greek theater, declare it to be one of the privileges of the ruling classes, irrelevant to their concerns and lives.

Indeed, in its primary sense of "limit" or "boundary," the term perhaps structures the entire problematic of the play, since what is at stake is precisely the question of the boundary: between kingdoms, families, right and wrong action, justice and violence, the rulers and the ruled, the divine and the human, the animal and the human. The primary significance of the term seems to be spatial; it comes from *maryā:* a mark, limit, or boundary; something that gives a clear or legible sign of the division of space. The term is thus perhaps essentially related to property and might indeed give shape to the relation between property and propriety. As boundary mark, *maryādā* produces an area that may be enclosed; that gains its identity from being thus enclosed. That is why it can also function as a figure for restraint: *maryādā* demands that one recognize the limits proper to oneself and let those limits guide one's actions. Bharati's work, however, gives us very little indication of how these limits may be set or known. Moving a bit too quickly and crudely, we could perhaps say that whereas the question of respecting or transgressing limits is, in the text of the epic, too often and too inextricably related to the structure of caste—something that determines *in advance* one's position in a social system—in Bharati's text, caste is replaced by the apparently more "liberal" term *maryādā*. *Maryādā* is neither the affirmation nor the negation of caste. While the logic of caste provides an explanation—however offensive it might be—of what one's limits are, and how they are determined, *maryādā* keeps intact the idea of the limit but internalizes it without providing the measure, ground, or logic of the limit.

The play itself draws our attention to the connection between *maryādā* and caste/class. A glimpse of this connection appears in one of the dialogues between two gatekeepers:

1: *Maryādā!*
2: Loss of faith!
1: Mourning for sons!
2: The future!
1: All these are for the glory of royal lives.
2: He, whom they all call their lord *(prabhu)*
  Takes responsibility for all of them.
1: But this our life—
  spent in desolate corridors.
2: Who will take responsibility for this?
1: We did not transgress *maryādā*
  Because we never had any *maryādā.*
2: The loss of faith never shook us
  Because we never had deep faith.
1: We did not bear sorrow
2: We did not know pain
1: Desolate as these corridors, our life has also passed.
2: Because we are servants.
1: We only carried out the commands of the blind king.
(GV 3, 373–74)

By assigning *maryādā* to a particular class, the two servants appear to be commenting bitterly on the deep division between royalty and servants. It is not surprising that the Marxist critic Namwar Singh singles them out as being the most striking characters of the play. Citing a part of this very dialogue in his book *Kavitā Ke Naye Pratimān* (New Models of Poetry), he claims that its effectiveness derives largely from the fact of its being a *dialogue* and not a monologue. As a monologue, it would have become so weighed down by gravity as to lose meaning. But as a dialogue, it is able to convey a self-mockery that in fact deepens the shadow of tragedy. Concluding his discussion of this passage, Namwar Singh writes, "*Unknown to the poet,* this poetic fragment reveals the mockery, if not the meaninglessness, of the '*maryādā*' and 'faith' established by the poet himself at the end."[8]

Namwar Singh is right in noting that the doormen's self-mockery is part of the implicit criticism of *maryādā* advanced by the passage—one becomes the vehicle for the other. But their self-mockery also blunts and perhaps negates their criticism. Because *maryādā* is successively aligned in this passage with faith, the capacity for mourning, and indeed the capacity for sorrow itself, it cannot simply be considered simply a luxury for the wealthy. The self-mockery of the doorkeepers, their presentation of themselves as mechanical beings and as creatures *deprived* of cultural attributes makes it unclear whether the text's criticism is directed at a culture of *maryādā* that excludes the lower classes, or at the lower classes themselves for their passivity and apathy.

This is perhaps why Namwar Singh insists that in this passage, criticism of *maryādā* reveals itself "unknown to the poet." That is to say, it has to be seen in isolation from its context for it to make a mark. Indeed, Bharati's own commitment to this concept is obvious not only from the conclusion of the play but also from his other writings, which demonstrate that it continues to remain politically and ethically significant for him. However, once we begin investigating what the play might suggest "unknown" to the poet—once we become attentive to various tensions within the text itself—we may go further. I began this section by noting that the play appears to frame violence as the transgression of *maryādā,* and hence as inseparable from it. Here, let us return to the central topos of this transgression: Asvatthama's wrath and his desire for revenge.

The Emergence of the Animal

Bharati's Asvatthama ascribes the emergence of the animal within him to Yudhisthira's "half-truth," to the way Yudhisthira confused, in his own words, the animal with the human. It is this confusion or transgression, this monstrous conflation of categories, that constitutes the original breach of *maryādā,* according to Asvatthama, and thus produces his own, performed degeneration from human to animal. The language connecting animality to blindness and violence makes a striking appearance in the second act of the play. Focusing on Asvatthama's desire for revenge, this act is titled *Paśu kā uday* (The Emergence of the Animal). Here Asvatthama himself presents us with an account of his desire for revenge:

> My father was indefatigable
> With a half-truth
> Yudhisthira killed him.
> Since that day,
> Whatever within me
> Was auspicious, soft,
> Has been aborted

By Yudhisthira.
He, the King of dharma, said:
"man or animal."
He did not separate
The human from the animal.
Since that day
I am a mere animal:
A blind, barbarian animal.[. . .]

I will stay alive
Like a blind, barbarian animal—
May the words of the King of dharma come true!
May I grow two claws
Beneath my ribs . . .
Killing, only killing, only killing
Become the last meaning
Of my being. (GV 3, 380–82)

Thus Asvatthama explicitly relates the violence of his actions to the violence of Yudhisthira's words. Yudhisthira's "half-truth," which is no truth at all but rather a mockery of truth, figures here as a potent weapon, capable of killing not just particular human beings but "humanity" itself. In fact the entire play vacillates between two distinct conceptions of violence: violence as the excessive application of physical force and violence as the transgression of law (of propriety, integrity, right, truth, and so on). The two are certainly connected, as is manifest even by my own use of the word "excessive," suggesting that some applications of force may not be violent. But in reading the play we are also forced to consider that if, conceptually, violence can only be defined as violation and transgression, and hence as inseparable from the idea of limit or *maryādā,* such a definition, by itself, cannot provide the basis for a political or ethical denunciation of violence. Once defined as transgression, violence can only function in relation to a concept of the proper, of propriety and essence, or a concept of "truth." The play dramatizes this opposition when it pits Asvatthama's murderous intent against Sanjaya's dedication to truth. This is emphasized when, in the passage following the one cited above, Sanjaya both echoes and reverses Asvatthama's confession: "Truth alone, Truth alone, Truth alone / Is the last meaning / Of . . . [my being]." But there is another side to this, for violence as transgression inevitably carries the glow of glamour, of agency and action. This ambivalence pervades the entire play.

Sanjaya, however, is not Asvatthama's true opponent, for at the end he too is presented as an emblem of weakness. If Asvatthama is the one who commits the most egregious breach of *maryādā*, Krishna is the one who is presented as the protector of *maryādā*. At the end, it is Krishna who, in dying, becomes a Christ-like figure, taking on the sins and the sorrow of the world. His final victory is the conversion, so to speak, of Asvatthama, who has been his sworn enemy before. This is not a surprise, since the prologue had already informed us that Krishna is the only one with the courage *(sāhas)* to disentangle the tangled thread of *maryādā*. But who is Krishna for Bharati?

Krishna in *Andhā Yug*

At the very end of *Andhā Yug*, we are told that as he lay dying, Krishna proclaimed that he would become active and alive in certain moments: moments of new creation, courage, fearlessness: in maryādāyukt ācaraṇa, action in accordance with *maryādā*. Krishna thus becomes a figure for an orientation toward the world, toward oneself and others, and it is this figure that is presented as the resistance to violence. But Bharati's Krishna is not Gandhi's Krishna. It is crucial to note that Krishna can only be presented in this play as someone who wages a just war, and not as someone who advocates nonviolence.

While Krishna is addressed as "lord" *(prabhu)* by his followers, and while he is invested with a distinct aura of divinity, he is also presented as the most beautiful example of human potential. The old supplicant in act 1, whose prediction about the victory of the Kauravas has proven false, refers to Krishna as his example when he argues that human beings indeed control their own destiny:

> I do not know
> Whether he is god *(prabhu)* or not
> But that day it was proven
> Whenever any human being *(manuṣya)*
> Remaining unattached, challenges history
> That day the stars change course.
> Destiny is not pre-established.
> Every moment, human decisions make or erase it. (GV 3, 372)

Thus the play implies that to be human can mean, in effect, to be divine: to remain unattached, to make destiny, just as falling away from these ideals may turn one into an animal. On this account, the play may be read as an unambiguous moral allegory. Alok Bhalla, who has published an excellent English translation of the play, follows this thread and argues that the text presents a fairly clear solution to the problems it raises. In his introduction to the translation, Bhalla writes that there is no ambiguity in the play's valorization of Krishna as the embodiment of the ethical possibility. Criticizing earlier English translations for erasing the nuances of the Hindi text, he claims that in the original Hindi the play is not ambivalent in its portrayal of the characters but instead maintains a clear distinction between delusion and right ethical decision: even the Pandavas' many violations of the law are to be read as "the coarse and brutal face of justice that sometimes must be revealed."[9] He proposes that the play, until the very end, holds on to the figure of Krishna as the embodiment of righteousness and justice: "In Bharati's play, Krishna is the man of justice and truth we can all become. He is the advocate of all created things, and their finest embodiment. If I am right, then the primary concern of *Andhā Yug* is to reveal that the ethical and the sacred, that Krishna represents, is always available to human beings even in the most atrocious of times."[10]

But though one strain in the play does present Krishna as the "man of justice we can all become," other strains, repeatedly drawing attention to his many acts of deception and treachery, also articulate a rather severe criticism of his actions. It seems to me, therefore, that despite the moral tone of the play, and despite its conclusion, the text as a whole is more troubled than Bhalla would allow. The force of the text emerges from the questions it raises—about violent action, treachery, and truth—and none of these questions is really addressed by the conclusion. Asvatthama is "converted," but the doubts he had voiced about Krishna's role in the battle still linger over the stage, partly because of the power and attraction of Asvatthama himself as a transgressive figure.

We should thus read Krishna also as a symptom of the play's ambivalent representation of violence. Though clearly related to the Krishna of the *Mahābhārata,* Bharati's Krishna is a modern god: that is to say, a compassionate and loving deity. A brief comparison of the sections of the *Mahābhārata* and of *Andhā Yuga* where Krishna responds to Queen Gandhari's accusations shows that the desire to turn Krishna into a modern human figure—a figure who would be acceptable as an ideal to modern Hindus—runs up against the text of the *Mahābhārata* in curious ways, producing some contradictions that can only appear in the play as a sort of repressed confusion.

In the *Mahābhārata,* after seeing the bloodied corpses of her sons on the battlefield and witnessing the demented grief of their wives, Gandhari is overwhelmed and pronounces a curse on Krishna: "Since you ignored the kinsmen, the Pandavas and the Kauravas, as they killed each other; therefore you too will be the killer of your kinsmen" (Streeparvan, 25.43). She predicts that after thirty-six years Krishna will die an unheroic death after killing his own family and sons, and that the women of his family will then be as grief-stricken as are the women of her family now. The curse reiterates a theme that runs through the *Mahābhārata:* suffering produces the desire to cause suffering to others; it is almost indissolubly connected to revenge. In pain or distress, one seeks to locate in some other the cause of one's own sorrow and then to inflict pain on that other. One's perception of one's own state is inextricably implicated in one's perception of the state of others, and the pleasure of causing pain to an enemy ameliorates one's own pain.[11]

Krishna in the *Mahābhārata* responds to Gandhari by depriving her of this pleasure of revenge. His own clan, he says, is not capable of being killed by anyone else, not even the gods; thus he was already aware that his kinsmen would die by killing each other. Moreover, he accuses her of being responsible for the deaths of her sons, claiming that her own indulgence brought about their deaths, an admonition that is then "softened," as it were, by the pronouncement that like animals, humans of different classes are born for different ends: a Ksatriya woman bears sons so that they may be killed (in battle). The couplet that ends the dialogue proceeds thus:

> Then, hearing the disagreeable *[apriyaṃ]* words of Vasudeva repeated,
> Gandhari was silent, her eyes agitated with grief. (Streeparvan, 26.6)

Let us compare this to the corresponding scene in Bharati's play. Here, Gandhari's curse ends with invoking the divine/bestial dichotomy that is part of the figural structure of the play: "You may be god, but you will die like an animal." Krishna's response is as follows:

> Mother!
> Whether divine or transcendent
> I am your son, and you, my mother. (GV 3, 432)

He then goes on to say that it was he alone who died and suffered on the battlefield for eighteen days as the carnage was waged; being himself (the principle of) both life and death, he accepts Gandhari's curse. The scene ends with Gandhari bursting into tears of regret and self-recrimination as Krishna reiterates that she should consider him as her son, in an obvious effort to comfort her for the loss of her many sons.

The god who, in the epic, conceives of motherhood only in terms of production—explicitly bracketing the emotional weight of the relation as he reminds Gandhari that a Ksatriya princess bears sons for the purpose of slaughter, just as a cow produces draft animals and a Śudra woman servants—becomes, in the twentieth-century poem, a god who sanctifies the mother-son relation in the most intimate terms. Reaffirming a pattern that has apparently provided erotic gratification to generations of modern Indians, the scene of Bharati's play presents us with a mother who becomes worthy of worship to the precise extent that she herself worships the son-god.

The distant and strategic god of the epic, whose function is largely to iterate the necessity of war, thus gives way to an altogether different figure. The modern god also proclaims the necessity of war but does so in a tone of compassion and sorrow, as though he too were subject to a law that bewildered him. The harshness of the epic god—his fundamental link to the structure of caste and the principle of war—is erased and in his stead emerges a god/human who identifies with the ethical dilemmas of liberal modernity. We may trace a similar impulse in Bharati's long poem *Kanupriyā* (1959). The poem, written in the voice of Krishna's beloved Radha, describes both Radha's young and tender love for Krishna and her later pain and confusion, occasioned by the war he fought. In one of the last sections of the poem, Radha describes a dream about Krishna, sleeping in the midst of the ocean, his head on her breast. His lips move and in sleep, he says, "Svadharma! [one's own duty/dharma] . . . Finally, what is svadharma for me? . . . Justice-injustice, truth-falsehood, reason-unreason—what is the criterion? Finally, what is the criterion?" (GV 3, 261)

It is not that the questions Krishna asks here are entirely foreign to the *Mahābhārata;* indeed they occur repeatedly, for instance in the *Śāntiparvan,* when Yudhisthira questions the dying Bhisma about the basis for action and the duties of kingship. However, by presenting Krishna as the one who may ask rather than answer those questions, the work transforms Krishna into a figure with whom modern readers may identify. Thus, though the play is fundamentally based on the idea of the continuing relevance of the epic narrative, it also implicitly affirms that it cannot transport the god of the epic into twentieth-century India; it affirms that such a transportation would be at odds with its own ethical or aesthetic ideals.[12]

But though Krishna has been transformed into a reluctant and compassionate advocate of violence, that does not mean that violence as the antidote to injustice has lost its appeal. If Asvatthama remains for Bharati "the real, the smouldering question" posed by the play,[13] it is precisely because he, more than any other character, embodies this desire to respond to injustice with violence. Thus, though the play does present war as the field of deception and death where no one wins, and though it shows, as well, the final punishment and spiritual defeat of Asvatthama, it also remains enthralled by the idea of revenge as redemptive violence. The moral condemnation of violence cannot sever itself from a deep investment in violence as a singular form of political action. Bharati's writings about contemporary South Asia, and in particular his response to the Bangladesh war of liberation, enable us to place the play's political concerns in a broader frame. Here as well, a pious and almost habitual denunciation of political violence is recurrently interrupted by an evidently intense desire for revolutionary violence.

Violence and Modernity

In a late essay written after the assassination of Prime Minister Indira Gandhi in 1984, Bharati expresses his despair at the violence that has cast its shadow over so many aspects of Indian political life. He voices a familiar—and in many ways inspiring—conviction: that democracy is incompatible with violence, being built on the foundation that difference of opinion must be confronted or addressed without recourse to the gun. Those who call for the destruction of their enemies—whether they be religious leaders, politicians, mobsters, or philosophers—are the enemies of not only democracy but all human civilization. Such a person wishes to "reverse the cycle of a human civilization developed over thousands of years, and to return the human being to the man-eating beastly state of the cave man" (GV 6, 328). By the end of the essay, there is no doubt that the highest and most complete human being is the one who is the ideal citizen—the *civil* citizen, or the civilian par excellence—of the nation-state.

We could of course read such statements simply as exhortative utterances that seek to awaken public repugnance toward the political uses of violence. But it may nevertheless be important to understand the conceptual frame that underlies them, since that frame so often informs the tenor of public discourse even today. It assumes that the history of human life is a history of progress and civilization and reads violence as an atavistic excrescence: the characteristic sign of the barbarian or the animal. This premise is perhaps the twin or the double of the premise underlying some of Gandhi's statements about violence, which, in reverse form, present violence as integrally connected to the amoral freedom of modernity. Each of these perspectives maps a moral condemnation of violence on a temporal axis, without noting significant differences between the figures and conceptions of violence in antiquity and modernity.

Within the Indian state, Bharati condemns all kinds of violence in the same breath: violence in the name of caste, region, language, and religion, as though violence as such were the obstacle to an enlightened polity. But that does not mean that he is consistently opposed to the exercise of violence in political life. This becomes apparent in his writings on the Bangladesh war of liberation, where he expresses his deep admiration for those who fought against the political control of Pakistan in the name of language and custom.[14] Within the state, violence is a sign of regression; elsewhere it may be a sign of political awakening. Thus we may detect, underlying the pious invocations of nonviolence and democracy, the survival of a thinking that compulsively conflates action with violence. Such thinking feeds on a historical link between revolution and democracy—or more precisely, on a seductive narrative that welds the two together. Indeed, that link itself may be only one aspect of a pervasive logic that establishes a facile continuity between transgression, action, and violence. This is precisely the continuity that Hannah Arendt sought to interrupt when she wrote that as the ability to act in concert ceases, violence becomes a substitute for action.[15]

In 1971, Dharamvir Bharati traveled to Bangladesh with the Mukti Vahini, the Bangladesh Liberation Army, and wrote a four-part account of his travels for *Dharmayug*, the popular weekly magazine he was editing at that time. It is in many ways instructive to read that account alongside *Andhā Yug*. Bharati's admiration for the Liberation Army shines through his words. He describes the young soldiers with sympathy and respect, most notably when they speak heatedly of their hatred of the Pakistanis and their desire for revenge. In a characteristic passage, he relates a conversation with a young soldier who expresses a passionate desire to "wipe Lahore off the map" in order to avenge the massacres in Dhaka. Bharati is stunned at the soldier's sudden outburst: "His dark face is flushed, and from behind his glasses, hatred is boiling over in his eyes . . . I say nothing, keep standing, with my hand on his shoulder, somewhere in my interior I feel a new closeness to him . . . As I have been bowing my head toward absolute love, so too, somewhere, have I been giving deep respect to supreme hatred. If I did not have faith in the indomitable power of this pure *[sātvik]* hatred, perhaps I would not have been able to establish Asvatthama standing thus before Krishna, with his head raised" (GV 7, 155).

Here, the soldier, like Asvatthama, personifies pure hatred. In Bharati's text, the capacity to feel such hatred is first linked to the capacity to perceive injustice and be outraged by it, and then to the capacity for love: in the following passage Bharati writes that only the one who can feel deep hatred is capable of deep love. Hatred becomes a sign of passion as such, and the desire for violence becomes a manifestation of the desire to translate passion into action. If we pay attention to the implications of this—to the coupling of passion with action—it becomes apparent that the desire for violence manifests, in its most spectacular form, a desire for immediacy. The spell cast by these categories—violence, passion, action—is the spell of the immediate; they all find their place in the fantasy of a consciousness that coincides perfectly with its content and produces acts that reflect it, without distortion, slippage, or residue.

There were many reasons for the immense significance of the Bangladesh war for Indians of Bharati's generation, including, of course, the war's resurrection of Pakistan as the rightful recipient of anger and hatred and of India as the protector of (Bengali) Muslims. Bharati's writings, however, also suggest a more complex reason. In his work, the Bangladesh war of liberation becomes an example of the ideal war of liberation and as such a bitter reminder of the war that India never fought against the British. On this account, India nationalism remained unable to translate its passion into action in such a way as to deliver a legible sign of its depth and an adequate fulfillment of its potential. That Bharati's admiration for the Bangladesh war of liberation in part evinces a frustrated desire for this unwaged war may be gathered from several parts of his work, both in this narrative and elsewhere. He is full of admiration when he describes the participation of both farmers and soldiers in the battle in Bangladesh—all citizens dedicatedly carrying out the duties assigned to them and thus participating in the battle for the country's independence.[16] In contrast, the scene of Indian independence appears humiliating: "How dull, in comparison," he writes, "must have been the arrival of Mountbatten, in uniform, on the carpets of the governor's residence, and, in the doom-filled shadow of savage riots, his leaving of the alms of government in our spread-out [begging] palms" (GV 7, 167). In Hindi, the phrase used by Bharati to describe these alms is remarkably strong: sattā kī bhīkh. The implication, of course, is that while Hindus and Muslims massacred each other, the British coolly divided the country in two and left with their majesty intact.

When he writes about the Bangladeshi rage against Pakistan then, Pakistan has become a figure that combines in itself both the internal and the external enemy; both the traitor and the imperialist. Describing his first vision of free Bangladesh, Bharati writes:

> Since March '71 when Sheikh Mujib started his campaign, I have lived day and night with the dream that I might one day see free Bangladesh with my own eyes. Not just I, but my whole generation has suffered one blow after another. In the course of the confused nonviolent and Satyagraha movement, one wave of true youth revolt rose in 1942. That was crushed. The second great phase was that of the Azad Hind Fauj [Subhash Chandra Bose's Indian Liberation Army]. That was betrayed. The wonderful revolt of the Royal Indian Navy was eaten up by our habit of compromising. Now, in the declining time of life, may this revolution, this revolution in Bangladesh, be successful!" (GV 7, 126)

Violence and revolution are inseparable in this story. This is not a story about respecting limits but about the transgression of limits. Once we detect the force of this story molding Bharati's writing, we cannot but return to *Andhā Yug* with a different ear. Not only does the play present Asvatthama as the one who is most acutely aware of the injustice of the war and the one whose questions remain, until the end, essentially unanswered; it also displays, at several moments, a deep fascination with violence as a desirable response to "injustice." We sense this in those passages that dwell upon the broken limbs, the sliced tongues, the dismembered bodies of the warriors, and also in Queen Gandhari's astounding thirst for all the details of the carnage caused by Asvatthama in the Pandava camp. Sanjaya recounts Dhristadyumna's death for her in the following way: "Quick as lightning, dragging him beneath the bed, [Asvatthama] crushed him with his knees. With his paws he strangled him; from the cavity of his eyes both pupils leapt out, like stones squeezed from unripe mangoes; black blood boiled in each hollow pit" (GV 3, 415–16). Surely such descriptions, recurrently repeated in the text, do not indicate an aversion to violence; in their very insistence on detail, they also betray a kind of pleasure.

Thus the unjust violence of the war is answered by Asvatthama's revenge—and by the seduction and satisfaction of that revenge. Any reading of the play would have to reckon with the fact that it is Asvatthama who is at the center of the play: not Yuyutsu or even Krishna. *Andhā Yug* is an exemplary modern text because it exposes so clearly the complicity between a moral condemnation of violence on the one hand and an abiding faith in violence as passionate (or "true") action on the other, in violence as the most compelling manifestation of action. Violence as the transgression of *maryādā* must of course be condemned, but its lure runs deep. An ambivalence concerning violence may be found in the pages of the *Mahābhārata* as well; indeed, it is precisely this ambivalence that makes the epic profoundly significant for modern readers. But its context and significance may be quite different.

Mahābhārata: Droṇaparvan

In presenting Asvatthama's violence as horrifying, but nevertheless desirable or even "just" in a certain way, Bharati's play follows the implicit argument of the *Mahābhārata.* In a persuasive argument about Asvatthama as the representative of a specifically Brahminical violence, David Shulman draws attention to the "text's insistence that Asvathāman is carrying out a supremely necessary role, however repugnant it may appear."[17] Drawing on Hiltebeitel's analysis, which presents parallels between Asvatthama's story and the Dakṣa myth (where Siva, initially excluded from Dakṣa's sacrifice, ultimately destroys and hence completes the sacrifice), Shulman foregrounds the moment in the *Sauptikaparvan* when Asvatthama is explicitly connected to Siva, the god of destruction. Asvatthama's violence, Shulman claims, must be seen as the justified violence of the idealist: "Both Asvatthāman and Rudra-Śiva exemplify the deeply Brahminical passion for refusing to come to terms with an imperfect, tragically limited world."[18] According to this analysis, the role of Brahmins, like that of Siva himself, is bifurcated in traditional Hindu thought: on the one hand they are sacrificial priests, responsible for the survival of a dharma dependent on violence, and on the other, symbols of nonviolence and transcendence.[19] Asvatthama embodies, in its extreme form, the sacrificial drive that arises out of resentment to wipe out injustice.

Indeed, the overarching description of the battle as a sacrifice is a powerful indicator that the poets wished to depict the violence of the battle as a necessary and sanctioned violence. Conversely, it also allows us to see that doubts regarding the battle may correspondingly be read as doubts concerning the legitimacy of the sacrificial order. To cite Tamar Reich: "The anxious suspicion that sacrifice and, by extension, the Brahman socioreligious order, dharma, is faulty because it is unavoidably founded on violence permeates . . . the *Mahābhārata* as a whole."[20] An attentiveness to the epic narrative reveals that a distinct pleasure in violence must be acknowledged as part of the same text that also often voices deep anxiety and concern about war. Its countless extended descriptions of the acts of the warriors on the battlefield carry an air of excitement and glory that has perhaps more in common with Hollywood and Bollywood action films than many earnest readers would like to admit. Though in the *Sauptikaparvan* Asvatthama's brutality is narrated in grisly details, in many instances, war is not presented as horrifying but instead as the arena that stages the appearance of skill, heroism, and courage. As we have noted before, the epic text often makes it a point to emphasize the *nonviolatory* or legitimate nature of the acts of the warriors. The *Droṇaparvan* (which, along with the *Sauptikaparvan,* provides the basis for the plot of Bharati's play), often describes the warriors as being pure of soul and pure of action (shudhātmānah shudhavrittā) who fight impelled by the desire to conquer one another: a conquest inseparable from the achievement of excellence. The desire to excel cannot be distinguished here from the desire to defeat and conquer, and this desire is celebrated when the warriors are admiringly described as being *"parasparajigīṣvaḥ":* desirous of conquering one another (for example, *Droṇaparvan,* 190.9).[21] Indeed, we are told many times that the battle did not violate any rules of dharma or righteousness; in so far as it was fought in accordance with the established rules of war, it was a just war (164.9).

The attraction of violence, however, does not only lie in its being an instance of necessary, heroic, or right action. It carries other attractions, which may be gleaned from the elaborate similes describing the battle and the evident pleasure of the narration itself. Violent acts are often depicted as beautiful acts and the poets seem to revel in their descriptions of wounded and broken bodies as much as in their blow by blow account of the war. The two armies clash like rivers swollen in the rainy season (*Droṇaparvan,* 16.49); the mace of a warrior, when struck by his enemy's mace, resembles a tree lit up by fire-flies (*Droṇaparvan,* 14.18); the heroes themselves, smeared with blood, are repeatedly compared to flowering trees. The battlefield is often compared to a river: elephants are like its alligators, human heads its stones, swords float on it like fish, blood forms its water, and it carries soldiers to the land of death. Severed heads, resembling the rising sun, the lotus, or the moon, fall to the earth. The warriors, inflamed with rage, scatter arrows like the sun.

In these, and numerous other similes, the power of the warriors, and particularly the power of wrath, takes on the quality of a force of nature. The battlefield, where soldiers arrogate to themselves the power of life and death and where they stake their own lives in a mighty game, becomes the place where the human world rivals nature. The poets delight in this representation of battle, inviting us to view the battlefield through a kaleidoscope that transforms each grisly scene into a different landscape: a landscape of flowing rivers, flowering trees, and flaming sun. In the course of the narrative, the "natural" world itself is steadily infected until it becomes indistinguishable from the battle, as though a severed head had forever imprinted its outline on the rising sun, and all rivers had exposed a potential for carrying corpses in their flow.

Although the narration reads at times like a sports commentary, moving from blow to blow, movement to movement, we must recall that the poets are not in fact "seeing" the battle they describe, any more than is the listener in the tale, the blind king Dhritrashtra, to whom Sanjaya describes each event. Indeed, the poets' aim may be to generate in their audience a response similar to the king's when he says that upon hearing these amazing accounts of duels, he is envious of those with eyes (spṛhayāmi sacakṣuṣām), and always desirous of hearing more. (*Droṇaparvan,* 14.1). Like the blind king, we only have access to the narration, and like him, we are seduced into believing that the narration is mimetic, descriptive of events that someone else may in fact have seen.

In such a frame, where acts of war are repeatedly represented as acts of nature, the figure of the animal cannot but be different from the figure that appears in Bharati's play. Examining this figure may allow us to perceive some of the specific features that underlie the epic's celebration of violence. In the *Mahābhārata,* though Asvatthama articulates a harsh condemnation of Yudhisthira, he blames Yudhisthira simply for lying and cheating, and not for conflating him with an animal. Calling Yudhisthira "false-speeched," Aswathamma mockingly says:

> He who through deceit caused the teacher [Drona] to forsake his
> weapons
> Today, the earth shall drink the blood of that just and righteous
> King
> [Yudhisthira] (*Dronaparvan,* 166. 27).

Since the warriors on the battlefield are often compared to bulls, lions, and elephants, the generic concept "animal" cannot function as a pejorative concept in the epic. The term *paśu* that Bharati uses in *Andhā Yug* does occur as a derogatory term in the Asvatthama episode in the *Mahābhārata,* but in a striking reversal, Asvatthama uses it not to describe himself, as in Bharati's text, but instead to describe his father's killer, Dhristadyumna, whom he later kills in a gruesome nocturnal massacre at the Pandava camp.

> Kathaṃ ca nihataḥ pāpaḥ pāncālaḥ paśuvanmayā
> Śastrāhavajitāṃ Lokānprāpnuyāditi me matiḥ

> How will that depraved Panchala [Dhristadyumna], killed by me
> like a [sacrificial] animal *[paśu]*
> Obtain the worlds of those conquered by arms in battle—such is my
> thought. (*Sauptikaparvan,* 5.34)

And later the narrator Sanjaya, describing Dhristadyumna's death, also says that Asvatthama tried to kill him with his bare hands and feet, as if he (Dhristadyumna) had been an animal *(paśu) (Sauptikaparvan,* 8.18). As for himself, Asvatthama proclaims that he does not care if, after having killed his father's killer, he is born in his next birth as a worm or an insect (5.27).

Thus we encounter several classes of animals with different symbolic values: lordly ones such as lions and bulls; despicable ones such as insects and worms; and then the *paśu.* We may recall here that the word *paśu* comes from the root *paś:* to fasten, bind, or tether, and that in its primary meaning it refers to animals that are tethered—to cattle or kine, domestic or sacrificial animals. Opposed to *mṛga,* the wild animal, the *paśu* is the one who is brought under the control of the human and within the ken of the human world. To kill someone like a *paśu* thus implies killing in such a way that the other is given no ability or opportunity to defend himself: to kill as though the other were a fastened animal—destined for killing or for sacrifice. Here the *paśu,* far from being the one who is himself violent (as in Bharati's text), is in fact the one who is most susceptible to "bare" violence; to violence against which he has no defense. To kill with a weapon appears to be a sign of respect, on the other hand, perhaps because it implies that the opponent cannot be killed by one's own force.

The ability to kill with one's own hands is, correspondingly, a mark of the killer's great strength, as is evident in descriptions of the great Pandava hero Bhima, who is known for his ability to fight with his bare hands. But though killing someone like a *paśu* is obviously a way of degrading him, both in his death and in his afterlife, it is not an act that may be carried out with impunity. Asvatthama imagines that he will be held accountable in his own "next birth" for this act, because he will not kill Dhristadyumna on the battlefield, under the protective shade of the rules of war. The animal here is not an undifferentiated figure, as it is for Bharati, and neither is it aligned with the barbarian. The complexity of animal hierarchy suggests a different relationship to the animal world. If the *paśu* is despised, it is certainly not because of its potential for violence but because of its weakness; correspondingly the *mṛga* is to be emulated because of its power. In men as in animals, what is valued is the display of power and the ability to conquer or subdue others.

Indeed, in the descriptions of battle, "nature" itself is not something to be overcome in a moral sense but rather in the sense that "natural" things—including forests, animals, and even appetites—are constructed as things to be defeated and conquered: those against which one may test one's strength, as against an enemy. We may note in this context that the very law of the Ksatriya is sometimes presented, not as a prescription that one may avoid or abandon, but as a natural law to which one is inescapably bound. This reaches back to an originary tension in the concept of dharma: a concept that constantly vacillates between the prescriptive and the descriptive and often seeks to ground its injunctions in the realm of nature.[22] Indeed, it seems that in the classical texts, including the epics and the *Manusmṛti,* the desire to articulate the dharma or the innate nature of things is often inseparable from the desire to provide a ground for the hierarchy of social order. Dharma as innate nature—the law of one's being—becomes the alibi for dharma as the law of separation and hierarchy. To cite a famous example, we read in the *Manusmṛti* that "to protect this whole creation, the lustrous one made separate innate activities for those born of his mouth, arms, thighs, and feet,"[23] followed by a list of the assigned activities for the four *varnas.*

Clearly the naturalization of law often serves to render it immune from scrutiny or interrogation. Paradoxically, however, it also sometimes enables the articulation of a resistance to violence. For example, in the *Mahābhārata,* such naturalization of the law (dharma) of the Ksatriya occasionally has the rhetorical effect of turning the warrior into an object of pity. The warrior becomes the one who is compelled to fight, burdened and shackled by the duty of war, as by an immutable force. Even Duryodhana, the eldest of the Kauravas, and the one most often held responsible for the events that led to the war, is at times presented in this light. Facing his old friend Satyaki, who is now fighting on the Pandava side, Duryodhana is filled with nostalgia and sorrow:

> Dhik krodhaṃ dhiksakhe lobhaṃ / Dhikmohaṃ dhigamarṣitaṃ
> Dhigastu kṣātramācāraṃ / Dhigastu balamaurasaṃ
> Yattvaṃ māmabhisandhatse tvāṃ cāhaṃ shinipungava
> Tvam hi prāṇaiḥ priyataro mamāham ca sadā tava
> Smarāmi tāni sarvāṇi balyevrittāni yāni nau
> Tāni sarvāṇi jīrṇāni sāṃprataṃ no raṇājire. (*Droṇaparvan,* 164. 23–25).

> Damn anger, my friend, damn greed, damn avarice and intolerance.
> Damned be the Ksatriya code of conduct, and damned be our strength.
> Since I am your target, and you mine, O Bull among Shinis!
> You are dearer to me than life itself, as I have always been to you.
> I remember now our childhood—all those acts of old, which the battlefield has deprived of meaning.

Though Duryodhana mentions greed and anger, what shines through is his love for Satyaki. The warrior is here presented as fighting not because of his intense hatred of injustice (as in Bharati's text), but because he is bound by a code. He almost fights, as it were, *against* his (true) passion, against his love and a history of friendship. Such passages occur frequently enough to provoke us to think about their meaning and function. Indeed, once we notice the regularity with which they occur, we may speculate that they are simply examples of a narrative convention: a convention of pathos periodically staged before the detailed—and equally conventional—descriptions of duels. Such conventions, however, may be the only means by which the sorrow of war can be articulated. The resistance that momentarily emerges through the matrix of convention may be our only access to the values of compassion and nonviolence that were redefining the meaning of "life" in early India in fundamental ways.

Bharati and the *Mahābhārata*

Bharati himself read the *Mahābhārata* as an exemplary modern text. In an essay originally published in *Paśyanti,* he writes that the consciousness of crisis and the consciousness of modernity—of perceiving one's own historical time to be fundamentally different from the past—usually arise together and may in fact be considered to be two aspects of a single historical experience. Indeed, the *Mahābhārata* is, for him, singular in its evocation of crisis: "Never in our ancient history did such a deep cultural crisis arise as during the time of the *Mahābhārata*. For the first time it seemed that all those systems which have been passed down from the timeless past have been shattered."[24] According to him, it was this consciousness—a modern consciousness—that gave rise to the widespread idea that an era had passed, and that a new age, the Kaliyug, had now descended.

But this does not imply that the consciousness of modernity emerges in every age as mere repetition; the cyclical return of the same. On the contrary, Bharati writes that his own era's sense of its modernity is unprecedented in history. As my discussion of Mohan Rakesh in Chapter 2 suggests, in this regard Bharati's views are not very different from those of several other writers of his generation. From Bharati's perspective, the singularity of his own epoch arises both from the intensity of its consciousness of change and from historical factors:

> Such deep consciousness of a pervasive cultural crisis, such unchecked anarchy caused by disintegrating values, and moreover, knowing that this historical turn is the most important turn in human destiny; that in this moment of crisis it is our responsibility to take some decision, and that whatever decision we take, whether it be right or wrong, will be forever and ever the final decisive turn for human kind—on the one hand, such colossal disintegration and on the other, such a profound responsibility of contemporaneity—these are aspects of modern consciousness which have never before arisen in history. (GV 4, 478)

As we read further, we learn that the singularity of this moment has a lot to do with developments in science. These developments have created a paradoxical situation: on the one hand, they have liberated human beings from blind faith and superstition and established the ideals of liberty, equality, and fraternity; but on the other, by explaining not only the movements of the planets but indeed the movements of the human soul and consciousness in mechanical terms, they have in fact robbed us of freedom. Via a wide-ranging discussion that includes references to Marx, Nietzsche, and Yeats, Bharati claims that the challenge of his time is to hold on to the conviction that the human being is distinct from both the machine and the animal; that this being is neither controlled entirely by the laws of physics and of the unconscious nor entirely at the mercy of the same instincts for self-preservation that guide animals: "The human being is different from the animal *[paśu]* and machines *[yantra]*, he is neither the inactive witness of history, nor a mere straw fallen in its flow; he has to be established again in the form of the maker of history; he is himself the center from which history, having strayed, is disintegrating" (GV 4, 488). He critiques those ideas and beliefs that present the human as being, in essence, an animal who blindly struggles for his own existence. Such ideas, he writes, have encouraged the belief that there is no criterion or basis for values except the struggle for self-preservation.

It is not difficult to concur with Bharati's perception of crisis: he is struck by the crisis of an age that seems to have eroded the conceptual ground of the very categories that it most urgently needs. We may also understand his desire to turn to Sanskrit texts for exemplary models, for the postcolonial context confronts us, in very stark ways, with the crisis of models. But in establishing a correspondence between the crisis depicted in the *Mahābhārata* and the crisis of his own time, Bharati's work also exposes the metaphorical range of the terms it employs: the referents of several terms have changed quite fundamentally, though the terms themselves continue to function as though they could provide a story of continuity.

The *Mahābhārata*'s anxieties about war arise in a frame where nationalism, patriotism, or colonialism could not have provided a moral sanction for war. That may partially explain why the question of justice cannot really be posed in terms of the ends of the war but only in terms of the actions of the warriors: their conformity to, or transgression of, the code of war. Karma, work or action, acquires for Bharati and his contemporaries a significance related to the rise of the individual as political actor. The individual's action is seen as the external manifestation of an internal feeling or decision, and violence is implicitly or explicitly valorized because it seems to be a means of translating passion into effective action. This concept of action, however, bears only a superficial resemblance to the action that is valorized in the Sanskrit texts, for there action always carries the trace of ritual or caste action.[25] We recall that in the *Gītā* Arjuna is explicitly cautioned not to conceive of himself as the source of his actions.[26]

For Bharati and many of his contemporaries, however, the *Gītā* became particularly significant precisely because it seemed to advocate action in the modern sense, as originating in will, and as that which changes the conditions that bring it forth. In a telling moment, soon after independence, Bharati writes an essay implicitly pitting Subhash Chandra Bose against Nehru. He criticizes the latter for famously describing the moment of Indian independence as a "tryst with destiny." Blaming India's desolation during the Middle Ages on apathy and a widespread reliance on "destiny," he writes that those who wished to change the sad condition of the country had realized that they must inculcate in the common people a new faith in hard work *(karmaṭhta)* and activity. That is why the *Gītā*, which extols action *(karma)*, became an exemplary text for so many nationalist leaders, and that is why so many new commentaries on the *Gītā* were written.[27] "After the proclamation of action, from all four directions, and after all the work *[karma]*, struggle, and sacrifice of more than a hundred years, what do we attain but 'destiny,' over which we have no control, but having made a 'tryst' with which, we are to be happy and content" (6:114).

Modern Indians often seized Sanskrit texts and terms in an attempt to counter the ills of modernity, but what they seized were words that had already been charged with contemporary ideals and politics and divested of their earlier significance. It is not surprising that in comparison to Nehru, Bharati saw Bose, the leader of the Indian National Army, as the better, more true heir of the *Gītā*. Bharati's writings show us that at least part of the *Mahābhārata*'s appeal for (Hindu) Indians during the mid-twentieth century can be traced to an unfulfilled fantasy of war: a widespread fantasy of forming a victorious army against two differently "illegitimate" rulers and curiously twinned enemies, Britain and Pakistan. As is congruent with whatever we can decipher of the logic of colonialism and neocolonialism, only one of those remains today in the position of the enemy.

5

Poetry beyond Art

The themes of poetry, like the nature that creates worlds, do not decay, even when bound by the thousand efforts of a thousand poets.

—Anandavardhana, *Dhvanyāloka*

In the preceding chapters, we have noted that in attempting to invest Sanskrit texts with contemporary relevance, modern Indian readers often found it necessary to endow the characters (and sometimes writers) of these texts with an interiority that would display some of the dilemmas and desires of their own time. Engagement with such an interiority, which enables characters to emerge as individuals and not as types, emerges as an essential aspect of the pleasure of reading for modern readers. The most frequent complaint voiced against Sanskrit literature, and especially the literature of the "classical" period, is that it is too conventional, too limited by its adherence to stereotypical characters and scenes. Such complaints appear most frequently when modern readers assess Sanskrit poetry: that is to say, when they assess these texts *as* poetry, whether the texts are lyric, dramatic, or epic. Their own familiarity with romantic and modernist lyric poetry prompts such readers to search for something resembling the distinct and individual "voice" of the poet, and in such a quest they are often disappointed. A poem that does not communicate the touch of an experience in a manner that allows readers to recognize and apprehend something of their own inner life seems scarcely a poem at all. Is "poetry" an idea that has been understood in absolutely different, perhaps incompatible, ways in different periods? What distinguishes the texts that appear as "poetry" *(kāvya)* in Sanskrit?

The term that often embodies the most discernible threat to poetry, for modern readers, is "art" *(kalā)*. It indicates everything that would limit or betray the spontaneity, originality, or immediacy of the experience that modern readers wish to glimpse in poetry. On the other hand, Sanskrit poetic theory often focuses on the conscious, deliberate use of a distinctive language in its attempts to locate the specificity of poetry. What seems to be valued, above all, is not what is said but how it is said; that is what renders an utterance poetic. Sanskrit poetic treatises highlight the significance of *alaṃkāra*, ornamentation, *rīti*, style, or *vakrokti*, indirect or "crooked" speech. Poetry is distinguished by its uncommon way of designating things, events, and experiences. But though it may be "uncommon" in comparison with quotidian speech, indirect or ornamented speech in Sanskrit poetry often makes use of a rather predictable set of resources, and this is what modern readers find hard to appreciate. Taking as my starting point the tension between art and poetry, I will discuss in this chapter how this tension guides modern Indian readers in articulating their relation to Sanskrit poetry and to poetry itself. The readers I will focus on are Hazariprasad Dvivedi (1907–79), an enormously influential Hindi scholar, novelist, and essayist, head of the Hindi department at Banaras Hindu University and then at Punjab University, whose work on Kalidasa I discussed in earlier chapters; his contemporary Buddhadeva Bose (1908–74), the head of the first comparative literature department in India at Jadavpur University and one of the most acclaimed poets of the "post-Tagore" generation in Bengal; Ram Chandra Shukla (1882–1942), widely regarded as the first historian of Hindi literature, who was also the head of the Hindi department at Banaras Hindu University from 1937 until his death in 1942; and Jaishankar Prasad (1889–1937), dramatist, poet, and one of the four "pillars" of the *Chhāyāvād* (romantic) school of Hindi poetry. All four are literary stalwarts on the landscape of north India whose work evinces a particularly strong relation to Sanskrit texts. I will not attempt to discuss their work as a whole, but in each case I will focus on closely reading a representative text that shows us how they framed, contained, or redefined the tension between poetry and art, and the avenues that this tension opened for each of them. This tension becomes, in each case, the node through which other political and literary concerns can be articulated. As their relation changes and as the frame for it changes, "poetry" and "art" themselves also change. I am particularly interested in the ethico-political questions that sometimes come to the fore as modern writers articulate their relation to Sanskrit poetry.

The last section of the chapter will turn to Anandavardhana's landmark ninth-century treatise, the *Dhvanyāloka* (The Light of Suggestion). Perhaps preeminent among Sanskrit texts on poetic theory, the *Dhvanyāloka* already presents a strong argument against the primacy of ornamentation *(alaṃkāra)* in poetry and instead proposes a new concept, that of resonance or suggestion *(dhvani)*, which it presents as the characteristic mark of poetry. The subordination of *alaṃkāra*, which is also a project for modern readers of Sanskrit, already emerges as a concern for Anandavardhana's work. It opens a path that enables him to reflect not only about the specificity of poetic language but, more significantly, about the very possibility of a future for poetry. Understood at its fullest (or most suggestive) sense, *dhvani* may open new paths for both the writing and reading of poetry.

The Language of Sanskrit Poetry

Theoretical discussions of poetry, of its functions, aims, or desires, produce poetry as the figure that vacillates between two opposing conceptions of language: on the one hand, language as that which reveals the truth—whether it is the truth of things in the world, of feelings, or even of some communal or ideological aberrations—and on the other, language as that which seduces, beguiles, and creates, as it were, convictions that have no relation to truth. Whenever poetry appears to put into play the second conception, whenever it appears to carve out for itself a sphere that has a deviant relation to truth, it arouses suspicion. Sanskrit poetry, which frequently arouses such suspicion, also sometimes elicits, for that reason, a curiosity about its historical function and task. Such a curiosity becomes evident in Hazariprasad Dvivedi's work as he examines the sociocultural context for poetry in early India.

Noting that Sanskrit poetry appears to be based on certain conceptions that no longer correspond to what modern readers expect from poetry, Dvivedi attempts to explain this phenomenon by looking at the task assigned to poetry by traditional texts and by reflecting on the historical connection between poetry and art. He begins his essay "Kāvya-Kalā" (The Art of Poetry) by making an apparently innocuous statement: "Poetry is also an art" (Kāvya bhi ek kalā hai).[1] The essay is an attempt to understand what this means, and Dvivedi's aim is to demonstrate that the conception of poetry as art belongs to an early age and that such a conception was in fact overcome or surpassed even within the Sanskrit tradition. He begins by observing that both Jain and Buddhist texts often mention sixty-four arts, and that number is frequently quoted in later texts as well. Often these are specifically mentioned as the arts of women, though that is not always the case. In looking at the lists of arts in early texts, it seems that "art" refers to any kind of knowledge that requires some cleverness *(caturāyī)*. Among the arts are included such diverse subjects as grammar, meter, law, or statecraft, as well as "skills" such as swordsmanship, horse riding, drama, poetry, the art of make-up, clothes dyeing, and so on. However, the repeated appearance of the number sixty-four leads Dvivedi to believe that it must originally come from Vatsyayana's *Kāma Sūtra*, which includes, in its list of arts, not only the arts of love but also the literary arts of eloquence, verse, and narration. "Art" in this text seems to mean the gratification and seduction of women, and its end is diversion and enjoyment. Poetry, writes Dvivedi, certainly had a place in this list.

He thus identifies poetry as a specifically urban practice in early India, noting that at least since the time of Gautama Buddha, the arts had become a necessary part of urban life in India. Poetry is the art that enables its practitioner to gain acclaim at the court, to please refined men, and to seduce women. "Actually, the poems that became the means of pleasure in poetry societies and assemblies were [instances of] wonder in speech" *(ukti-vaicitrya)*.[2] Unusual or wonderful speech indeed was considered the essence of poetry *(kāvya)* as attested by the aesthetic theories that focus on *vakrokti* (crooked, oblique, or indirect speech). Dvivedi goes on to say that in courtly culture, even when *rasa*—the emotion or mood of poetry—was valued, it signified, for the most part, only one *rasa*, the erotic. Whether defined in terms of *vakrokti* or *rasa*, poetry was considered an art: either an art of speech, celebrated in public gatherings, or a part of the art of love, as described by Vatsyayana in the *Kāma Sūtra*. Its aim, like the aim of the art of love, was to win either the heart of the "heartful" one: the *sahṛdaya*, the sensitive man of refinement, or the body of the beautiful woman. Like other arts, it required concentration and practice, and, correspondingly, talent or inspiration was not deemed terribly important. With a touch of humor, Dvivedi notes that though treatises on poetry don't quite claim that they can teach a donkey how to sing, they do suggest that, with diligent endeavor, even a person of little talent may acquire enough skill to win acclaim at the court.

In this way, the essay presents us with an image of the poet as seducer whose main goal is to convey pleasure, to create a certain effect, and, indeed, to hide rather than faithfully represent his own feelings or thoughts. The aim of poetry in this particular context was to produce a specific social effect that would be advantageous to the poet. We are thereby invited to consider a historical conceptual connection between the art of seduction, which relies on a degree of charming ambiguity, and the indirect speech *(vakrokti)* valued in poetry. Both rely on skill in order to produce the effect of emotion—in other words, both may be understood as instances of the technical or mechanical "production" of emotion. More obviously, both have as their aim the diversion or pleasure of the man of refined taste.[3] Dvivedi sees no reason to disavow this aspect of the Sanskrit tradition, though he presents it as an earlier stage in the history of aesthetics: a stage that would be surpassed with the progress of time. The essay concludes with the following paragraph:

> In this way, the poem capable of engrossing the mind of the *sahṛdaya* can certainly obtain a place in Vatsyayana's art of female-gratification and seduction. In fact at the time when poetry was called an art, the importance of these two virtues alone was indicated: 1) variation and wonder in speech *(ukti-vaicitrya)* and 2) delighting the heart of the *sahṛdaya (sahṛdaya-hṛdya-ranjan)*. As the field of experience *(anubhav)* and the field of thought *(vichār)* expanded, the definition of art also expanded, and the field of poetry likewise continued to expand.[4]

The essay thus suggests that poetry as eloquence and seduction may be an integral part of the genealogy of poetry in India. Though Dvivedi does not pretend to admire this conception of poetry, he nevertheless attempts to frame it in a way that would render it comprehensible. Poetry emerges as an urban and social skill; as a kind of linguistic dexterity whose value derives from its ability to successfully manipulate hierarchical relations. Of course, it is important for Dvivedi to present the association between eloquence and seduction as a phase to be overcome in a progressive history.[5] That is why he wants to keep Kalidasa's work distinct in this regard, by observing that long texts like *Meghadūta* and *Kumārasaṃbhava* were probably not among the texts that gained courtly admiration.

Though Dvivedi's erudition and genuine curiosity are evident throughout, also implicit in the essay is the claim that urban, courtly culture in early India was a superficial culture, and that the association of poetry with art could only gain popularity in such a culture. Poetry would gradually progress to a stage when *rasa* (aesthetic emotion) rather than *alaṃkāra* (ornamentation) would be recognized as its true distinction.

Dvivedi's contemporary Buddhadeva Bose (1908–74), though also an admirer of Kalidasa, is more aggressive in his response, to both Kalidasa and Sanskrit poetry in general. Struck by the disjunction between the received image of Sanskrit poetry and the actual experience of reading this poetry, Bose discusses this disjunction in an unusually frank manner in the introduction to his translation of Kalidasa's *Meghadūta*. Originally published in 1957, the introduction has now been translated from Bangla into English by Sujit Mukherjee and published as a separate volume titled *Modern Poetry and Sanskrit*

Kavya. Apparently questioning the easy conjunctive of the title, Bose begins by declaring that "an estrangement has come about these days between Sanskrit Poetry and our selves."[6] He writes that although several scholars of Sanskrit may still be found in India, and although the vocabulary of Rabindranath Tagore, "the founder of modern Bangla," was greatly enriched by his knowledge of Sanskrit, yet "among those who generally read Rabindranath, it is doubtful whether more than one in a thousand has read a few pages of Sanskrit poetry" (Bose, 13). As a matter of principle, it is generally recognized that the study of Sanskrit is important for the study of Indian languages and literatures; yet something about the actual moment of contact stifles the interest of the modern Indian, and available writings about Sanskrit literature are remarkably uninspiring in kindling the curiosity of the reader:

> The fact is, we feel somewhat uneasy when faced with Sanskrit. Even when our interest is aroused about its literature, reading about it cannot sustain such interest. What we read is often mere facts—and these too rather debatable facts—or outbursts of enthusiasm or the expression of a petrified mentality labeled as Hindu which has ignored the passage of time and remained stationary in its own self-esteem . . . The truth is, no real connection has been established between our way of life today and Sanskrit literature. (Bose, 14)

Initially, Bose discusses this lack of connection in terms of the history of modern India. Modern Indians have usually learned about Sanskrit texts through the work of Western scholars, whose erudition, even when truly remarkable, has not been touched by "the soul of literature." On the other hand, the Indian scholars who have written about these texts have bestowed on them such uncritical appraisal that their very veneration at times becomes a reason for aversion. Rabindranath Tagore's work on Sanskrit literature is, for Bose, an example of this kind of scholarship. Bose remarks that when writing about Sanskrit texts, Tagore seemed to fall into a "trance of delight" that led him to disregard several crucial aspects of the texts he discussed. Sanskrit literature has thus been systematically deprived of contact with the modern literary critical sensibility. That is why it is the most petrified and neglected of all classical literatures. "In the whole world," writes Bose, "only Sanskrit has been turned into a huge and respected corpse, which cannot be approached without our first having mastered the technique of dissection. This is the main reason of our alienation from Sanskrit poetry" (Bose, 20).

However, as we read on, we discover that there may be a deeper, more constitutive reason for the lack of connection between Sanskrit literature and the life of modern Indians. It is not that Sanskrit poetry *no longer* represents, or speaks to, the intimate concerns of its readers but rather that it has *never* done so. Indeed, underlying much of Bose's argument is the idea that the most significant change has occurred in the ideal of poetry itself. Sanskrit poetry is "comprehensively artificial" in a way that the modern reader, fed on a steady diet of Romantic ideals, finds difficult to appreciate.

> We cannot but be amazed to learn today that poetry could have been composed in a language in which children did not make their first attempts to speak, in which husband and wife did not quarrel or speak words of love to each other . . . But it will not take us long to understand that this strange situation was possible on one condition—the poetry should be removed as far as possible from 'life' or 'the natural'; that no unlettered person will have any right to it; that directness and spontaneity will be eschewed; that instead of an appeal to the heart, a preponderance of skill, contrivance, and other employments of the intellect will prevail. (Bose, 30)

Drawing on Schiller's distinction between naive and sentimental poetry, Bose proposes that while one might find a few examples of what Schiller calls "naive" poetry in the Sanskrit tradition—poetry that shares an immediate and unselfconscious relation with nature—most of Sanskrit classical poetry cannot be considered naive. The classical Sanskrit poets seemed to be at home not in nature but rather in convention and tradition. The invocation of Schiller is instructive, for it shows us how powerfully Bose's relation to the past, and to poetry itself, is underwritten by romantic categories. For us, reading Bose's work today, it may be useful to recall, at the same time, Philippe Lacoue-Labarthe's claim that Schiller's work (like Nietzsche's, discussed in Chapter 3) arose in response to a modern question that had become inextricable from a national question: the question of Germany's relation to Greece. Lacoue-Labarthe proposes that the distinction between naive and sentimental poetry represents an attempt to identify the Greek as a "being of nature":

> But what does "a Greek" mean to the era?
>
> It means, in the wake of Winckelmann and his variations on the "Greek body," and after the divisions introduced by Rousseau, what

> could be imagined and posited as a being of nature. Which is also to say, correlatively, what the modern beings of culture could no longer even hope to become again, however powerful their nostalgia, since, as Schiller said, "nature in us has disappeared from humanity." Thus, one considers Greek, or "naive," the poet who *is nature,* who "only follows simple nature and feeling, and limits himself solely to the imitation of actuality"; on the other hand, the poet who *seeks nature* or desires it, as though called by the lost maternal voice, is modern, or "sentimental."[7]

Schiller's essay is fundamentally concerned with thinking about the very possibility of modern art and in locating its distinctive task and potential. His "decisive gesture," according to Lacoue-Labarthe, lay in dividing and *historicizing* the Aristotelian definition of art—*techne*—that conceived of art as both an imitation and a completion of nature. This definition is now mapped onto a temporal axis. Schiller thus makes the argument that while Greek (naive) art is mimetic, an imitation of nature, the task of modern (German) art is not to imitate the Greeks in their imitative relation to nature. Instead, the task of German art is to complement or rather *supplement* nature; to accomplish that which nature is not capable of doing. Schiller thus provides a narrative whereby, though the moderns may lack the immediacy of the Greek world, they are nevertheless compensated for that lack, for they also have the opportunity to go beyond the Greeks, "to surpass or surmount them," in Lacoue-Labarthe's words.

Such a narrative would not be particularly useful to Bose; for him, the central question is not how modern Indian poets are to surpass the Sanskrit poets, or how they are to be worthy heirs of this tradition, but rather how they are to acknowledge these somewhat embarrassing ancestors as part of their lineage. On the one hand, Sanskrit poetry, apart from some religious texts, offers few examples of "naive" poetry, and on the other, it cannot be granted the distinction of being modern, of being "sentimental" in Schiller's terms, or "romantic" in Goethe's. Whereas modern poets, Bose writes, including T. S. Eliot and the Bengali poet Sudhindranath Dutta, may be called "romantic" since they belong to the "bands of alienated rebels" who experienced their social world as a burden, the so-called classical poets of Sanskrit belong in some strange purgatory; they have fallen out of nature into (mere) convention: "But those whom historians have included in the 'classical' age of Sanskrit literature—such poets dislodged from the 'lap of nature,' yet were not ready for truly personal utterance" (Bose 32–33). Highly self-conscious and predominantly concerned with artistry and skill, their poetry cannot move us, or offer us anything we might consider truly thoughtful. The classical treatises on poetry that have been preserved in India manifest similar tendencies. "Why is it that poetics came to be called *'alaṃkāra-śāstra'* [the study or science of ornamentation] in Sanskrit? The word *alam* means adequate or sufficient; hence *alaṃkāra* [that which makes enough] means that which has brought about adequacy. That which has not been provided with *alaṃkāra* is not complete and fully or adequately expressed—this seems to be the starting point of Sanskrit poetics" (Bose, 33). That is why, Bose says, even when these treatises laud the suggestive quality of poetry, the examples they provide seem curiously stilted and unappealing to modern readers.

At the end of the essay, Bose proposes that in attempting to bridge the distance between Sanskrit poetry and the modern reader, translation of Sanskrit texts into modern Indian languages is the first requirement. Presented in more familiar apparel, this strangely decadent and artificial poetry could at least be divested of the garb that so vividly announces its inadequacy for the modern world. Since the essay was written as an introduction to Bose's own translation of *Meghadūta,* it is not altogether surprising that Bose would end by emphasizing the significance of translation. However, read in terms of Bose's concerns, this emphasis acquires a deeper dimension. Translations, Bose contends, are necessary in every age, for they enable the ancient poets to "speak in our language" and hence keep them alive (Bose, 100). A dearth of good translations accounts for the modern Indian's estrangement from Sanskrit; in Europe, on the other hand, varied translations of Greek and Latin texts have been produced in every age. "This must be one of the reasons, " Bose writes, "why the pre-Christian heritage continues to flow without any break in the life-stream of modern Europe" (Bose, 100).

The focus on translation at the end of the essay responds to an idea first expressed at the beginning of the essay: the idea that the deficiencies of Sanskrit poetry may partly be traced to the Sanskrit language. Considering the special features of Sanskrit vocabulary and grammar, Bose proposes that the force of the language may be hampered by a syntax in which "there is no definite place for the nominative" (Bose, 28). The subject of any given sentence is not clearly announced; freedom of syntactical construction means that the relation between the subject of a construction and his or her action (the verb) may be indirect and hard to decipher.[8] Moreover, Sanskrit suffers from an excess of synonyms; its words cannot be an effective means of expression because they are too easily interchangeable. Gain in variety is paid for by loss of precision. In Sanskrit poetry, for example, several words with varying connotations may be used to refer to a woman, he writes, but since poets use them interchangeably, their specific connotations are usually lost. Modern Indian languages are more economical and hence more effective as well: "This particularity of effect created by each word, which we today accept as the life of poetry, is not possible in Sanskrit. There, in order to present an idea or an image, one word replaces another mainly to answer some metrical need, fulfill some word-compounding (as in samdhi or samasa) requirement, or merely to enhance the resonance in sound. No word is incongruous, but none is inevitable or unique" (24).

The essay thus proceeds by way of highlighting a series of gaps. Perhaps we could put it in this manner: in reading Sanskrit poetry, we first discover a gap between the poet and the reader (29) since the poem does not convey to the reader the particular experience of the poet. Second, Sanskrit syntax, which allows for extremely flexible word order, creates another gap: that between the actor and the action, both of which could be located quite far from one another in a verse (29). And finally, the most egregious gap, that between a word and its meaning: words themselves no longer designate something specific but are used to convey something other than their meaning: a rhythm, a meter, a sonic effect. Thus we may summarize the central weakness both of the Sanskrit language and, correspondingly, of Sanskrit poetry: it does not communicate; or what it communicates is something other than meaning as the personal, individual thought or experience of the speaker. It is, perhaps, *too much* language. As language, it aspires to too much: too much power, too much freedom, too much flexibility, so that what speaks in it is the language itself rather than the speaker who wishes to appropriate it: "If we note carefully we shall see that those Sanskrit words seem inapt for modern use which have not been able to give up their ambition for owning more than one, two, or more unrelated meanings" (26); "A modern poet . . . does not want the word itself to convey some special meaning of its own; he does want the word to act as a carrier but the meaning must be his very own . . . While the modern poet strives to get the most work out of each word, the Sanskrit poet seeks to bestow upon each word the same independence and similar distinctions" (27–28).

While this shows us why Bose believes that Sanskrit poetry must be translated anew in each age in order that it may communicate something to its modern readers, it is not entirely clear *what* it would communicate. Indeed, perhaps we should question the essay's assumption of the very possibility of translation, since it is clear that *kāvya* or poetry itself is the thing that has proved most resistant to translation, for the essay implies that the concept of poetry itself has changed quite radically from the ancient to the modern world. From this perspective, one might in fact say that the very question posed by the essay is a question of translation; the question succinctly presented in Ernst Robert Curtius's book *European Literatures and the Latin Middle Ages* that Bose might even have read:

> What do the English "poetry," the German "poesie" and "Dichtung" mean? The words give no indication of the essence of the thing, because they are late and derivative. In Homer the poet is the "divine singer," the Romans call him vates, "soothsayer." Herodotus uses *poiema* ("a thing made") for goldwork, *poiesis* ("making") for making wine.[9]

Curtius thus draws our attention to the ways in which the figure of the poetic is enmeshed in a matrix of associations and references that differ from language to language. What it "means" in each language is exactly what is lost in translation. Bose's question is related to this, insofar as he asks: How do we read Sanskrit poetry as poetry, if it fails to provoke the intellectual and emotional response that draws us to poetic language; in other words, if it fails to fulfill our expectations about poetry or *kāvya,* as we understand that word. His response, which calls for more translations in modern Indian languages, suggests that only in translation can we encounter Sanskrit poetry as "poetry." Though Bose's work thus situates modern Indian languages as the rightful inheritors—indeed, as the future—of Sanskrit, my sense is that today in the age of "world literature," we should perhaps also be wary of a position that reaffirms, in a way, the increasing monolingualism of modernity.

Kāvya, Alaṃkāra and *Kalā* in Modern Hindi Criticism

Though their work is also concerned with the relation between art and poetry, the directions taken by Jaishankar Prasad and Ram Chandra Shukla are different. The question addressed by both of them seems to be the following: How can the figure of poetry be *reclaimed* from Sanskrit texts in order to provide a new conceptual basis for modern Hindi poetry? Literary concerns are entirely intervowen in their discussion with ethico-political concerns. Directly engaging with the context of modernity and colonialism, Prasad's and Shukla's work seeks to chart out the moral and intellectual responsibility of the poet. To this end, in different ways, both attempt to disavow the perceived association of poetry with *alaṃkāra* (ornamentation) and, in Prasad's case, with art as such.

For many Hindi writers of the early twentieth century, the linguistic and literary lineage of Sanskrit became significant as a means of distinguishing Hindi from Urdu and thus presenting a genealogy of "Indian" poetry that emphasized both a linguistic and a spiritual continuity.[10] Exclusionary and chauvinistic on the one hand, the narrative of this continuity also participated in a powerful nationalist and anticolonial discourse. These are familiar and abiding paradoxes. Even in the late colonial period, the number of people who actually knew Sanskrit poetry was relatively small, and so one may assume that when references to Sanskrit poetry surface in literary essays, these are not directed only at those few but instead are part of a larger public polemic. The subordination of *alaṃkāra* and *kalā* (art) in the work of Prasad and Shukla has to be read as part of such a political context. Their work is powerfully shaped by a desire to present a history of intellectual thought that has been forgotten by its heirs. Remembrance—right recollection—of the Sanskrit tradition is offered as a cure to the trauma of alienation and deracination effected by colonialism.

Shukla's seminal essay "Kavitā kyā hai" (What Is Poetry? 1903)[11] advances the argument that in order for poetry to grasp as its essential task the fabrication and protection of a world for modern human beings—that is to say, a realm where a relation to the human and the nonhuman other is possible—it has to disengage from the spell of *alaṃkāra*. The essay seems to be throughout animated by an anxiety about the isolation of the human being. It begins with the premise that ordinary or nonpoetic language has shown itself incapable of providing a home for human beings, of making for them a world of relation. The very first line of the essay makes apparent the disjunction between *manuṣya* (human being, mortal man) and the rest of creation: "Poetry *(kavitā)* is the means *(sādhan)* by which the human beings's emotional [or passionate] connection to the rest of creation *(śeṣ sṛṣti)* is protected and sustained" (65). But the first paragraph also makes it clear that the human being Shukla has in mind belongs to a particular era; this human being lives in a world where new things surround him, such as warehouses, factories, engines, and airplanes. The newness of these things is likewise jarring for a particular reason: *they do not have a history of figurative association with the (figure of) the human.* Only such a history of association—a history that fabricates a web around and between the linguistic being of things—is capable of providing human beings with a world in which they feel at home. Poetry, he writes, is the profession of those basic originary instincts that appeared at a very early age in human beings, as a result of their emotional experiences within living creation *(sajīv sṛṣti).* The thread of these instincts gives human beings the experience of identifying with the rest of creation. This creation includes not only "natural" things such as forests, mountains, lakes, trees, animals, and stars but also the field, hut, and plough—all those things that have been human companions for many centuries. "The emotional impress of these companions is secured in a radical form in human interiority because of long tradition *(dīrghparaṃparā)*" (65).

On his own, the human being is not concerned about others—not even about other human beings. This great disease *(mahārog)* that keeps the human being enclosed within his own concerns can render even his own life deathly. Poetry provides the cure for this disease. That is why it is important for Shukla to emphasize that poetry creates an appropriate or right relation among humans, and between humans and things. It now becomes clear that the essay is addressed to those Hindi poets who consider poetry a means for expressing and communicating only pleasure; who focus on love poetry and on the one sentiment or rasa of *śṛngāra* (erotic love). In doing so, they turn poetry into a mere resource for pleasure and lust. Shukla's aim is to recall these poets to another conception of poetry, one he claims to find in Sanskrit texts. In early Sanskrit poetry, such as Valmiki's and Kalidasa's, he finds a representation of nature that is powerful precisely because it is quite free of *śṛngāra.* The weaknesses of Hindi poetry may then be attributed to the fact that it arose at a time when Sanskrit poetry itself had fallen from its earlier ideal.

Why does Shukla, like many of his contemporaries, feel the imperative to cleanse the self-consciously suggestive and sensuous poetry of Kalidasa from the taint of *śṛngāra?* I would suggest that Kalidasa has to be safeguarded, as it were, from the general image of classical Sanskrit poetry, precisely because the subsequent fall of Sanskrit poetry is a necessary part of its narrative. Only such a narrative can allow the modern theorist of poetry to present himself as the true heir of the "true" originators of Sanskrit poetry and poetic theory. In Shukla's essay, *śṛngāra rasa* becomes almost seamlessly aligned with *alaṃkāra* itself, since both *śṛngāra* and *alaṃkāra* imply "adornment," they both reduce the "communication" of poetry to the communication of sensuous enjoyment, the inferior and debased pleasure of the senses.

In order for modern Hindi poetry to join in the work of creating community, however, it must be "recalled" to a new duty: that of rendering moral categories beautiful. Poetry must be given the task of making us sensible to "inner" beauty, the task of creating and sustaining a realm of interiority that at once depends upon and negates the external, visible, or sensible realm to which it remains bound. In this sense, the text implicitly claims that the ideological production of an interiority susceptible to aesthetic categorization is essential for any vision, however minimal, of a "just" or equitable social life.

In this way, the project of "democracy," conceived as the project of a minimally equitable and moral community, becomes part of the project of metaphysics. Both demand that poetry (or language more generally) be first perceived as that which itself has interiority—a hidden, invisible, nonsensuous, but nevertheless all-powerful interiority—a soul that belongs to a different order from its body. That is why Shukla has to distinguish between *rasa* and *bhāva* (emotion) as the *prāṇa* (breath, life) of poetry, and *alaṃkāra* as the mode of description. The *constitutively* figurative and polysemic status of language, which comes to the fore in the discourse we usually call "poetic," is thus parsed into the division visible/invisible or body/soul, so as to transform poetry into the primary agent of moral community.

Let us be more clear. "The fact is," Shukla writes, "that poetry does not want to see the distinction between beauty and virtue or dutifulness [. . .] Poetry is the harvest of a high-intentioned, generous and selfless heart. The true poet is the one who causes beauty to flow in the heart of the human being. In his gaze, the king and the pauper are all equal. He doesn't consider them anything except human" (70–71). The peculiar quality of language that renders it unable to "see"—to mark or note—the distinction between the several figurative uses of a word (a word such as "beauty" for example), becomes in this polemic a sign of its inherently "democratic" and virtuous character.

But what is the relation between inner and outer beauty—in poetry itself and in the "life" produced by poetry? This is the question that the text attempts to answer, in several ways, and the question against which it finally crashes, if we may put it in this way. Like Dvivedi, Shukla claims that though for a brief period *alaṃkāra* (ornamentation) became the defining criterion for Sanskrit poetry, that period passed, and the recognition that *rasa* is indeed the soul of poetry reasserted itself. Indeed, older scholars, he writes, always considered *rasa* to be the most significant element in poetry. *Alaṃkāra* was considered useful only insofar as it served *rasa*. It was only later that *alaṃkāra* itself occupied a position of prominence. But then again a reversal took place, and thoughtful people realized that *rasa* is the soul of poetry.

This temporal vacillation should be read as a symptom of a constitutive problem. In Shukla's discussion of poetry, appearance or visible (external) form is at once significant as a symbol and a guarantee of interiority *and at the same time* is arbitrary, detachable, and inessential. This contradiction guides the entire essay and allows its various arguments to be presented. First, Shukla writes that poets have frequently employed the intersection of inner and outer beauty because poetry doesn't see the difference between beauty and purity: Ram's beauty and Ravana's ugliness are images or reflections, *pratibimb,* of their interior *(antahkaran).* The outer here is the mimetic sign of the inner, its own visible and authentic image. But toward the end of the essay, a familiar figure, that of the ugly adorned woman returns to complicate the argument: "Just as an ugly [lit. 'ill-formed'] woman cannot become beautiful by wearing ornaments, unnatural, ugly and contemptible emotions cannot be rendered beautiful and attractive by the use of *alaṃkāra*" (75). Shukla's aim is obviously to prescribe a limited and subordinate role for *alaṃkāra,* to underscore that it is only effective to the extent that it remains faithful to what it represents. But the analogy also draws our attention to several related problems. Not only does it take the category of "ugliness" as self-evident rather than as the outcome of an act of judgment, it also refuses to consider, in this instance, that the woman's ornaments may function as the real indication of her true (inner) beauty. Most specifically, it prompts us to ask: if figures of speech really function as ornaments, what is the body they adorn? Is not the "ugliness" or "unnaturalness" of emotions an effect of precisely the rhetoric that describes them, rather than something that exists prior to such description?

We can identify the problem faced by text: on the one hand, it recognizes that rhetorical language, the persuasive (and historically infused) language of poetry, is indispensable for producing moral categories as necessarily and originally linked to aesthetic qualities, and thus for creating community. That is, in effect, the burden of the entire essay and the ground of Shukla's defense of poetry. On the other hand, this recognition has to be masked, if it is to be at all effective, for drawing attention to the rhetorical production of moral values is precisely to undermine their power, which lies in their self-presentation as natural and universal. The term *alaṃkāra* proves very useful in this context, for it announces itself as a detachable addition to an already given body of meaning—of which it simply happens to be the only perceptible or intelligible sign—*even as it itself conjures the body to be adorned. Alaṃkāra* is, by definition, exteriority, and its task is precisely the production of the division between the exterior and the interior, or between the figurative and the literal.[12]

Shukla attributes the overvaluation of art and adornment in Hindi poetry to a misrecognition of its true ends: the assumption that it is merely a means of diversion. His argument appears to be directed against those poets who have taken as their model the figure of the urban poet described by Dvivedi and who consider poetry either as a means of self-promotion or of sensual indulgence. To such poets, who have chosen as their models the most degenerate aspects of the Sanskrit poetic tradition, Shukla proposes other models: those "true" Sanskrit poets (Valmiki and Kalidasa) who saw as their task the recognition and celebration of inner beauty. Read as a moral struggle, the debates between the proponents of *rasa* and *alaṃkāra* in the Sanskrit tradition are recast in order to prescribe the sociopolitical role of poetry in modern India.

We have thus seen how Dvivedi, Bose, and Shukla all exhibit varying degrees of anxiety about the role of art or ornamentation in Sanskrit poetry. Whereas Dvivedi and Shukla argue that this was by no means the dominant strain in Sanskrit poetic thought, Bose traces such excessive rhetoricity to the Sanskrit language itself and claims that only by displacing the language—by translation—can Sanskrit poetry be "liberated" from such excess.

The argument advanced by Jaishankar Prasad (1889–1929) in his canonical essay "Kāvya aur Kalā" (Poetry and Art) is in some ways the most radical of all. Grasping the bull by the horns, as it were, Prasad argues that the association between poetry and art does not belong to the Sanskrit tradition at all and that Hindi critics who think that poetry can only be considered in terms of art have in fact internalized a philosophical taxonomy learnt from European theorists. In order to make that argument work, he has to present his own account of the taxonomy practiced by the Sanskrit tradition and the place of poetry in that taxonomy. As we may imagine, the tradition he speaks of comes to stand for the precolonial past of India. Prasad's essay may thus be read as presenting a postcolonial intervention, for its main concern is to question the pervasive influence of Western conceptions of poetry in the modern world and to present the Sanskrit tradition as a fundamentally different knowledge system. Though he begins by discussing the relation between modern readers and Sanskrit literature, the history he seems most concerned with is the history of European cultural domination, which has affected the way all traditions are read in the modern world.

In reading the essay today, we are struck by the urgency of its concerns. It is as though Prasad were foreseeing the possible obliteration of premodern, non-Western traditions of thought. It seems to me that his desire is not simply for preservation or even for the remembrance and safeguarding of difference. Instead, following a logic that has by now become familiar to us, Prasad presents his reading of early Indian thought with the express purpose of situating it as the organic and proper ancestor of a modern Indian literary movement, in this case, *Chhāyāvād* (Romanticism). He protests against those who are too quick to declare something "un-Indian" or opposed to Indian cultural thought, without taking the time to study the various turns and changes that have occurred over time in this tradition. Most critics, he writes, habitually credit everything new in Hindi literature to the influence of the West, never pausing to consider that there may well be antecedents for several modern elements within early Indian texts.

Thus, in Prasad's work—as in the work of some of the other writers discussed in the preceding chapters—the call to remember Sanskrit texts functions as a way of opening these texts to the modern world and reorienting them toward a postcolonial modernity. With this aim in mind, Prasad argues that Hindi critics, influenced by Western thought, have forgotten the fundamental principles of Indian thought concerning poetry. The disturbing liaison of poetry with art functions as the nodal point of the analysis. The classification of poetry as art, Prasad contends, is not a feature of the Indian conception of poetry but of the Western aesthetic tradition. From Plato to Hegel, Western writing about poetry is marked by this conception, and it is a conception essentially connected to Western metaphysics. In the Indian tradition, on the other hand, poetry has always been conceived as fundamentally distinct from art. In a sentence extensively quoted by later Hindi poets and critics, Prasad, drawing on his reading of various Sanskrit texts, defines poetry as the decisive perception of the soul (Kāvya ātmā ki sankalpātmak anubhūti hai).[13]

The point is to emphasize that poetry is a form of knowledge *(vidyā)* rather than a sub-knowledge, an art, or a skill. Prasad contends that the Indian tradition divided knowledge into two kinds: knowledge of the *śāstras*—treatises on religious observances, law, and morality—and poetic knowledge. The status of poetry as a branch of knowledge is what chiefly interests him, and that is what he wishes to revive in a world where Western conceptions of knowledge have become hegemonic:

> In the classification of knowledge *(gyān)*, the cultural difference in [aesthetic] taste *(ruci)* between the east and the west is remarkable.

> Because of the prevalent education system, western influence on the development of our thought *(chintan-dhārā)* is pervasive today, and that is why we are bound to perceive our knowledge-related symbols from that perspective. It may be said that we do not engage helplessly in this kind of discussion, but nobody can keep himself untouched by the thought-stream *(vicār-dhārā)* of the world, [especially] since new means are available for the exchange of ideas. As a consequence of this awareness, we should make a return to our [own] tastes and inclinations. Because our own fundamental knowledge-symbols are not weak.[14]

It is a complicated passage, and difficult to translate. Rhetorically dexterous, it is concerned with what we often call "globalization." Precisely because means of exchanging ideas are more accessible in the modern age, Indians must return to their own traditions, so as not to remain helpless or empty-handed participants in this discussion. The thought stream of the world turns out not to be in fact *of* the world but one that only appears to speak of and for the world. So as not to be overpowered by it, Prasad advises a return to a local tradition whose strength is not recognized by modern Indians.

In the very next paragraph Prasad substantiates this argument. The Hindi criticism of his day, he writes, begins with invoking art. In doing so, it follows the Hegelian classification of art as being divided between the material and the immaterial (the embodied and the unembodied; *mūrta aur amūrta)* and judges the value of art accordingly. In this system, music and poetry are considered abstract arts, though poetry is accorded a higher status than music. Prasad presents two arguments against this classification. First, even in the terms of Hegel's own classification, poetry should be considered a material rather than spiritual art since it becomes visible in its written form. Indeed, he writes, the alphabet originated in many countries as a form of art, and hence the distinction between literary and visual art may not be entirely clear. The Tantric texts of India have presented elaborate theories about the letters of the alphabet, proposing that they might have an essential, rather than conventional, connection to forms of consciousness and expression. Therefore, since the alphabet is integrally connected to poetry, poetry too could be considered a sensuous and material (embodied) form of art.

His second argument is more far-reaching in its critique, aimed not at a particular aspect of the Western taxonomy he has been discussing but at its premises and implications. He claims that a system of classification that relies on the distinction between the material and the immaterial becomes in the last analysis a means of relegating poetry (as art) to a lower sphere than religion and philosophy. In an ultimate, astute move, he contends that the aim of the hierarchy implicit in this system is to preserve the authority of philosophy—and, moreover, of a philosophy that has defined itself as the exclusion or the overcoming of poetry.

The Sanskrit tradition, on the other hand, has followed a different path from the very beginning. Here, the poet is not only regarded as synonymous with the seer or the *ṛṣi* but the *ṛṣi*/poet is also regarded as one who "sees" the poem or the mantra. Exploiting the term *darṣana,* which suggests vision and revelation but is also the term closest to "philosophy," Prasad thus points to a fundamental untranslatability between Western and Eastern metaphors of knowledge. Poetry is a form of knowledge in India, and yet it has been figured as something embodied and concrete. Indeed—and this is Prasad's main argument here—the very distinction between material and immaterial belongs to a hierarchical system that became, over time, pervaded by Christian beliefs. Oppositions between the subtle and the gross, the abstract and the concrete, heaven and hell are ultimately all expressions of the assumption that the human world is inferior to the disembodied and pure heaven of God. In contrast, he asserts that in the Indian tradition, the embodied and the disembodied, the transient and the eternal are all considered forms of the divine. Even the abstract is cognized as being endowed with form and as being unrecognizable in the absence of form. Prasad writes that from this perspective, the distinction between the concrete and the abstract is not significant for the Indian tradition. Indeed, as far as aesthetic theory is concerned, without reference to form, the very perception of beauty becomes meaningless (Sīdhī bāt to yeh hai ki saundarya-bodh binā rūp ke ho hi nahīn saktā).[15]

Imagining poetry as distinct both from art *(kalā)* and from religious/moral doctrine *(śāstra),* the Sanskrit tradition has instead conceived of it as a particular and unique form of knowledge. Whereas *śāstra* is concerned with transcendental ends, poetry *(kāvya)* is concerned with both the transcendent and the mundane and is hence implicitly superior to *śāstra. Śāstra* compiles the empirically gathered principles of human society; such principles, like those of science *(vigyān),* reach their limit in their utility. Poetry or literature, on the other hand, is engaged in constantly disclosing the ever-new mystery of the experience-perceptions *(anubhuti)* of the soul (kāvya yā sāhitya ātmā ki anubhutiyon kā nitya nayā-nayā rahasya kholne men prayatnasheel hai).[16] Prasad accepts that in the interval between the poet's perception and its verbal expression, something we call art may have some impact, yet, like Shukla, he insists that its role remains secondary. Indeed, he wishes to claim that in poetry, the perceptive experience *(anubhuti)* remains of primary significance; it alone determines the power and beauty of the expression *(abhivyakti).*

Needless to say, Prasad has to present a determinedly selective version of the Indian tradition to make his argument. Thus he quotes more extensively from the *Upaniṣads* than from the Sanskrit treatises on poetry, and in the rare instance where he provides an example of poetry, he refers to the *Ṛgveda.* All this must be read as part of the essay's project. Starting by excoriating narrow definitions of "Indianness" *(bhārtiyatā)* that have arisen in response to the influence of Western thought, it wishes to open the path to another kind of nationalism—a nationalism that highlights, instead, the parochialism of Western thought. Here indeed, if we may use the much-vaunted term, is a project of "provincializing Europe." The distinction between poetry and art—though presented through a series of tropes that may seem worn to us today—can itself be read as a trope, a rhetorical device, whose most important function, I would argue, is nothing less than depriving the West of poetry. In other words, the essay implies that the West's peculiar mistake—a mistake, that is, however, entirely in accord with the structure of its entire philosophical self-presentation—isn't just that it has classified poetry as art. The mistake is that in doing so, it has missed, as it were, the essence of poetry. And therefore it has missed something crucially significant about human experience and human language. By classifying poetry as art; by conceiving of it as one among the arts, the West reveals that in fact, it knows *only* art. It has failed to discover the particular form of "knowing" represented by emotional perception.

I have attempted to indicate here that the figure of Sanskrit poetry—the figure of poetry itself in early India — becomes a highly charged figure as modern Indian writers consider their own relation to this figure and consider, as well, the context that has shaped that relation. Though the four writers I have discussed here ultimately have different projects and arguments, they all respond, in some way, to the perceived dominance of "art" in poetry. As we may expect, this dominance is variously read as a sign of a lapse, a weakness, or a mistake to be overcome: whether in the evolution of a classical and courtly language, the moral fiber of a culture, or the theoretical underpinnings of an imperial, European civilization. That interests me less than the powerful fecundity of the tension between art and poetry. In each case, this tension becomes, as it were, the pretext that allows these writers to engage with some of the most resilient questions that have emerged, over the centuries, with regard to the strange category of poetry: questions about its social and historical functions, as also about the ethical and political foundations of poetic languages. Hackneyed as it may seem, this tension thus provides the opening for modern writers to perform the difficult postcolonial task of constructing a literary-philosophical tradition—however precarious, fractured, and exclusionary it might be.

The Danger of Art and the Future of Poetry

Poetry clearly engages language in a distinct way. For Sanskrit writers this distinction was most broadly characterized as the ability to cause pleasure. If what makes an utterance pleasurable is its "beauty," where does this beauty lie? Is it caused by the beauty of the sentiment or moral that is conveyed, or by ornaments of speech? Thus poetry's relation to ornamentation and rhetorical figures occupied Sanskrit theorists as well, and debates among them often focus on the question of poetic language with the aim of isolating the particular features that render language "poetic." These debates are complex and usually exhibit a technical attention to linguistic operations. I will not comment here on those aspects of the debates. Of greater interest to me is an allegory of poetry that appears frequently in early texts. This allegory presents poetic language as a feminine figure that captivates by means of its ornaments *(alaṃkāra),* and, over the centuries, it gives rise to extended discussions about ornamentation and figural language, robing and disrobing, art and artifice, poetry as amusement and poetry as knowledge.

We find a very early appearance of this figure in a hymn in the *Ṛg Veda* that sings of the origin of *vāc,* poetic language. I translate *vāc* as "poetic language" rather than simply language or speech partly because this particular figure of the hidden, and feminine, *body* of truth is a figure that later becomes often conflated with the figure of poetry. I have elsewhere attempted a detailed commentary on this hymn; here I will simply cite the verse relevant to our present purposes:

> And one, seeing *vāc,* did not see; and one, hearing, did not hear her.
> To one she reveals her body, like a young wife, beautifully clothed
> and desirous, to her husband.[17]

There is thus a manifest and an unmanifest form of language: it reveals itself only to the select few, and this revelation is like the revelation of a wife to her husband, the privileged one who will be granted access, beyond and beneath adornment.

That this scene of the revelation of knowledge or meaning is also a scene of seduction catches the imagination of later writers. In the prologue to a famous seventh-century work, Bānabhatta's *Kādambarī*, we find the following verse:

> A novel story, charming with sparkling conversations and love-
> sportings,
> Which takes its form of composition from its mood,
> Creates in the heart pleasure heightened by curiosity:
> Just as a new bride,
> Seductive with scintillating coquetries and sweet speech,
> Who, at love's urgings, comes of her own accord to her lord's couch,
> Creates in the heart passions stirred by anticipation.[18]

Here it is no longer a question of marking the difference between the ordinary purveyors of language and the few who are initiated into its hidden mysteries. Rather, it is a matter of describing the erotic delights of well-crafted stories that create passion by inciting the anticipation of passion. Here, as in the verse from the *Ṛg Veda*, a discovery is anticipated, but instead of being a discovery of "truth," it is simply the discovery of how the plot of the story will unfold.

The idea that kāvya makes possible a distinct relation to knowledge—a pleasurable relation—appears in several texts. Early in his commentary (the *Locana*) on the first part of Anandavardhana's *Dhvanyāloka*, Abhinavagupta approvingly cites a statement attributed to Bhattanayaka: "It is the man who relishes [what he reads], not he who learns it nor he who obeys it, [who is eligible] for [reading] poetry."[19] A few lines later, having mentioned that poetry is generally considered to impart both joy and instruction, Abhinavagupta adds:

> Nevertheless, of instruction and joy, joy is the chief goal. Otherwise, what basic differences would there be between one means of instruction, viz., poetry, which instructs after the fashion of a wife, and other means of instruction, such as the Vedas, which instruct after the fashion of a master, or history, which instructs after the fashion of a friend? (71)

In contrast to Dvividi, who attributes the association of poetry with *śringāra-rasa* to the superficiality of urban culture, Abhinavagupta suggests that there is something essentially erotic about linguistic beauty so that even when it instructs, it does so via the path of romantic love. It is perhaps this notion of the sensuous beauty of poetic language that facilitates its relation to ornamentation. The very characteristic that distinguishes and privileges poetic language can thus also function as a sign of its frivolity. As we have seen, this frovolity becomes a source of unease for modern critics, and they respond by privileging those Sanskrit texts that refute the centrality of *alamkāra.* Of those texts, the *Dhvanyāloka* is itself the most well-known and influential.

The *Dhvanyāloka* occupies a singular place in the history of Sanskrit aesthetics, both because of its own interventions in current debates about the characteristics of poetic speech and because of the further interventions of the renowned scholar Abhinavagupta, who wrote an extensive commentary *(Locana)* on the *Dhvanyāloka. Dhvanyāloka* is usually translated as "the light of suggestion." Since *dhvani* primarily means "sound" (even noise or roar), and *ālokah* primarily means "seeing" or "beholding," "the light of resonance"—or even "the beholding of resonance"— might be a closer translation. Obviously the title itself presents us with a curious metaphor, an example of syneasthesia, importing the property of light onto sound and employing an example of the very *alaṃkāra* that *dhvani* will attempt to assimilate within its larger scope. Evidently in response to a complex and long debate in the aesthetic tradition, the text presents a powerful attack on the primacy of *alaṃkāra.*

Anandavardhana does this by advancing a new idea about the specificity of poetic language. He claims, in brief, that the best kind of poetry is one where the conventional meaning renders itself subordinate to the suggested meaning *(dhvani).* The complexity of the argument arises from his desire to claim that suggestion is different not only from denotation but also from indication; it is thus different from *both* the literal and the figurative or the implied meaning. Indeed, all through the text one detects a desire to locate a quality of language that hovers at the very edge of semantic meaning. *Dhvani,* relying on *vyañjakatva,* or suggestion often approaches what we may call today "significance," that which may be signified but not "meant" by an utterance. As I will discuss later, Anandavardhana draws at least some attention to the essentially contextual quality of *dhvani,* and most importantly, he marks it as a specific feature of *mortal* language—of language that cannot be the embodiment of truth and that necessarily fails to provide correct or adequate representation. Thus two powerful ideas are challenged: that poetic language provides privileged access to truth, and that it is distinguished chiefly by its dependence on figures of speech. Instead, Anandavardhana proposes a thesis regarding the singularity of the poetic word.

Many centuries earlier, as though anticipating Bose's criticism, he argues that the word that conveys this suggested meaning is unique and irreplaceable; it conveys a beauty that other words are incapable of conveying (1.15). This does not mean that only particular *words* are capable of resonance; the meaning of an utterance may also be resonant, fundamentally *unstable* in its suggestibility. These resonances, though based on the two recognized powers of language, denotation and indication, are nevertheless distinct from them and in order to be truly effective require their subservience. Thus the *Dhvanyāloka* advances the argument that *dhvani*—suggestion or resonance—is the soul of poetry.

The suggested meaning itself may be of various kinds: the suggestion of a thing or idea, the suggestion of a figure *(alaṃkāra),* or the suggestion of a *rasa* (an aesthetic emotion), the last being the one most valued by the text. In other words, *alaṃkāra* is most definitely not *alam-kāra* (lit. 'that which makes enough') where poetry is concerned; it is not that which completes or finishes the work of poetry, or which is the most essential characteristic of poetry. In making this argument, Anandavardhana is clearly arguing against theorists who believed that *alaṃkāra,* or more broadly, *vakrokti* (oblique or indirect speech), is the very essence of the poetic.[20]

There are several passages in the text where its subordination of *alaṃkāra* becomes clear. For instance, after already having claimed that *dhvani* is the true measure of poetry and that it is distinct from *alaṃkāra,* at the beginning of the second section, Anandavardhana writes that even a *rasa,* if it is not predominant in a verse, occupies the same place as *alaṃkāra:*

> Pradhāne anyatra vākyārthe yatrāngam tu rasādayah
> Kāvye tasminnalamkāro rasādiriti me matih. (2. 5)[21]

> When another significance is primary, and the *rasa* and the rest are parts [only]
> In such poetry *rasa* and the rest are *alaṃkāra,* in my opinion.

The explanatory remarks following the verse are even more explicit. The writer notes that when *rasa* is the most important aspect of the verse—that is to say in the best kind of poetry— then it cannot possibly be considered an *alaṃkāra,* since an *alaṃkāra* is only known to be a means or a cause *(hetu)* of beautification. However, nothing can be itself the instrument of its own beauty. Therefore when the *rasa* itself is the most significant aspect of the verse—when it is the soul of the verse—then it cannot be considered an *alaṃkāra.* The point is that *alaṃkāra* is *by definition* in a subordinate, external or attributive position.

Rasa, on the other hand, is not subordinate by definition. It is clearly superior to *alaṃkāra* but not as privileged as *dhvani.*[22] Related to the verb *ras* (to taste or relish; to feel, perceive, be sensible of), the noun *rasa* means both the juice of a fruit, and the best or finest part of an object, its essence or marrow.[23] In the words of V. K. Chari, "Reduced to its simplest form, the *rasa* theory states that the aim of poetry is the expression and evocation of emotions and that a poem exists for no other purpose than that it should be relished by the reader. Aesthetic experience is this act of relishing or gustation."[24] That a theory of aesthetic pleasure that started its career by foregrounding the sensual apprehension of the world—linking itself to the cultivated satisfaction of the tongue[25]—should become, in time, the means of emphasizing the more spiritual and emotional aspects of poetry is not without irony, yet this has precisely been the itinerary of *rasa.*

In the *Dhvanyāloka,* at times it seems that the subordination of *alaṃkāra* and the corresponding partiality for *rasa* and *dhvani* may be related to a privileging of spontaneity and passion in poetry. For example, in the third section, we are told that an *alaṃkāra* can only become part of the *rasa* conveyed by the verse, and hence a part of its *dhvani* or resonance, if it is "thrown" by the *rasa* itself in the path of the verse, requiring no additional effort on the poet's part (3. 16). The explanation following the verse emphasizes this idea. It tells us that we know that the *alaṃkāra* has been employed as a part of *rasa* when we see that no separate effort *(prithagyatna)* has been made on the poet's part. Certain tropes such as puns are thus incapable of becoming part of the *rasa,* since they so obviously require an effort that would distract the poet from his immersion in the *rasa.* Thus the problem with ornamentation is that it indicates the poet's conscious manipulation of language; it makes explicit his instrumental attention, if you will, to his work.

But perhaps the stakes are higher. Poetry seems to have already become an institution, and a moribund one at that. It is the representation of a static world whose themes and conventions are already limited and familiar. It now emerges that the aim of the text is not simply to provide "another" manner of judging and evaluating poetry but rather to think about the future of poetry. *Dhvani* becomes the concept that will open a path to the future of poetry. It is in this light that we should read the text's insistence that wonder in speech *(ukti-vaicitryam)* remains an essential aspect of poetry, or its indication that *dhvani* itself must take over the function of "ornamenting" speech, thereby rewriting the idea of ornamentation, this time from the perspective of *dhvani.* This becomes most apparent in the fourth and shortest section of the *Dhvanyāloka,* which explains the significance of *Dhvani* not only for the perceptive listener of poetry—the *sahṛdaya*—but indeed for poetry itself. Here Anandavardhana makes a remarkable claim: that *dhvani* is what allows new poetry to come into being.

> Therefore speech *(vāni)* that has been ornamented *(vibhuṣita)* by any of these kinds [of *dhvani*]
> Attains newness even if it was [earlier] arranged according to an old meaning. (4. 2)

The text goes on to explain that such speech, "ornamented by" one of the different kinds of *dhvani,* attains newness *(navatvam)* even if it touches the meaning formed by older poets.

In his commentary on this verse, Abhinavagupta reiterates that because of the wonder in speech *(ukti-vaicitryam)* these meanings become endless, ever susceptible to being renewed. We might think, at this point, that though the *Dhvanyāloka* wishes to establish a new principle for judging poetry, yet it does not depart so radically from the older view that poetry is distinguished primarily by its language, that is to say, by a particular choice of vocabulary and syntax. However, as we read on, we discover that the conventional meaning of *ukti-vaicitryam* is also challenged by Anandavardhana. Verse 7 and its accompanying explanation offers the argument that poetry never presents objects in their general or objective form but always in some particular or special aspect. That is why poetry did not end with the first poet, Valmiki. After all, Valmiki had already written about all the objects that future poets write about; there would be nothing left for them to say if Valmiki had already presented all these objects in their general (universal) aspect. One might say that what new poets bring to their verses is *ukti-vaicitryam,* but, asks Anandavardhana, what exactly is this *ukti-vaicitryam (kimidamuktivaicitryam)?* In response, he argues that wonder in speech arises not only from the novelty of description but indeed from the novelty of the *object* (referent) of utterance as well. In other words, it indicates both a new description and a new object. In making this argument, Anandavardhana relies on an older linguistic postulate. The two—what is to be spoken (described) and that which (in language) speaks or describes—*vācya* and *vācaka*—share an inseparable relation; hence the novelty of one is inextricably connected to the novelty of the other. Since objects that appear in poetry are presented in the context of a particular place and time, they can never be assumed to appear in their *sāmānya* or general form. This is what ensures the limitlessness of poetic utterances. New poets may borrow freely from earlier poets and yet be able to compose a new work. Like nature that has endless potential to create new objects and new worlds, he writes, poetry too can never come to an end, even if thousands of masters of poetry were to constantly engage in the effort to write.

Ramsagar Tripathi, who has written a Hindi commentary on the *Dhvanyāloka,* discusses the significance of *ukti-vaicitryam* when he says that poetic themes and objects can only appear in a specific form, conditioned by time, place, and other contingencies, and never in a general or objective form. Those who accept the principle of newness or wonder in speech (those who accept that this is possible) will have to accept that the described object or theme also changes with new descriptions. In fact, he writes, there is no way for them to avoid this conclusion.[26] Therefore there is no censure for the poet who borrows themes from earlier poets, for in each instance something new is bound to appear.

Keeping this in mind, I would propose that the fourth section of the treatise reveals the question that sets in motion the entire enterprise. This seems be the most simple, yet profound, question: What makes (new) poetry possible? As we have seen, Anandavardhan's response to this question evokes the idea of singularity. The singular perspective that each poet brings to the object enables the object to appear new and to be described with wonder or strangeness. This idea is closely connected to the idea of *dhvani* itself—indeed the two are symmetrically related. In the third section of *Dhvanyāloka,* Anandavardhan has already claimed that whereas the relation between the word and its meaning is fixed and eternal, the scope of *dhvani* (suggestion) is not determined but conditional. Because of its indeterminate nature, it must be regarded as a separate property of words, distinct from their denotative or indicative qualities. Here he has also presented one of the most striking theses of the treatise. Even the Mīmāṃsakas, who believe in the absolute authority of the Vedas, must believe in this indeterminate quality, Anandavardhana writes, otherwise they would have no means of distinguishing between mortal and immortal speech. For mortal speech always carries not only the object or idea that is to be conveyed but also the intentions and desires of the speaker.

It is thus conditioned by its context, by place, time, and other limits, and can hence never be a guarantee of its own truth. In this, it is unlike nonhuman or eternal speech, which is itself the guarantee of its truth. Something else, something having to do with the context of the utterance and the wish or desire of the speaker, intrudes in mortal speech and thus enables it to have the indeterminate property of suggestion (3.32).

In his thoughtful discussion of Anandavardhan's work, the Sanskrit scholar V. K. Chari draws our attention to some of the technical problems posed by this thesis. He asks whether it is correct to consider *dhvani* a third kind of semantic activity, if it is largely a contextual function, sometimes dependent on the relationship between words as well as between the utterance and its context. Moreover, he writes,

> All meaning is in fact contextual. So what point is gained by assigning it to a special verbal activity called suggestion? . . . Since all suggested meaning is contextual meaning, it should follow that all contextual meaning is suggested meaning. But, at this rate, the protagonists of the *dhvani* will have to admit that implications of the most prosaic and trivial sort are also instances of poetic suggestion. They do in fact realize this difficulty. But the solution they offer is unconvincing and circular. They argue that, although all cases of secondary meaning involve a suggestive element, they are not all instances of poetic suggestion because they lack the element of beauty. It is no doubt recognized by them that beauty in poetry consists of *rasa* evocation. But, in saying this, one is only abandoning the case for suggestion.[27]

As we may gather, Chari wishes to uphold the primacy of *rasa* in his own argument about poetry and is suspicious of some of the arguments offered by the *dhvani* theorists. We might rephrase Chari's question in the following way: If mortal language, or the unabsolute and indeterminate nature of mortal language, is essential for poetry, why is all mortal language not poetic? Instead of reading this as a weakness of Anandavardhan's argument, perhaps we could look at it another way. Rather than assuming that the idea of *dhvani* is presented only to account for the beauty of poetic language, we could perhaps understand it as Anandavardhana's response to a vision of the world as the home of unchanging universals. In such a world, where the general form of experience always remains the same, there would be, in a sense, nothing new for language to do. Indeed, in the passages I have been discussing from book 4, one of Anandavardhana's imagined opponents makes just this argument, claiming that it is only the "general" (universal) form of experience that is able to enter language, and such experience has already been described by ancient poets. Only on account of their (false) pride do modern poets (those of "today") claim originality when they only present a particular variation (of the universal) (4.7 *vritti*).

Anandavardhana argues, on the contrary, that *dhvani* enables both the objects of the world and human language to acquire new dimensions. He specifically says that suggestiveness should not be considered only a verbal power but one that has a wider scope—capable of affecting everything whose significance can change with time and place (3.33 and 4.7–10). What I find most surprising in reading such passages is the burden of modernity that the Sanskrit poetic tradition evinces. Already the ancient poets seem to tower behind, having said and done everything. Anandavardhana's remarks seem to be aimed against a common perception of the world as a static place, where there is nothing left to say or discover. The earlier theorists' emphasis on *alaṃkāra* becomes aligned in Anandavardhana's work with dread of death and fear for the end of poetry. In response to this fear, Anandavardhana seems to have reflected on the mortality—that is to say, the finitude or the inherently limited nature—of human language. His genius lay in turning this very finitude into a means for ensuring the future of poetry. According to him, poetry is possible because the realm of truth or absolute literality remains beyond human language. This inherent necessity of always conveying the different-from allows language to acquire *dhvani* or suggestiveness, which is the "soul" of poetry. If we take this idea seriously, and also take seriously his references to the contextual element in determining the significance of an utterance, may we not understand his work as also opening new possibilities for the *reading* of (old) poetry? In several parts of this book, I have drawn attention to how modern readers of Sanskrit poetry have apprehended and transformed its emphases. It is intriguing to consider that Anandavardhana himself may have given us, via his theory of language, a frame for understanding the inevitability, and indeed, the necessity, of such transformations.

Epilogue: Poetry and Justice

Plato did the decisive thing by casting poetry out. "We must take a lesson from the lover who renounces at any cost a passion which he finds is doing him no good."[1] Like this lover, who is never so in thrall of passion as to lose sight of the good, the citizens of Plato's republic must renounce poetry, for she is ever the advocate of passion—that is to say, of the regime of the senses, of pleasure and pain. As Socrates goes on to say to Glaucon: "Much is at stake, more than most people suppose: it is a choice between becoming a good man or a bad; and poetry, no more than wealth or power or honours, should tempt us to be careless of justice and virtue."

How exactly does poetry tempt us from justice? I will cite a significant passage from book 10:

> Let me put the case for you to judge. When we listen to some hero in Homer or on the tragic stage moaning over his sorrows in a long tirade, or to a chorus beating their breasts as they chant a lament, you know how the best of us enjoy giving ourselves up to follow the performances with eager sympathy. The more a poet can move our feelings in this way, the better we think him. And yet when the sorrow is our own, we pride ourselves on being able to bear it quietly like a man, condemning the behaviour we admired in the theatre as womanish. Can it be right that the spectacle of a man behaving as one would scorn and blush to behave oneself should be admired and enjoyed, instead of filling us with disgust?
>
> No, it really does not seem reasonable.
>
> It does not, if you reflect that the poet ministers to the satisfaction of that very part of our nature whose instinctive hunger to have its fill of tears and lamentations is forcibly restrained in the case of our own misfortunes. Meanwhile, the noblest part of us, insufficiently schooled by reason or habit, has relaxed its watch over these querulous

> feelings, with the excuse that the sufferings we are contemplating are not our own and it is no shame to us to admire and pity a man with some pretensions to a noble character, though his grief may be excessive. The enjoyment itself seems a clear gain, which we cannot bring ourselves to forfeit by disdaining the whole poem. Few, I believe, are capable of reflecting that to enter into another's feelings must have an effect on our own: the emotions of pity our sympathy has strengthened will not be easy to restrain when we are suffering ourselves.[2]

A prodigious analysis of the delights of aesthetic compassion—itself exposed as nothing but a ruse, and indeed, a training, for self-pity. Under the guise of lamenting the misfortunes of another, we give ourselves up to the enjoyment of lament, armed "with the excuse that the sufferings we are contemplating are not our own." The passage suggests that by a circuitous route, poetry allows us to contemplate our own sufferings. In so doing, it acts in complicity with a part of our nature that we otherwise keep in check: the lament machine, always hungry for more tears.

For man to act justly, a veil must be drawn over his contemplation of his own wretchedness. Poetry removes that veil: it allows a man to represent to himself his own condition as lamentable and, moreover, to give expression to his grief, as a woman might. It is worth recalling that Plato's staging of sorrow as a hunger and a passion is remarkably close to the one we find in the Homeric poetry indicted here,[3] as is his representation of mourning itself as a kind of deceit—an act of substitution. For instance, we may recall the moment in book 19 of the *Iliad* when we hear the lament of Briseis at the death of Patroklos.[4] Not only does the passage suggest that in lamenting Patroklos's death Briseis is in fact recounting to herself—and thus mourning—all the losses that have befallen her; it is also then followed by these provocative lines: "So she spoke, lamenting, and the women sorrowed around her / *grieving openly for Patroklos, but for her own sorrows/each.*"[5] The death of Patroklos provides an occasion for each woman to grieve for her own sorrows and to shed the tears held in abeyance so far. The "open" profession of grief is openly described as an excuse or a covering for a secret, inner, or "closed" communion with grief, for which there is no room in public life.

Plato's account repeats this narrative but with one significant difference: poetry in his account substitutes for death. If in Homer it is death that provides an excuse to mourn, in *The Republic* it is poetry that provides such an excuse. But perhaps it would be more accurate to say that each case brings to our attention the opening of a particular kind of public space; the space of mourning, like that of the poetic theatrical performance, is a space where one is allowed to weep. In *The Republic* this space appears as the antithesis of the ideal space of the city, exhibiting everything that is repressed in the city's "waking" life. In reading Plato and Homer together, we notice how poetry enters into a kind of secret partnership with death; together, they provide mortals respite from the relentless demand for fortitude that public life makes on them. But precisely the contagion of grief is the nightmare for Socrates, for such contagion would dissolve all those boundaries on which the city of reason depends: boundaries between self and other, man and woman, adult and child.

Plato's accusations are aimed at two different capacities of poetic language. The first is its capacity to move—to effect an emotional change by means of a representation—and the second, which complicates and blights the first, is the capacity to engender a kind of transference. The emotions that cannot be directed toward the self—that have been held in check—may be transferred onto another, an apparently more worthy recipient. What is primarily indicted thus is the capacity of poetry to engender connections whereby the self and the other become interchangeable; the experience of sorrow becomes a means of identification and, moreover, a means of giving expression to a mingled sense of dejection, grief, and dissent, which is at once one's own and another's. The poetic *communication* of sorrow is an obstacle on the path of justice and virtue, because, finally, it allows men to be compassionate spectators of their own sorrows—perhaps thus allowing them to face a darkness which the life of the city cannot dispel—and hence, it presumably mitigates their ability to judge in an impartial way. Sound judgment must preclude compassion.

In the Sanskrit tradition too we find a scene that explicitly connects poetry with lament. Indeed, this is not simply one scene among others but the scene often recalled as illustrating the beginning of poetry itself: the dramatic moment that produced the first poet, the *ādikavi*, Valmiki. The scene occurs in the second *sarga* of the Valmiki *Rāmāyaṇa.* The sage Valmiki is going to bathe in the Tamasa River when he sees a pair of sweet-voiced Krauncha birds:

10. But even as he watched, a Niṣāda hunter, filled with malice and intent on mischief, struck down the male of the pair.
11. Seeing him struck down and writhing on the ground, his body covered with blood, his mate uttered a piteous cry.

12. And the pious seer, seeing the bird struck down in this fashion by the Niṣāda, was filled with pity.
13. Then, in the intensity of his feeling of compassion, the Brahman thought, "This is wrong." Hearing the kraunca hen wailing, he uttered these words:
14. "Since, Nisada, you killed one of this pair of krauncas, distracted at the height of passion, you shall not live for very long."
15. And even as he stood watching and spoke in this way, this thought arose in his heart, "Stricken with grief for this bird, what is this I have uttered?"
16. But upon reflection, that wise and thoughtful man came to a conclusion. Then that bull among sages spoke these words to his disciple:
17. "Fixed in metrical quarters, each with a like number of syllables, and fit for the accompaniment of stringed and percussion instruments, the utterance that I produced in this access of *śoka*, grief, shall be called *śloka*, poetry, and nothing else."[6]

Two cries are uttered: first, the cry of the bird, *(karuṇā gir)*, and then the cry of the sage, the *śloka*, or verse. The bird cries on seeing its mate struck and writhing on the ground, and the sage utters his verse after hearing the cry of the bird. Ch. Vaudeville has read this passage closely in his essay on this episode.[7] Commenting on the movement of *karuṇā*—usually translated as "compassion"—in this passage, he remarks, "And it is the *karuṇā gir*, the mournful song or pathetic lament of the Kraunci which awakens *karunyam*, pity or sympathy, in Valmiki's soul, and which impels him to curse the sinful Nisada in the famous verse."[8] In a note he adds that "the word *karuṇā*, which occurs three times in the passage, is from the root *kṛī:* 'to pour out, scatter'; the primitive sense of *karuṇā* is 'lamentable,' that which draws out an expression of pain or compassion."[9]

Karuṇā is what is poured out, cries or tears, in response to the violence of life. Here again, it is the sharing of passion or pain—the element of compassion—that seems significant: precisely the act of "entering into the feelings" of another. In that sense, one may read the poet's voice as *giving voice to* the inarticulate cry of the bird. Yet we must also notice something else: the poet's words are not simply a lament. Indeed, what they indicate is first an act of judgment; the poet thinks, "This is wrong." And that thought is then followed by a statement that may be read as a curse; a dispensation of justice as revenge.

Here the poet is the one who is first drawn into the sorrow of the other, the bird. The passage in fact suggests that this may be what makes him a poet. The impulse toward justice is preceded by compassion. The passage thus enables a connection between compassion, poetry, and justice that does not seem possible for Plato. But we must also ask what kind of justice this is. For the passage also reveals something that may be hidden in the Platonic indictment of poetry: the potentially violent element engendered by the sharing of grief. Though arising out of sorrow, the poet's words take the form of a punishment, vindictively seeking to inflict pain on the agent of pain. In this scene, the poet thus appears as the double of *both* the bird and the hunter: his cry imitates the cry of the bird insofar as it arises out of sorrow, and it imitates the act of the hunter in so far as it seeks to inflict injury. It thus stages a confluence of *karuṇā* (compassion) and *hiṃsā* (violence), where each becomes the alibi of the other.[10] What does this origin narrative suggest in terms of the *Rāmāyaṇa* itself?

Since the *sarga* is widely regarded as a later interpolation, and since the originary integrity of the epic in any case, cannot be attested, we can only conjecture here about the *effects* of this narrative in the context of the *Rāmāyaṇa* as a whole. Vaudeville argues in his essay that the *sarga* performs a significant function: it indicates that the main theme of the *Rāmāyaṇa,* in its early form, may have been the sorrow of Sita, separated from her husband Rama, and thus connects the *Rāmāyaṇa* to an earlier tradition of folk poetry, sung by lower-caste musicians *(kuśilavas).* Drawing on a line in verse 39 that refers to the singing of a *śoka* (rather than a *śloka*) with four *padas,* he surmises that *śoka* itself might indicate not simply grief or lament but in fact a genre of folksong, a particular kind of lament. He further suggests that the famous verse beginning "*mā niṣāda . . .*" may itself be a *citation* from a well-known ballad of this genre. In this vein, he translates and comments on verse 39 as follows:

> "The lament [of the *kraunci* bird] sung by the great *ṛṣi,* by being repeated after, gained the nature (or attained the status) of *śloka* (lyrical utterance)."
>
> What seems to be alluded to in this verse is the passage from a form of folk-song *(śoka)* to lyrical poetry of a high order *(śloka)* such as is found in Valmiki's noble work. The *Krauñca-vadha* episode does not explain the birth of the *śloka* meter, but it clearly suggests that Valmiki derived his inspiration from a type of folk-ballad sung in the pathetic mood.[11]

Vaudeville's commentary develops a significant hypothesis that would place the lament song of the lower castes at the origin of the martial epic. The scene could then be read as a disclosure of what the epic may have repressed about its own sociopolitical genealogy. At an inaugural moment—a moment commemorated as inaugural—we perhaps find staged precisely a conflict regarding the origin.

The passage from *śoka* to *śloka* is also, as we have noted, the passage from curse to poetry. The poet who identifies with the grief-stricken bird also inadvertently identifies with the hunter. The transmission of *karuṇā* becomes also the transmission of what *karuṇā* protests against. Perhaps that is why Valmiki wonders at what he has uttered and consecrates it with the name of a poetic meter rather than allowing it to remain simply a curse. Thus "poetry" as metrical form is both related to, and distanced from, the judgmental and powerful forms of speech that precede it. In the movement of *śoka* to *śloka* the desire for revenge is not simply evinced, it is also staged and dramatized, put within quotation marks, so to speak. Poetry emerges when a scene of wild identification is safely channeled into a form of language that will henceforth be distinguished chiefly by its rhythmic repeatability.

We may read the privileging of *karuṇā* at the inaugural moment of Sanskrit poetry as a possible (albeit tangential) response to Plato. As we have noted, this passage from Valmiki exposes the identificatory and potentially violent force of lament, even as it contains that force by domesticating it in a new generic home. But instead of reading poetry-as-lament as a distraction from the path of justice, it positions it at the threshold of that path. By doing so, it establishes a relation between poetry and justice, at the same time as it also exhibits the intersection between justice-as-revenge and violence. Condensed in this moment is the ambivalent relation between violence, compassion and justice that will be played out through the epic, as Rama, the ideal king, responds both to the appeal of compassion and to that of violent "justice." Though it may be tempting to privilege poetry's role here as a critic of violence, it appears, at the same time, as its instigator. Whether or not the *sarga* describes the origin of poetry, it thus appears to legitimize epic poetry's own celebration of war. The celebration of war (in epic poetry)—like war itself (the act of "counter"-violence)—is perhaps seductively prefigured here as the spontaneous outpouring of (violent) compassion in a world populated by defenseless birds and malicious hunters.

Nevertheless, Vālmiki sets something in motion. Once evoked, so strikingly and succinctly, the deep thread of *karuṇā* cannot be simply reabsorbed into the fabric of the epic. In Valmiki's *Rāmāyaṇa,* that thread appears to mark the figure of Rama only in sporadic and uncertain terms, but later writers (including Anandavardhana) have attempted to draw out its significance more powerfully, as something that may be foundational, both for poetry and for justice. Among such attempts, the play *Uttararāmacarita* by the seventh-century poet Bhavabhuti deserves special mention. Indeed, the entire play may be read as an exploration of the effects of *karuṇā* since it asks what kind of a hero Rama would be if he were primarily governed by compassion. Though the "plot" of the play remains dependent on the text of the Valmiki *Rāmāyaṇa,* its focus is quite different. Focusing on the last parts of the epic, which describe the banishment of Sita, the play presents a Rama who is deeply grieved about this separation; the emphasis is on a sensitive and emotional protagonist rather than a king known for his valor and martial skill. In this respect, Bhavabhuti's play follows the dramatic model established by Kalidasa's love plays: the plot depends on an external constraint that produces the separation of lovers, and the sorrow of separation becomes the medium through which love may be rehearsed and performed as memory and loss.

If we read the play in this manner, paying attention to the structural similarities the play shares with Kalidasa's plots, we might conclude that *karuṇā* in this play functions simply as the idealization of *kāma* (desire)—the means by which *kāma* makes its appearance. The relation between *karuṇā* and *kāma* is indeed important, but reading *karuṇā* merely as a more elevated substitute for *kāma* may not do justice to Bhavabhuti's work. Because the play is not about any king but about Rama himself, the ideal and most virtuous king, the emphasis on *karuṇā* has a profound political impact. *Karuṇā* in the play functions as the force capable of questioning the very conception of virtue that upholds the "ideal" kingdom. In *Uttararāmacarita,* as in the epic narrative, Rama, after having fought a battle to regain his abducted wife Sita, in the end banishes her because his subjects consider her virtue tarnished. The difference between the two texts lies in Rama's reaction to this act: in Bhavabhuti's play, though he follows the wishes of his subjects, the intensity of his reaction forces the reader to question the justice of those wishes. Whereas in the epic narrative, the banishment serves to demonstrate Rama's virtue (as the ideal king, he disregards his own happiness in order to respect the values of the community), in Bhavabhuti's play, it demonstrates instead the cruelty of those values.

The political critique mounted by the play becomes most explicit in the passage that makes a connection between the banishing of Sita and the slaying of a Śudra ascetic. The lower-caste ascetic must be slain because in practicing religious austerities he is acting in a manner forbidden to his caste, and this transgression is considered responsible for the untimely death of a Brahmin boy. In the play—as in the famous epic episode to which it alludes—Rama does slay the low-caste ascetic. He thus conforms to the actions "prescribed" for him by earlier poets. But here, as in the banishment of Sita, he acts with great reluctance, calling into question the morality that apparently binds him. Thus when he describes his own act of killing the Śudra ascetic as an act "befitting Rama" (kṛtaṃ rāmasadṛśaṃ karma, 2.10),[12] his words are not just self-critical, a sign merely of a character's interior scrutiny. Their full impact becomes apparent only if we read them as also articulating criticism of the *legendary* Rama, the very Rama whose "role" is reluctantly performed by Bhavabhuti's shadow king.

It is only in this context that we understand the pivotal role of *karuṇā*. In the play, *karuṇā* seems to be the most powerful available means of expressing dissent. In the passage alluded to above, when Rama castigates his right hand, which has not only beheaded the Śudra ascetic but also banished Sita, he mockingly wonders whence such a hand may learn compassion (karuṇā kutaste). His fault, therefore—or rather, the fault of the legendary Rama—-is lack of compassion. On this account, we could say that *karuṇā* functions in the play as a political virtue, insofar as it becomes the basis on which a criticism of exclusions and hierarchies may be articulated. However, for Bhavabhuti, *karuṇā* was also the highest among the aesthetic emotions, or *rasas*. How would the political virtue of *karuṇā* relate to the aesthetic emotion of *karuṇā*, also famously extolled by the play?

I would suggest that we attempt to read the oft-cited verse in act 3 that proclaims the primacy of *karuṇā* among *rasas* in light of our preceding discussion. The verse goes as follows:

Eko rasaḥ karuṇ eva nimittabhedād
Bhinnaḥ pṛthakpṛthagivāśrayate vivartān
Āvartabudbudataraṅ gamayānvikārān—
Ambho yathā salilameva tu tatsamagram. (3.47)[13]

The one rasa of *karuṇā*, divided by the difference of causes
Takes shelter in several forms
As water appears different, in whirlpools, waves, and bubbles,
But yet is all water.

Among the eight primary *rasas* defined by the first-century treatise on drama, the *Nāṭyaśāstra*, Bhavabhuti declares *karuṇā* to be the most fundamental. Indeed, it is the only *rasa*, the only one of substance, since the others (erotic love, fear, revulsion, heroism, and so on) are simply different forms of this. *Karuṇā* is as different from the rest as substance is from form. But what does this *karuṇā* represent in the language of the *rasas?* Viraraghava's commentary on the *Uttararamcharita*, glossing this verse, defines *karuṇā* as "the excessive sorrow (dukha) born of separation from loved ones." M. R. Kale's further gloss provides a clarification: this excessive sorrow *(śoka)* is the *sthāyibhāva* of *karuṇā*.[14] We are thus reminded that in the system of the *rasa* theory, each *rasa* corresponds to a *sthāyibhāva*, the stable or lasting emotion that is both expressed and communicated by the *rasa*, and *śoka* is the *sthāyibhāva* of *karuṇā*.

As the sorrow born of separation from loved ones, *karuṇā* becomes thus the primary sign of emotional relation between beings, the sign that the absence of a (loved) other is experienced as a loss. This sorrow is in turn communicated to the reader or spectator, who is invited to participate in it. *Karuṇā* thus attests, above all, to the communicability of sorrow. Bhavabhuti suggests that without this prior communicability, no emotional or aesthetic relation would be possible. If he presents *karuṇā* as central to both poetry and justice, it is perhaps in order to indicate that both depend on the capacity for lamenting and for sharing lament. To read Bhavabhuti seriously would mean that we think about what this may propose not only in terms of its departure from the Platonic conception of the community of justice but also in terms of its possible implications for our own thinking about justice and poetry. Perhaps his work prompts us to think that no community is possible without the ability to recognize death as an incommensurable loss and to communicate one's deprivation in the face of such loss. Going further on the path opened by Valmiki's and Bhavabhuti's texts, we could say that placing lament at the origin of justice means that justice cannot think of itself as redress, revenge, or compensation; it begins instead with the consciousness of death, of that which it can never redress. It begins with an absolute sense of incommensurability.

I am not sure about any of this. From another position, it is also possible to decide that the link made by Bhavabhuti between justice, compassion, and poetry is too weak, or perhaps even a way of *evading* some crucial political questions. After all, Bhavabhuti's Rama does not finally change his actions but only his responses. It is at moments like these that we as readers are called upon to make decisions. To be sure, we could (and should) read Bhavabhuti's work more extensively, and be more attentive as well to its historical context. But finally, it is up to us to seize moments such as these, and to amplify what may be hovering around them, or hesitating in them. Reading Bhavabhuti would remain a trivial act if we did not at least make an effort to take his thinking further along the path he has already indicated.

Attempts to find a radical ethico-political justification for poetry periodically arise to answer the charge of poetry's frivolity—even in the Sanskrit tradition, which is so often criticized for its focus on art, skill, and sensuous beauty. We glimpse such attempts in Valmiki's and Bhavabhuti's work as we do in the work of modern Hindi writers such as Shukla and Prasad. All these attempts can of course be read in terms of the possible historical pressures that produced them: whether the pressure of Buddhist thought on Hindu beliefs, or the pressure of a wider, insistent discourse of nonviolence, or the pressure of nationalist aspirations and demands. To be sure, if we disregard those pressures, we would not be able to gauge the significance or the singularity of such attempts and would risk conflating and thus weakening them. But at the same time, we cannot *reduce* them to these pressures, or read them entirely in terms of a historical context that we have, in advance, determined for them. This has, in effect, been the argument of this book, even as I have struggled to come to terms with its various premises and implications. If we read Sanskrit texts today, we have to do so with the sense that they are not entombed in a dead age but that they can, in some way, break through to our world and exert, in turn, a certain pressure on it. We have to read them not for their knowledge but for their thought—for that which continues to be thought in them. They can only be exposed to our time if we too are, in some fleeting but inescapable way, exposed to them.

Notes

Introduction

1. U. R. Anantha Murthy, *Samskara: A Rite for A Dead Man,* trans. A. K. Ramanujan (Delhi: Oxford University Press, 1978), 82.

2. I use the word "reading" not in an analytic sense here but to refer broadly to all the ways in which the words of a text may be sequentially followed by someone, whether by the mouth, the eye, or the ear.

3. I am partly referring here to Michel Foucault's discussion of the distinguishing characteristics of modern conceptions of reading, especially in *The Order of Things.* See Foucault, *The Order of Things: An Archaeology of the Human Sciences* (New York: Vintage Books, 1994).

4. Anantha Murthy, *Samskara,* 2.

5. Walter Benjamin, "The Task of the Translator," in *Illuminations,* trans. Harry Zohn (London: Fontana, 1982), 75.

6. Peggy Kamuf, *Book of Addresses* (Stanford, Calif.: Stanford University Press, 2005), 70.

7. There are of course exceptions. Sanskrit folktales mention the embarrassment of kings and princes when confronted by (upper-caste) women who know the grammatical language and are more learned than the men. See, for example, Somadeva, *Tales from the Kathāsaritasāgara,* trans. Arshia Sattar (London: Penguin, 1994).

8. Ashok Aklujkar, "The Early History of Sanskrit as Supreme Language," in *Ideology and Status of Sanskrit: Contributions to the History of the Sanskrit Language,* ed. Jan E. M. Houben, 70 (Leiden: E. J. Brill, 1996).

9. Robert P. Goldman and Sally J. Sutherland Goldman, trans. *The Rāmāyaṇa of Vālmīki: An Epic of Ancient India,* vol. 5, *Sundarakāṇḍa* (Princeton, N.J.: Princeton University Press, 1996), 192.

10. Madhav M. Deshpande, *Sanskrit and Prakrit: Sociolinguistic Issues* (Delhi: Motilal Banarsidass, 1993), 25.

11. Ibid., 73.

12. Giorgio Agamben, *The End of the Poem: Studies in Poetics,* trans. Daniel Heller-Roazen (Stanford, Calif.: Stanford University Press, 1999), 54.

13. Ibid., 55; my emphasis.

14. Lynn Zastoupil and Martin Moir, eds. *The Great Indian Education Debate: Documents Relating to the Orientalist-Anglicist Controversy, 1781–1843* (Surrey: Curzon Press, 1999), 111. Hereafter cited in text as *Education Debate,* with page numbers.

15. G. N. Devy, *After Amnesia: Tradition and Change in Indian Literary Criticism* (London: Sangam Books, 1992).

16. Alok Rai, *Hindi Nationalism* (Hyderabad: Orient Longman, 2000).

17. Sumathi Ramaswamy has provided an eloquent account of Tamil's "contest" with Sanskrit. See in particular chapter 2 in Ramaswamy, *Passions of the Tongue: Language Devotion in Tamil India, 1891–1970* (Berkeley: University of California Press, 1997). Two contemporary personal narratives provide different responses to Sanskrit's upper-caste history and status: Kancha Ilaiah, *Why I Am Not a Hindu: A Sudra Critique of Hindutva Philosophy, Culture and Political Economy* (Calcutta: Samya, 1996), 12–17, and Kumud Pawde, "The Story of My 'Sanskrit,'" in *Subject to Change: Teaching Literature in the Nineties,* ed. Susie Tharu, 85–97 (Hyderabad: Orient Longman, 1997).

18. Benedict Anderson, *Imagined Communities: Reflections on the Origin and Spread of Nationalism* (London: Verso, 1991), 36.

19. Jean-Luc Nancy, *The Inoperative Community,* trans. Peter Connor, Lisa Garbus, Michael Holland, and Simona Sawhney (Minneapolis: University of Minnesota Press, 1991), xl.

20. Simon Gikandi, *Writing in Limbo: Modernism and Caribbean Literature* (Ithaca, N.Y.: Cornell University Press, 1992), 4.

21. C. R. Devadhar, ed., *Mālvikāgnimitram of Kalidasa* (Delhi: Motilal Banarsidass, 2002), 2.

22. Han Robert Jauss, *Toward an Aesthetic of Reception,* trans. Timothy Bahti (Minneapolis: University of Minnesota Press, 1982), 21.

1. *Smara*

1. Rabindranath Tagore, *Selected Writings on Literature and Language,* ed. Sisir Kumar Das and Sukanta Chaudhuri (New Delhi: Oxford University Press, 2001), 241.

2. I use the word "postcolonial" to indicate that which is critical of the colonial, or in Ania Loomba's words, as "the contestation of colonial domination and the legacies of colonialism." See Loomba, *Colonialism/Postcolonialism* (London: Routledge, 1998), 12.

3. Tagore, *Selected Writings on Literature and Language,* 239.

4. Tagore, "Nationalism in the West," *Nationalism* (Calcutta: Rupa and Co. 1992), 55.

5. For an insightful reading of this "loss," see Lalita Pandit, "The Psychology and Aesthetics of Love: *Sringara, Bhavana,* and *Rasadhvani* in *Gora,*" in *Rabindranath Tagore: Universality and Tradition,* ed. Patrick Colm Hogan and Lalita Pandit (Madison, N.J.: Fairleigh Dickinson University Press, 2003).

6. M. R. Kale, ed., *The Abhijñānaśākuntalam of Kālidāsa,* 10th ed. (Delhi: Motilal Banarsidass, 1969), 12. Hereafter cited in text with act, verse, and page number. All translations from this and other Sanskrit texts in this chapter are mine, unless part of another text. In some instances I have made only minor modifications to Kale's and Barbara Stoler Miller's English translations. I have also been helped by Shrikrishnamani Tripathi's Hindi translation and accompanying commentaries. See also Shrikrishnamani Tripathi, ed., *Abhijñānaśākuntala of Mahakavi Kalidasa, edited with the "Vimla," "Chandrakala" Sanskrit and Hindi Commentaries* (Varanasi: Chaukhamba Surbharti Prakashan, 2003).

7. Barbara Stoler Miller, "Kalidasa's World and his Plays," in *Theater of Memory: The Plays of Kalidasa,* ed. Barbara Stoler Miller, 38–39 (New York: Columbia University Press, 1984).

8. V. S. Apte, *The Practical Sanskrit-English Dictionary* (Delhi: Motilal Banarsidass, 1965).

9. *Bhaṅga* carries multiple connotations; it may mean breaking, shattering, or splitting; a break, fracture, breach; separation, analysis; fall, downfall, decay, ruin.

10. Kalidasa's play is based on an episode recounted in the *Mahābhārata.* The tension between two representations of the king—one as the guardian of peace and prosperity, and the other as a cruel and rapacious hunter—is particularly obvious in the *Śakuntalā* narrative in the *Mahābhārata.* See *The Mahābhārata,* trans. J. A. B. van Buitenen, book 1: The Book of the Beginning (Chicago: University of Chicago Press, 1973), sections 62–69 (155–71), and especially section 63 (157–58)

11. Narayan Ram Acharya, ed., *Raghuvaṃśa of Kalidasa.* With Commentary Sanjivini of Mallinatha, extracts from the Commentaries of Vallabhadeva, Hemadri, Dinkara Misra, Caritravardhana, Sumativijaya, *Raghuvaṃśasāra,* critical and explanatory notes, various readings and indexes (Varanasi: Chaukhambha Orientalia, 1987).

12. Mallinatha probably lived in the second half of the fourteenth century. He is widely believed to be the standard traditional authority on Kalidasa; his commentaries still guide modern interpreters and are often included in scholarly editions of Kalidasa's works.

13. Kalidasa, *Raghuvaṃśa,* 9.64.

14. Hazariprasad Dvivedi, *Granthāvalī,* vol. 8 (New Delhi: Rajkamal Prakashan, 1981), 146.

15. Acharya Jagdishchandra Mishra, ed., *Saundarananda Mahākāvya of Śri Aśvaghoṣa* (Varanasi: Chaukhamba Surbharati Prakashan, 1991), 82.

16. M. R. Kale, ed., *Kumārasambhava of Kālidāsa* (Delhi: Motilal Banarsidass Publishers, 1999), 93.

17. In her study of Hinduism, Madeleine Biardeau makes a similar claim: "And so it is legitimate to say that the perfect woman, the sati—who appears in nineteenth century English literature as the widow who throws herself on the her husband's funeral pyre—has love as her first duty, or to use a more homogeneous language,

love as her *svadharma.* Of course, a woman's dharma is not usually expressed in this way. Her duty is summed up in a formula: to serve her husband as her principal god. However, when one knows the central place of amorous desire in the marriage bond, the deduction is self-evident and is in no way theoretical." See Biardeau, *Hinduism: The Anthropology of a Civilization,* trans. Richard Nice (Delhi: Oxford University Press, 1989), 47.

18. Stephanie Jamison, "The Classical Moment in India," in *The Classical Moment: Views from Seven Literatures,* ed. Gail Holst-Warhaft and David R. McCann (Lanham, Md.: Rowman and Littlefield, 1999), 41.

19. Romila Thapar, *Śakuntalā: Texts, Readings, Histories* (New Delhi: Kali for Women, 1999), 39, 38.

20. Historical evidence suggests that Chandragupta I, usually considered the founder of the Gupta empire, married a Lichchavi princess, and that the alliance contributed to his prestige. Of Chandragupta II we know that the Shakas (Scythians) who ruled over parts of western India were defeated during his reign, and a popular story about his "rescue" of—and subsequent marriage to—the captured wife of his older brother tells us something about the way protection (of women) became an early trope in the emperor's arsenal. We also know that Chandragupta II entered into matrimonial alliances with several kingdoms—through either his own marriages or the marriages of his children. See, for instance, D. N. Jha, *Ancient India in Historical Outline* (New Delhi: Manohar, 1999), 149–51.

21. Dvivedi, *Granthāvalī,* vol 8, 237.

22. Ibid., 220.

23. Ibid., 221.

24. Wendy Doniger, *Asceticism and Eroticism in the Mythology of Siva* (Delhi: Oxford University Press, 1973), 148.

25. Thapar, *Śakuntalā,* 58.

26. Ibid., 74.

27. Tagore, *Selected Writings on Literature and Language,* 245.

28. Thapar, *Sakuntala,* 59. While Thapar does not call Durvasa the double of Dusyanta, she suggests that he too might have wanted "a different kind of hospitality for which she [Sakuntala] was not willing"—an offering of sexual favors.

29. Among modern readers, two whose work I've found especially insightful are Barbara Stoler Miller and Charles Malamoud. See Stoler Miller, "Kalidasa's World and His Plays" in *Theater of Memory: The Plays of Kalidasa,* ed. Stoler Miller, 3–42 (New York: Columbia University Press, 1984), and Malamoud, "By Heart: Notes on the Interplay between Love and Memory in Ancient Indian Poetry" in his book *Cooking the World: Ritual and Thought in Ancient India,* trans. David White (New Delhi: Oxford University Press, 1998), 247–59.

30. The desire for such submission, which would make violent coercion redundant, may be glimpsed in those passages in *Abhijñānaśākuntala* and *Raghuvamsa*

that present explicit or implicit arguments against the hunt, in the king's own "transformation" into a lover of natural beauty, and in the valorization of the ascetic's (ostensibly unaggressive) relation to nature.

31. Thapar, *Śakuntalā,* 66.

32. Jamison, "The Classical Moment in India," 43.

33. Malamoud, "By Heart," 250; my emphasis.

34. See also Stoler Miller in this context: "In this Sanskrit literature, an act of remembering is a conventional technique for relating the antithetical modes of love-in-separation *(vipralambha-śṛṅgāra)* and love-in-union *(saṃbhoga-śṛṅgāra)." Theater of Memory,* 39.

35. *The Meghadūta of Kalidasa: Text with Sanskrit Commentary of Mallinatha, English Translation, Notes, Appendices and a Map.* Edited by M. R. Kale. 8th ed. (Delhi: Motilal Banarsidass, 1974), 13.

36. Tagore, *Selected Writings on Literature and Language,* 222–23.

37. Concerning "she": I am told that in Bengali the gender of both the reader and the beloved remains indeterminate.

38. Tagore, *Selected Writings,* 223.

39. Ibid., 225.

2. Literary Modernity and Sanskrit Poetry

1. Hazariprasad Dvivedi, *"Merā Kānchnār,"* in *Chune Hue Nibandh* [Selected Essays], ed. Mukund Dvivedi, 43–44 (Delhi: Kitabghar, 1996).

2. Ibid., 44. This and all other translations from Hindi and Sanskrit texts in this chapter are mine, unless part of another author's text.

3. Ibid.

4. Namwar Singh, *Dūsri Paraṃparā Kī Khoj* (Delhi: Rajkamal Prakashan, 1982), 82

5. The debate about the "other" tradition was later carried on with considerable verve and acrimony in the pages of the Hindi journal *Pūrvagraha* by Radhavallabh Tripathi and Wagish Shukla. See *Purvagraha* 91 and 94, 1989.

6. Namwar Singh, *Dūsri Paraṃparā Kī Khoj,* 93.

7. Srikant Verma, *Racnāvalī,* vol. 1, ed. Arvind Tripathi (New Delhi: Rajkamal Prakashan, 1995), 54–57.

8. Written in 1956, the poem is reminiscent of the work of the famous Urdu poet Faiz Ahmed Faiz. In poems such as *Mauzoo-e-Sukhan* and *Mujh Se Pehli Si Mohabbat,* the poet announces a similar break with a tradition of romantic poetry. The harshness of the real world, as well as its powerful appeal to the poet, are acknowledged while at the same time the sweetness of an increasingly irrelevant world of beauty and love is implicitly mourned.

9. Verma, *Racnāvalī,* 487.

10. Dharamavir Bharati, *Granthāvalī,* vol. 3, ed. Chandrakant Bandivadekar (New Delhi: Vani Prakashan, 1998), 73–74.

11. Mohan Rakesh, *Āṣārh kā ek din* (Delhi: Rajpal and Sons), 2000.

12. Jai Dev Taneja, *Lahron Ke Rājhans: Vividh Āyām* (New Delhi: Radhakrishna, 1975), 13.

13. Suresh Awasthi, Bhūmikā, [Introduction] to Mohan Rakesh, *Lahron Ke Rājhans* (Delhi: Rajkamal Prakashan, 2001), 9.

14. Aparna Bhargava Dharwadker, *Theaters of Independence: Drama, Theory, and Urban Performance in India since 1947* (Iowa City: University of Iowa Press, 2005), 165.

15. Ebrahim Alkazi, "Language in Hindi Drama," *Hindustan Times,* August 12, 1972; cited by Taneja, *Vividh Āyām,* 15.

16. Mohan Rakesh, *Mohan Rakesh: Sāhityik aur Sānskṛtik Dṛṣti* (Delhi: Radhakrishna Prakashana, 1975), 165.

17. Ibid., 164.

18. Mohan Rakesh, *Lahron Ke Rājhans* (Delhi: Rajkamal, 2001), 19.

19. Rakesh, *Mohan Rakesh,* 26–27.

20. Ibid., 28.

21. Needless to say, Rakesh was not alone in thinking that he lived at a time that demanded a new kind of response. Aparna Dharwadker's *Theaters of Independence* provides a thoughtful and well-researched account of the many debates and polemics that shaped postindependence theater in India, including those generated by IPTA (The Indian People's Theatre Association). Dharwadker argues that this sense of historical responsibility in turn produced a momentous and charged urban theater: "Despite the apparent conformism of the 'modernists' and the radicalism of the 'nativists,' however, the field of post-independence urban theater is in all important respects a *historically unprecedented formation* in India. For the first time since the classical period of Sanskrit drama (ca. A.D. 400–1000), Indian theatrical practice is framed by fully developed, competing, even polarized theories of dramatic representation and reception, and participates equally in the cultures of (print) textuality and performance" (*Theaters of Independence,* 4).

22. See Jean-Luc Nancy, "Is Everything Political," trans. Philip M. Adamek, *The New Centennial Review* 2, no. 3 (2002): 15–22, 18.

23. Susan Stanford Friedman, "Definitional Excursions: The Meanings of *Modern/Modernity/Modernism,*" *Modernism/Modernity* 8, no. 3 (2001): 493–513, 503.

24. Nemichandra Jain, "*Āṣārh kā ek din: Samikṣātmak Viśleṣaṇa* [Critical Analysis]," in *Āṣārh kā ek din* (Delhi: Rajpal, 2000), 122.

25. Jai Shankar Prasad's play *Skandagupta Vikramaditya* had earlier also presented Kalidasa as Matrigupta, the ruler of Kashmir.

26. Rakesh, *Āṣārh kā ek din,* 93.

27. Ibid., 102.

28. Ibid., 97.

29. Ramesh Gautam, *Mithak aur Svantantryottar Hindi Nātak* [Myth and Post-Independence Hindi Drama] (Delhi: Nachiketa Prakashan, 1989), 58–59.

30. For a different reading, see Aparna Dharwadker's *Theaters of Independence.* In her analysis of the play, Dharwadker highlights the modernist and postcolonial aspects of Rakesh's work. "By refusing to create an ideal author to explain an ideal oeuvre, Rakesh follows the modernist dictum of separating the poet from his work; by placing the poet in deterministic institutional contexts, he inserts postcolonial into modernist perspectives" (242).

31. Rakesh, *Āṣārh kā ek din,* 12.

32. Ibid., 93.

33. Ibid., 104–5.

34. Mohan Rakesh, *Andhere Band Kamre* (Delhi: Rajkamal, 1991), 198.

35. Rakesh, *Mohan Rakesh,* 35.

36. Ashvaghosha, *Saundaranandaṃ Mahākāvyam,* ed. Acharya Jagadish Chandra Mishra (Varanasi: Chaukhamba Surbharati Prakashan, 1991), 4.39.

37. Ibid., 4.42

38. Ibid., 5.42.

39. Buddhadeva Bose, *Modern Poetry and Sanskrit Kavya,* trans. Sujit Mukherjee (Calcutta: Writers Workshop Books, 1997), 55.

40. See Taneja, *Vividh Āyām,* 21–24.

41. Mohan Rakesh, *Rāt Bītne Tak aur Anya Dhvani Nātak* (Delhi: Radhakrishna, 1998), 22.

42. In Rakesh's short story "Miss Pal," a female character appears in a similar role. But the representation of her indecision and conflict seems quite different from that of the male characters we have discussed. She carries a greater sense of failure than them, and the narrator's perspective seems markedly different as well, for she is presented as being pitiful in a way that the men are not.

43. Mohan Rakesh, *Lahron Ke Rājhans* (Delhi: Rajkama, 2001), 36–37. These lines seem to be repeated in several versions, including the first story Rakesh wrote based on Ashvaghosha's text.

44. Mohan Rakesh, *Ekatra,* ed. Jaidev Taneja (Delhi: Radhakrishna, 1998), 245.

45. In Rakesh's other works—those clearly situated within a modern context—the relation between gender and modernity becomes more complex. The novel *Andhere Band Kamre,* for example, suggests that the male characters, both Harbans and the narrator, are on the one hand attracted to women who appear to be independent and strong-willed—like Nilima and Sushma—but on the other are drawn toward women who are considerably younger and unassertive; women who conform to a more traditional image of domesticity, like Shukla. Indeed, the locus of male alienation and anxiety in the novel seems to be the "modern" woman herself: her desires, demands, and expectations. Similarly, in *Ādhe Adhūre,* Rakesh's last completed play, the female protagonist is at the end implicitly presented as being responsible for the incapacity, and even, in a sense, for the violence, of the male, to whom she apparently presents the image of his inadequacy. Nevertheless—and it is important to note this—in

Rakesh's work the "modern," more independent woman is not simply demonized, as she often is in the popular cultural texts of those decades. The relation between Harbans and Nilima in *Andhere Band Kamre,* and the narrator's ambivalence in judging this relationship, are significant in this regard. The narrator cannot *not* hear Nilima's story; he cannot just ignore her version of the events that occur. He notices—and records—how the source of the tension lies within Harbans himself, who on the one hand wants his wife to be a dancer and on the other cannot stand the thought that she might be a public artist who would want a career, recognition, and remuneration.

46. Dipesh Chakrabarty, *Provincializing Europe: Postcolonial Thought and Historical Difference* (Princeton, N.J.: Princeton University Press, 2000), 244.

47. Paul de Man, *Blindness and Insight: Essays in the Rhetoric of Contemporary Criticism* (Minneapolis: University of Minnesota Press, 1983), 148.

48. Ibid., 152.

49. Rakesh, *Mohan Rakesh,* 98.

50. Ibid., 101.

51. Rakesh, *Ekatra,* 111.

52. Rakesh, *Sāhityik aur Sānskṛtik Dṛṣti,* 140.

53. Ibid., 117; my emphasis.

54. Ibid., 117–18.

55. Rakesh, *Sāhityik aur Sānskṛtik Dṛṣti,* 61.

56. In this context, we might keep in mind that these views were not shared by many of Rakesh's contemporaries. For example, the Bengali writer, actor, and director Utpal Dutt (1929–93), who was also actively involved in thinking about new directions for Indian theater, believed that all the stage devices found in European theater could be innovatively used in Indian theater, and that the attempt to keep these devices cordoned off from Indian theater could only be a reactionary and ultimately futile attempt. See Utpal Dutt, "On Proletarian Myths," in *People's Art in the Twentieth Century* (Delhi: Jan Natya Manch, 2000), 321–36.

57. Rakesh, *Sāhityik aur Sānskṛtik Dṛṣti,* 50.

58. Ibid., 49–50.

3. Allegory and Violence

1. Although the wide range of 400 BCE to 400 CE is often considered the period of composition of the *Mahābhārata,* there is disagreement about these dates. Alf Hiltebeitel has suggested that the text might have been composed "between the mid-second century B.C. and the year zero." Hiltebeitel, *Rethinking the Mahābhārata: A Reader's Guide to the Education of the Dharma King* (Chicago: University of Chicago Press, 2001), 18.

2. The *Bhagavadgitāparvan* (the Book of the *Bhagavad Gitā*) is the sixty-third of the hundred minor books of the *Mahābhārata* and the third episode of the *Bhiṣmaparvan (The Book of Bhiṣma),* itself the sixth of the eighteen major books.

3. Friedrich Nietzsche, "On the Uses and Disadvantages of History for Life," in

Untimely Meditations, trans. R. J. Hollingdale, 78 (Cambridge: Cambridge University Press, 1983).

4. Ibid., 67.

5. See Philippe Lacoue-Labarthe, "History and Mimesis" in *Looking after Nietzsche,* ed. L. Rickels, (Albany: State University of New York Press, 1990), 209–31.

6. Nietzsche, "On the Uses and Disadvantages of History for Life," 122–23.

7. J. A. B. van Buitenen, ed., *The Bhagavadgitā in the Mahābhārata: A Bilingual Edition* (Chicago: University of Chicago Press, 1981), 64. Following van Buitenen, I provide line citations in text, ordered by book, chapter, and verse. Page numbers provided in the notes refer to van Buitenen's text. I have modified van Buitenen's translation in some instances.

8. Ibid., 123.

9. Ibid., 117.

10. Israel Selvanayagam, "Aśoka and Arjuna as Counterfigures Standing on the Field of Dharma: A Historical-Hermeneutical Perspective," *History of Religions* 32, no. 1 (1992): 59–75; Nick Sutton, "Aśoka and Yudhiṣṭhira: A Historical Setting for the Ideological Tensions of the Mahābhārata?" *Religion* 27 (1997): 333–41.

11. G. W. F. Hegel, *On the Episode of the Mahābhārata known by the name Bhagavad-Gitā by Wilhelm von Humboldt, Berlin 1826,* ed. and trans. Herbert Herring (New Delhi: Indian Council of Philosophical Research, 1995), 16–19.

12. G. W. F. Hegel, *Philosophy of Right,* trans. T. M. Knox (London: Oxford University Press, 1967), 114–15.

13. Judith Butler, *Antigone's Claim: Kinship between Life and Death* (New York: Columbia University Press, 2000), 2.

14. For example, "The general terms *proprium officium* and *milites* [in the translation], as in the foregoing *religio* and *impietas* put us at first *in a European way of looking at things,* they *deprive the contents of its coloration,* tempt us too readily to misunderstand the peculiar meaning and *to take the passages for something better than what they actually express.*—The above quoted is not at all based upon what we call duty, moral obligation, but only on natural destination." (Hegel, *On the Episode of the Mahabhāratā,* 25; my emphasis).

15. On Hegel's reading of the *Gitā,* see Gayatri Spivak, *Critique of Postcolonial Reason: Toward a History of the Vanishing Present* (Cambridge, Mass.: Harvard University Press, 1999), 37–67. Spivak's commentary proceeds along some of the paths I have pursued here but her aim is to demonstrate that "'Hegel' and the *'Gitā'* can be read as two rather different versions of the manipulation of the question of history in a political interest, for the apparent disclosure of the Law" (58).

16. The name of the place where the battle between the Pandavas and the Kauravas is fought.

17. M. K. Gandhi, *Hindu Dharma,* ed. Bharatan Kumarappa (Ahmedabad: Navajivan Press, 1950), 150.

18. Ibid.,160.

19. Pravachanacharya V. Panoli, ed., *Gitā in Sankara's Own Words* (Calicut: S. Paramasivan, 1975), 22.

20. Sri Aurobindo, *Essays on the Gitā, First Series* (Calcutta: Arya Publishing House, 1949), 73–74. The essays were originally published in the *Arya* from August 1916 to July 1918.

21. This law, along with the paradoxes it generates, is discussed in early texts from other traditions as well. For instance, we might recall here Plato's comments on civil strife in *The Republic:* "Observe, then, that in what is commonly known as civil strife, that is to say, when one of our Greek states is divided against itself, it is thought an abominable outrage for either party to ravage the lands or burn the houses of the other. No lover of his country would dare to mangle the land which gave him birth and nursed him. It is thought fair that the victors should carry off the others' crops, but do no more. They should remember that the war will not last for ever; some day they must make friends again." *The Republic of Plato,* trans. Francis MacDonald Cornford (London: Oxford University Press, 1945), 173.

22. See, for example, *Karnaparvan,* 8.49, in Vishnu S. Sukhthankar, S.K. Belvalkar, P. L. Vaidya, et al., eds., *Mahābhārata,* Critical Edition (Poona: Bhandarkar Oriental Research Institute, 1933-72). Hereafter cited in text by book, chapter, and verse number.

23. D. D. Kosambi, *Myth and Reality* (Bombay: Popular Prakashan, 1962),18–19.

24. Romila Thapar, *From Lineage to State: Social Formations in the Mid-First Millenium B.C. in the Ganga Valley* (Delhi: Oxford University Press, 1984), 132.

25. Alladi Mahadeva Sastry, *The Bhagavad Gitā with the Commentary of Sri Sankaracarya,* 7th ed. (Madras: Samata Books, 1977), 137 (4.21).

26. Van Buitenen, *The Bhagavadgitā in the Mahābhārata,* 112.

27. Ibid., 72.

28. Bimal K. Matilal, *Ethics and Epics,* ed. Jonardon Ganeri (New Delhi: Oxford University Press, 2002), 94.

29. David Gitomer, "King Duryodhana: The *Mahābhārata* Discourse of Sinning and Virtue in Epic and Drama," *Journal of the American Oriental Society* 112, no. 2 (1992): 222–32, 223.

30. Van Buitenen, *The Bhagavadgitā in the Mahābhārata,* 3–4.

31. Israel Selvanayagam, "Aśoka and Arjuna as Counterfigures Standing on the Field of Dharma: A Historical-Hermeneutical Perspective," *History of Religions* 32, no. 1 (August 1992): (59–75), 67.

32. Patrick Olivelle, *Samnyasa Upanisads: Hindu Scriptures on Asceticism and Renunciation* (New York: Oxford University Press, 1992), 54.

33. That the Ksatriya dharma itself had become associated with violence and greed is evident from other parts of the epic as well. Dhritrashtra's lament at the commencement of the battle evinces a similar sentiment: "Harsh is the Kṣatriya Dharma as laid

out by wise men; if we want the kingdom, having slain the Pandavas, or if they want it having slain their grandfather."

34. R. N. Sharma, ed., *Manusmṛti: Sanskrit Text with English Translation of M. N. Dutt* (Delhi: Chaukhamba Sanskrit Pratishthan, 1998), 7.99, 290. Similar ideas are expressed on several occasions in the *Mahābhārata* and explicitly in book 12, the *Śanti Parvan.*

35. Madeleine Biardeau, *Hinduism: The Anthropology of a Civilization* (Delhi: Oxford University Press, 1989), 113.

36. M. K. Gandhi, *Hind Swaraj and Other Writings,* ed. Anthony J. Parel (Cambridge: Cambridge University Press, 1997), 16.

37. Gandhi's approach here is markedly different from that of Bankimchandra Chattopadhyay. Sudipta Kaviraj has discussed how important it was for Bankim to present Krishna precisely as a historical figure: "Bankim's vindication of Kṛṣṇa is not aimed against other Hindu or Indian constructions of ideality, but the rational theology of Christianity . . . Christ was a historical figure. Bankim must, or at least he thinks he must, argue the historicity of Kṛṣṇa, not only his rational superiority as an ideal." See Sudipta Kaviraj, *The Unhappy Consciousness: Bankimchandra Chattopadhyay and the Formation of Nationalist Discourse in India* (Delhi: Oxford University Press, 1995), 88.

38. Gandhi, *Hindu Dharma,* 18.

39. Walter Benjamin, *The Origin of German Tragic Drama,* trans. John Osborne (London: Verso, 1998), 175.

40. Jacques Derrida, *Of Grammatology,* trans. Gayatri Chakravorty Spivak (Baltimore: Johns Hopkins University Press, 1974), 14.

41. The very first essay in Aurobindo Ghose's two-volume collection on the *Gītā,* titled "Our Demand and Need from the *Gitā,*" makes a similar argument, asking us to distinguish between two elements in every scripture: "one temporary, perishable, belonging to the ideas of the period and country in which it was produced, the other eternal and imperishable and applicable in all ages and countries." *Essays on the Gitā,* 5.

42. Gandhi, *Hindu Dharma,* 9.

43. Kosambi, *Myth and Reality,* 29.

44. Van Buitenen, *The Bhagavadgitā in the Mahābhārata,* 16.

45. Alf Hiltebeitel, *The Ritual of Battle: Krishna in the Mahābhārata* (Albany: State University of New York Press, 1990), 139.

46. Gandhi, *Hindu Dharma,* 145.

47. Philip Lutgendorf, *The Life of a Text: Performing the Rāmcaritamānas of Tulsidas* (Berkeley: University of California Press, 1991), 399.

48. Ronald Duncan, ed., *The Writings of Gandhi: A Selection* (New Delhi: Rupa and Co., 1990), 40.

49. Ibid.

50. M. K. Gandhi, *An Autobiography: The Story of My Experiments with Truth,* trans. Mahadev Desai (Boston: Beacon Press, 1993), 265.

51. Dennis Dalton, ed., *Mahatma Gandhi: Selected Political Writings* (Indianapolis: Hackett Publishing Company, 1996), 40.

52. In the context of the pervasive perception of Gandhi as a traditionalist, his reference to reason as the final arbiter is striking. As Anshuman Mondal notes in a recent article, "One cannot overlook the fact that he possessed a concept of rationality which, though qualified by his spiritualism, was nevertheless based upon a modern, scientific rationality . . . indeed, one cannot fail to notice throughout his discourse the lexicon of modern science: his naming of ashrams as 'laboratories,' or satyagrahi as 'moral scientists', his 'experiments' with truth and so on." See Mondal, "Gandhi, Utopianism and the Construction of Colonial Difference," *Interventions* 3, no. 3 419–38, 435.

53. Gandhi, *Hindu Dharma,* 34.

54. Ashis Nandy, *Traditions, Tyranny, and Utopias: Essays in the Politics of Awareness* (Delhi: Oxford University Press, 1987), 156.

55. Ibid., 320.

56. Ibid., 319–20.

57. Ibid., 325.

58. Ibid., 326, my emphasis.

59. Ibid., 321 (quote), 329.

60. Sisir K. Bose and Sugata Bose, eds., *The Essential Writings of Netaji Subhas Chandra Bose* (Delhi: Oxford University Press, 1998), 320.

61. B. R. Ambedkar, *What Congress and Gandhi Have Done to the Untouchables* (Bombay: Thacker and Co., 1946), 187.

62. See Jacques Pouchepadass, *Champaran and Gandhi: Planters, Peasants and Gandhian Politics,* trans. James Walker (New Delhi: Oxford University Press, 1999). Pouchepadass concludes that the main significance of Gandhi's intervention in 1917 in Champaran was "that it heralded the conjunction of the middle-class nationalist intelligentsia, which was in search of a mass following, with the dominant peasantry, whose economic rise since the 1860s and ascendancy over the lower classes of the countryside was about to find expression in the realm of modern-style institutional politics (232)." For a different argument about the appropriation of Gandhi's message by peasant groups in Uttar Pradesh and Bihar, see Shahid Amin, "Gandhi as Mahatma: Gorakhpur District, Eastern UP, 1921–2," in *Subaltern Studies III,* ed. Ranajit Guha, 1–61 (Delhi: Oxford University Press, 1984).

63. *Selected Political Writings,* 125.

64. *Hindu Dharma,* 135.

65. B. R. Ambedkar, *Annihilation of Caste,* ed. Mulk Raj Anand (New Delhi: Arnold Publishers, 1990). Hereafter cited in the text by title and page number. Gandhi's response is published in the same volume.

66. Rabindranath Tagore, *The Home and the World,* trans. Surendranath Tagore (London: Penguin Books, 1985), 153–54.

67. http://www.sabrang.com/cc/archive/2001/jan01/docu.htm.

4. The Lure of Violence

1. David Gitomer, "King Duryodhana: The *Mahābhārata* Discourse of Sinning and Virtue in Epic and Drama," *Journal of American Oriental Society* 112, no. 2 (1992): 231. For a different response, also contesting orientalist versions of literary history, see Patrick Colm Hogan, "Beauty, Politics and Cultural Otherness: The Bias of Literary Difference," in *Literary India: Comparative Studies in Aesthetics, Colonialism, and Culture,* ed. Patrick Hogan and Lalita Pandit, 3–46 (Albany: SUNY Press, 1995).

2. Romila Thapar, *From Lineage to State: Social Formations in the Mid-First Millenium B.C. in the Ganga Valley* (Bombay: Oxford University Press, 1984), 141.

3. Romila Thapar, *Interpreting Early India* (Delhi: Oxford University Press, 1992), 148–49.

4. On the one hand, "legitimate" violence depends on "illegitimate" violence, on violation, properly speaking, in order to justify its own existence, and on the other, it cannot keep itself distinct from such illegitimate violence and constantly appears akin to it. This idea has been frequently explored in political theory. For example, drawing on Walter Benjamin's analysis of the foundational violence of the law, Etienne Balibar writes, "Any violence, in the sense of *Gewalt,* that has to become legally or morally legitimate must present itself if not as retaliation, at least as correction and suppression of *violent forces*—whether they be rooted in human nature, social conditions, or ideological beliefs—which have destroyed or disturbed an originary ideal, originally peaceful, non-violent order, or threaten it with destruction." See Balibar, *Politics and the Other Scene,* trans. Christine Jones, James Swenson, and Chris Turner (London: Verso, 2002), 139.

5. The publication of the anthology *Tār Saptak* in 1943 is generally considered the inaugurating moment of what is called "New Poetry" in Hindi. A modernist movement, it is associated with formal, linguistic, and thematic experimentation. For responses and analysis, see Namwar Singh, *Kavitā Ke Naye Pratimān* (Delhi: Rajkamal Prakasan, 1968); Acharya Nand Dulare Vajpeyi, *Nayī Kavitā* (New Delhi: Macmillan Company of India, 1976); and Lucy Rosenstein, *New Poetry in Hindi* (Delhi: Permanent Black, 2003).

6. James L. Fitzgerald, ed. and trans., *The Mahābhārata: The Book of the Women; The Book of Peace, Part One* (Chicago: University of Chicago Press, 2004), 223.

7. Dharamvir Bharati, *Andhā Yug,* in *Granthāvalī,* vol. 3, ed. Chandrakant Bandivadekar (New Delhi: Vani Prakashan, 1998), 381. Hereafter cited in text as GV, with volume and page numbers. All translations from Bharati's work are mine.

8. Namwar Singh, *Kavitā Ke Naye Pratimān* (Delhi: Rajkamal, 1968), 174; my emphasis.

9. Alok Bhalla, "Defending the Sacred in an Age of Atrocities: On Translating *Andha Yug*," in Dharamvir Bharti, *Andha Yug*, trans. Alok Bhalla (Oxford: Oxford University Press), 7.

10. Ibid., 13.

11. Indeed, it is quite obvious that the entire narrative of the *Mahābhārata* is, in the words of Charles Malamoud, "a network of tales of vengeance." Not only does the desire for revenge—fueled most strongly by the image of Draupadi's initial humiliation at the Kaurava court—repeatedly appear as a reason for the Pandavas' decision to go to war but various unrelated encounters during the war also depict the settling of old scores. For example, it is no surprise when Dhritstadyumna kills Drona, because we already know that he has been born for the very purpose of killing him and hence avenging Drona's own killing of Dhristadyumna's father, Drupada. Malamoud writes that since most of these killings involve treachery, they cannot be read only as acts of eliminating one's enemy but must be read *specifically* as acts of vengeance, occasioned by the desire to commit "an act of violence that is the equivalent of—and, when possible, of the same order as—the violence one has suffered." Thus he claims that "the *Mahābhārata* shows us, in a thousand different ways, that the desire for vengeance is a vital ambition, an essential passion that needs no justification outside itself, being that which gives meaning to human action." Malamoud, "Return Action in the Sacrificial Mechanics of Brahminic India," in *Cooking the World: Ritual and Thought in Ancient India*, trans. David White (Delhi: Oxford University Press, 1998), 156.

12. Indeed, Bharati's work clearly demonstrates that Krishna can no longer appear as a *character* in the pages of either *Andhā Yug* or *Kanupriya*. In the former, he can appear only as a voice, a shadow, a play of light, and in the latter, as the object of Radha's recollections, questions, desires. In this way the works perhaps show us that the name of Krishna can only function in modern India as a memory, a reinflected and reoriented trace.

13. Dharamvir Bharati, "An Interview by Vasant Dev," in *Contemporary Indian Theatre: Interviews with Playwrights and Directors*, ed. Paul Jacob, 92 (New Delhi: Sangeet Natak Akademi, 1989).

14. Bharati, *Muktakṣetre Yuddhakṣetre*, in *Granthāvali*, vol. 7, 123–209.

15. Hannah Arendt, *On Violence* (San Diego: Harcourt Brace, 1970), 44.

16. We are reminded of Fanon: "But it so happens that for the colonized people this violence, because it constitutes their only work, invests their characters with positive and creative qualities. The practice of violence binds them together as a whole, since each individual forms a violent link in the great chain, a part of the great organism of violence which has surged upward in reaction to the settler's violence in the beginning. " Frantz Fanon, *The Wretched of the Earth*, trans. Constance Farrington (New York: Grove Press, 1963), 92.

17. David Shulman, "Aśvatthāman and Bṛhannaḍā: Brahmin and Kingly Paradigms

in the Sanskrit Epic," in *The Origins and Diversity of Axial Age Civilizations,* ed. S. N. Eisenstadt, 421 (Albany: SUNY Press, 1986).

18. Ibid., 422.

19. See also J. C. Heesterman, "Non-Violence and Sacrifice," in *Indologica Taurinensia* 12 (1984): 119–27. Drawing attention to the profound conflict concerning violence in Brahminical texts, Heesterman writes, "On the one hand there are the incontrovertible prescripts of Vedic ritual enjoining animal sacrifice; on the other hand the dharma scriptures in an equally strict fashion require *ahiṃsā* . . . The embarrassing point is that this killing is enjoined precisely by the most hallowed part of the tradition, the *śruti* which is the source of all dharma" (119–20).

20. Tamer C. Reich, "Sacrificial Violence and Textual Battles: Inner Textual Interpretation in the Sanskrit Mahābhārata," History of Religions 41, no. 2 (2001): 168.

21. Vishnu S. Sukhthankar, S.K. Belvalkar, P. L. Vaidya, et al., eds., *Mahābhārata,* Critical Edition (Poona: Bhandarkar Oriental Research Institute, 1933–72). Hereafter cited in text by book, chapter, and verse number.

22. For a succinct and excellent analysis of these aspects of dharma, see Wendy Doniger's and Brian K. Smith's introduction to *The Laws of Manu,* trans. Wendy Doniger with Brian K. Smith (London: Penguin, 1991), especially xxxix-xl.

23. Ibid., 12–13.

24. Dharamvir Bharati, "Ādhunikta arthāt saṃkat kā bodh," in *Granthāvalī,* vol. 4, 477.

25. See, for example, Madeleine Biardeau and Charles Malamoud, *Le Sacrifice dans L'Inde Ancienne* (Paris: Presses Universitaires de France, 1976), especially 125.

26. Jean-Pierre Vernant has observed that "in thought as expressed in Greek or ancient Indo-European there is no idea of the agent being the source of his action. Or, if I may translate that . . . there is no category of the will in Greece." See Richard Macksey and Eugenio Donato, eds., *The Structuralist Controversy: The Languages of Criticism and the Sciences of Man* (Baltimore: Johns Hopkins University Press, 1970), 152.

27. Bharati may have had in mind Tilak's extensive commentary on the Gītā, which emphasizes that *karma* must be understood not in the restricted sense of traditional texts but in a wider and more inclusive sense. All actions performed by men, Tilak proposes, should be understood as *karma.* See B. G. Tilak, *Śrimad Bhagavadgita-Rahasya,* 3rd ed. (Poona: Tilak Brothers, 1971).

5. Poetry beyond Art

1. Hazari Prasad Dvivedi, *Aśok ke phūl,* 20th ed. (Allahabad: Lokbharti Prakashan, 1998), 101.

2. Ibid., 104.

3. *Vakrokti* and *alaṃkāra* thus become aligned in some ways, not only because of their emphasis on the technical aspects of poetic speech but also because of the way they foreground the question of gender. Indeed, one of the oldest scenes in this

tradition is the scene where poetry, or indeed, speech *(vāc)* herself, "chooses" and seduces the one she loves best: the one who is most cultivated, most learned, or most artistic (*Ṛg Veda,* 10.71). Over time this scene changes quite dramatically: it is no longer about speech or poetry choosing the one she loves best but about the kind of beloved most valued by the discerning man of taste. In fact, as we may guess, the story is even more complicated. For it is not just a matter of the relative charms of the woman but of her status and intent. The language that, in early Sanskrit literature, borrows from the skills of the courtesan in order to captivate the heart of the connoisseur, turns out to be no fit ancestor for the language that nineteenth-century Hindi nationalists valued—for this language must now assert her wifely credentials against the new harlot on the block, Urdu. Alok Rai has given us a choice example of this strain in a quote from Sohan Prasad's 1886 poem *Hindi Urdu Ki Larhāi* (The Fight between Hindi and Urdu), where Hindi, the dutiful daughter of Sanskrit, thus chastises Urdu: "This is not fit conduct for a decent married woman, you harlot, you! / She who is forever bedecking herself is but a prostitute . . . / Consider well, such is not the conduct of a loyal wife." (Alok Rai, *Hindi Nationalism* (Hyderabad: Orient Longman, 2001, 94).

4. Ibid., 110.

5. Charles Malamoud has analysed the scene of seduction in Sanskrit literature with characteristic sensitivity. See "Seduction in an Indian Light," in *Cooking the World: Ritual and Thought in Ancient India,* trans. David White (Delhi: Oxford University Press, 1998), 130–43.

6. Buddhadeva Bose, *Modern Poetry and Sanskrit Kavya,* trans. Sujit Mukherjee (Calcutta: Writers Workshop, 1997), 13. Hereafter cited in text as "Bose" with page numbers.

7. Philippe Lacoue-Labarthe, "Holderlin and the Greeks," trans. Judi Olson, in *Typography: Mimesis, Philosophy, Politics* (Stanford, Calif.: Stanford University Press, 1989), 238.

8. Writing about the style of classical Sanskrit, the renowned French scholar Louis Renou makes some similar observations: "The word order, in poetry at least, is arbitrary; the sentence is lengthened and heavily burdened with dependent phrases, relative and other subordinate clauses, with descriptive matter and incidental stories . . . Metaphors and comparisons increase and multiply; words with a double meaning are favored . . . It is obvious that, in the circumstances, Sanskrit was drifting away from the status of a spoken language." Renou, *Indian Literature,* trans. Patrick Evans (New York: Walker and Company, 1964), 19–20.

9. Ernst Robert Curtius, *European Literatures and the Latin Middle Ages,* trans. Willard Trask (Princeton, N.J.: Princeton University Press, 1953), 145.

10. See Alok Rai, *Hindi Nationalism* (Hyderabad: Orient Longman, 2001).

11. Acharya Ram Chandra Shukla, *Pratinidhi Nibandh* (Delhi: Radha Krishna, 1971), 65–76.

12. I would not have arrived at this analysis if I had not read Derrida's work, and especially "White Mythology: Metaphor in the Text of Philosophy," in *Margins of Philosophy,* trans. Alan Bass (Chicago: University of Chicago Press, 1982), 207–71.

13. Jaishankar Prasad, *Kāvya Aur Kalā Tathā Anya Nibandh* (Varanasi: Prasad Prakashan, 1983), 64.

14. Ibid., 60.

15. Ibid., 62.

16. Ibid., 64.

17. I have attempted a more detailed analysis of this hymn in "Remembering the Veda: Accumulations of Interest," in *Jouvert: A Journal of Postcolonial Studies,* ed. Kenneth Reinhard and Julia Lupton Reinhard, "Special Double Issue: Religion Between Culture and Philosophy" 3, nos. 1 and 2, 1999. http://social-class.ncsu.edu/Jouvert/v3il2/sawhne.htp.

18. Gwendolyn Layne, trans,. *Kādambari: A Classical Sanskrit Story of Magical Transformations, by Bāṇabhatta* (New York: Garland Publishers, 1991), 4.

19. Daniel H. H. Ingalls, Jeffrey Moussaieff Masson, and M. V. Patwardhan, trans., *The Dhvanyāloka of Anandavardhana with the Locana of Abhinavagupta.* (Cambridge, Mass.: Harvard University Press, 1990), 70. Further references to this edition appear in the text by page number.

20. Kuntaka, considered by both Hazariprasad Dvivedi and the philosopher Bimal Matilal as being the most interesting exponent of this theory, composed his *Vakrokti-jivita* in the tenth century. He argued that *vakrokti* is in no way external to poetry, and that the relation between the "ornament" and the "ornamented" in poetry is thus unlike the relation between a body and its ornaments. See Bimal Krishna Matilal, *The Word and the World: India's Contribution to the Study of Language* (Delhi: Oxford University Press, 1990).

21. K. Krishnamoorthy, ed. and trans., *Dhvanyāloka of Ānandavardhana* (Delhi: Motilal Banarsidass, 1982), 42. I have used this edition wherever I have cited the Sanskrit text. Translations are mine, though I have been helped by Krishnamoorthy and others. Further references appear in the text by book and verse number.

22. In his introduction to the *Dhvanyāloka,* Ingalls makes a different argument, suggesting that *rasa* remains the goal of poetry for Anandavardhana: "Now the concept of *rasa,* it seems to me, is more important than that of *dhvani* in furnishing a criterion of beauty" (19). My own sense is that the significance of *dhvani* extends beyond providing criteria for beauty. This is what I have attempted to propose in this chapter.

23. Sir Monier Monier-Williams, *A Sanskrit-English Dictionary,* s.v. *"ras."*

24. V. K. Chari, *Sanskrit Criticism* (Delhi: Motilal Banarsidass, 1993), 12.

25. "But what is this thing called *rasa?* Here is the reply. Because it is enjoyably tasted, it is called *rasa.* How does the enjoyment come? Persons who eat prepared food mixed with different condiments and sauces, etc., if they are sensitive, enjoy the different tastes and then feel pleasure; likewise, sensitive spectators, after enjoying

the various emotions expressed by the actors through words, gestures and feelings, feel pleasure etc. This (final) feeling by the spectators is here explained as the (various) *rasas* of *nāṭya*." Adya Rangacharya, ed. and trans., *The Nāṭyaśāstra: English Translation with Critical Notes* (Delhi: Munshiram Manoharlal, 1996), p. 55.

26. Tripathi, ed., *Dhvanyāloka,* 590.

27. Chari, *Sanskrit Criticism,* 102–3.

Epilogue

1. Francis Macdonald Cornford, trans., *The Republic of Plato* (London: Oxford University Press, 1981), 340.

2. Ibid., 337–38.

3. For example, after Hektor's death, Priam says: "I wish he had died in my arms, for that way / we two, I myself and his mother who bore him unhappy, / might so have *glutted ourselves* with weeping for him and mourning." *The Iliad of Homer,* trans. Richmond Lattimore (Chicago: University of Chicago Press, 1951), book 22, 426–28, 446 (my emphasis). And in book 24 we read: "Then when great Achilleus had taken *full satisfaction* in sorrow and the passion for it had gone from his mind and body, thereafter he rose from his chair . . ." (24. 512–15, 488 my emphasis). One may find other similar examples.

4. "Patroklos, far most pleasing to my heart in its sorrows, / I left you here alive when I went away from the shelter, / But now I come back, lord of the people, to find you have fallen. / So evil in my life takes over from evil forever. / The husband on whom my father and honoured mother bestowed me / I saw before my city lying torn with the sharp bronze, / And my three brothers, whom a single mother bore with me / And who were close to me, all went on one day to destruction" (*The Iliad,* 19. 287–94).

5. Ibid., 400.

6. Robert P. Goldman, trans., *The Rāmāyaṇa of Valmiki, an Epic of Ancient India* (Princeton, N.J.: Princeton University Press, 1984), 127–28.

7. Ch. Vaudeville, "Rāmāyaṇa Studies I: The Kraunca-Vadha Episode in the Valmiki Rāmāyaṇa," *Journal of the American Oriental Society* 83, no. 3 (August–September 1963): 327–35.

8. Ibid., 331.

9. Ibid., 334.

10. In a conversation Namwar Singh called it the "first poem of curse and compassion." See Srikant Verma, *Racnāvali,* ed. Arvind Tripathi, vol. 1 (Delhi: Rajkamal Prakashan, 1995), 554.

11. Ch. Vaudeville, "The Kraunca-Vadha Episode," 334.

12. M. R. Kale, ed., *The Uttararāmcharita of Bhavabhūti* (Delhi: Motilal Banarsidass, 1993), 55.

13. Ibid., 97.

14. Ibid.

Index

SIMONA SAWHNEY is associate professor of South Asian literature and literary theory at the University of Minnesota.